Introduction to Information Systems

Judith C. Simon

The University of Memphis

ACQUISITIONS EDITOR	Beth Golub
MARKETING MANAGER	Jessica Garcia
PRODUCTION EDITOR	Ken Santor
COVER DESIGN	Suzanne Noli
COVER ILLUSTRATION	©Laertis/The Stock Illustration Source, Inc.

This book was printed and bound by R.R. Donnelley—Crawfordsville. The cover was printed by Phoenix Color Corporation.

This book is printed on acid-free paper.

The paper in this book was manufactured by a mill whose forest management programs include sustained yield harvesting of its timberlands. Sustained yield harvesting principles ensure that the numbers of trees cut each year does not exceed the amount of new growth.

ISBN 0-471-39390-8 (pbk)

Printed in the United States of America

10 9 8 7 6 5 4 3 2 1

PREFACE

Information technology has become an extremely important and increasingly complex component of business and professional organizations. Decisions related to information technology and the related information systems can be a major factor influencing an organization's survival.

A basic knowledge of information systems is a requirement for everyone working in various types of organizations today. For example, managers at all levels must make decisions about which systems are best for specific situations. The personnel within organizations today must have an understanding of the role of information systems, as well as appropriate methods for using the technology effectively. This text and the accompanying Web site are designed to provide an introductory level of understanding of these systems.

This printed text and its companion Web site are designed to complement each other and to be used together during the study of each chapter. For example, the Web site contains additional content for each chapter; student quizzes, links to related business and vendor sites, and business cases. In addition, the purchase of *Introduction to Information Systems* allows you four months of access to the nation's most-respected business news service: the Wall Street Journal Interactive Edition. Each chapter in this text has an Online Activities section tied to research activities using the *Interactive Journal*. Exploring this site for relevant topics raises awareness of the practical applications of information technology concepts.

This arrangement offers numerous advantages to students, including:

▼ lower cost of the printed text, because the quantity of printed materials can be reduced.

▼ availability of more up-to-date content after purchase of the text, because of the capability of updating and expanding the online content very quickly.

▼ flexibility of course content; e.g., students needing an emphasis only on basic content will be provided adequate materials, while other students who may need more thorough coverage of content, or a more extensive managerial emphasis, can find those materials at the Web site.

▼ the opportunity for practice in performing typical online activities rather than being limited to traditional text-based activities.

▼ becoming acquainted with the business reporting and features of the Interactive Journal through free access.

Materials for instructors are also provided on the Web site. Advantages to instructors of this design include the quick feedback possible from student activities and quizzes, the use of content that can be updated much more quickly than is possible with a traditional text, and the use of activities that are often of more interest to students, without the need for the instructor to design the Web site. Instructors who have Internet access in their classrooms could choose to display materials from the Web site in class, reducing the amount of preparation needed for class materials.

Although the materials in this text and related Web site are designed to focus primarily on effective business uses of information systems, the content is appropriate for people in all fields who need to develop an understanding of basic information technology concepts and the related systems developed to use the technology. Developing an understanding of how these concepts are used in business situations assists students in applying their knowledge to a variety of other situations. With the flexibility provided in the design of this text and companion Web site, and the *Interactive Journal* access, the materials can be used for a variety of student needs at either the undergraduate or graduate level.

The order of presentation of concepts is designed to start with topics that are most likely to be known by the reader or likely to be related to known topics. The order of presentation also allows the reader to move from the more external or computer-user topics to the more internal or system development and management concepts. The materials in this text are separated into four sections, as follows:

Part I provides an introduction to the topic of information systems, such as ways in which we are using this technology and the components of an information system, followed by descriptions of information systems in organizations. Beginning with Chapter 2 where these topics are introduced, each chapter contains a Management Perspective, a Global Perspective, and an Ethical or Social Perspective.

Part II describes the typical uses of the Internet for electronic commerce and related activities. It also includes a discussion of the types of communications technologies that are available and in use for communicating and conducting business transactions electronically.

Part III describes the software and hardware components of information systems. This section includes the software for traditional office applications as well as for managerial decision making. Also included is a discussion of system software, which has become a prominent aspect of business decisions related to software selection. The hardware component of information systems is described from the point of view of people who must make decisions about appropriate selections. This section does not delve into the internal operations in depth. The topics included are those aspects of the technology that are most important for making good decisions. A reader who wanted to obtain more detailed information about how these systems work could then go to numerous books designed for that purpose or could find additional information at the Web site for this text.

Part IV proceeds to a discussion of the development of information systems. As with other sections of this text, the topics are discussed from the point of view of people who must work with the developers. This text does not provide the depth that would be needed by an actual developer, but tries to provide an understanding of the process for those many people who will need to communicate with developers of their systems. This section ends with a discussion of the management concerns related to all the information resources, including the sometimes overlooked but essential topics of managing the human resources that are using the systems.

Appreciation is expressed for the assistance provided by all the hard-working staffs at Digital Springs, Inc. and John Wiley & Sons. Thank you Rick Leyh, Steve Welch, Camille McMorrow, and Jeanne Payne at DSI. Thanks to Beth Golub, Brent Gordon, and David Kear at JWS. Their guidance and continuing encouragement have made this text a reality.

CONTENTS

PART I: OVERVIEW OF INFORMATION SYSTEMS

Chapter 1 - Information Systems Overview 1
   Learning Objectives

Developments Leading to Today's Technology 1

Effects of Information Technology on Our Lives 2
   Changes in Business and Professional Activities 3
      Automobile Manufacturing
      Medical Diagnoses
      Aircraft Manufacturing and Use
      Disabled Workers
   Changes in Career Options

Components of Information Systems 6
   People
   Procedures
   Hardware
   Software
   Data

Additional Terms and Related Concepts 13
   Data, Information, and Knowledge
   Data/Information Flow

Summary 15

Questions for Review and Discussion 16

Selected References 17

Chapter 1 Key Terms 17

Online Activities 20

Chapter 2 - Information Systems in Organizations 21
   Learning Objectives

Common Types of Information Systems 21
   Transaction Processing Systems
   Information Reporting Systems
   Other Types of Information Systems

Strategic and Other Managerial Uses of Information Systems 26

Strategic Decisions Related to Information Systems 29

Functional Uses of Information Systems 29
   Human Resources Information System
   Accounting/Financial Information System

Marketing/Sales Information System
Production/Operations Information System
Cross-Functional Relationships

New Concerns Because of Information Technology 34
Global Concerns
Types of Organizations
Need for Global Awareness
Global Strategies
Ethical Issues
Privacy
Security
Accuracy
Ownership
Other Issues
Social Issues

Summary 41

Questions for Review and Discussion 41

Selected References 42

Chapter 2 Key Terms 43

Online Activities 46

PART II: ELECTRONIC COMMERCE AND RELATED TECHNOLOGIES

Chapter 3 - Electronic Commerce and Internet Technologies 51
Learning Objectives

Overview 51
Basic Communications Software Requirements and Features
Sources of Communications Software

Electronic Data Interchange 53

Introduction to the Internet 54
Advantages and Disadvantages of Commercial Internet Use
Internet Access
World Wide Web (WWW)

Business Examples of Internet Electronic Commerce 59

Security Issues of Internet Electronic Commerce 61

Expected Growth of Internet Electronic Commerce 61

Additional Internet Technologies 63
Electronic Mail and Telecommuting
File Transfer Protocol (FTP)

Newsgroups and Mailing Lists
Intranets and Extranets
Trends

Summary 70

Questions for Review and Discussion 71

Selected References 71

Chapter 3 Key Terms 72

Online Activities 74

**Chapter 4 - Data Communications and Networking
Considerations** 77
Learning Objectives

General Concepts 77

Characteristics of Communications Channels 81
Type of Service
Direction of Communication
Number of Data Paths
Number of Connections
Type of Signal
Speed of Transmission
Mode of Transmission

Data Communications Media 87
Wire Pairs
Coaxial Cable
Optical Fiber
Broadcast Radio
Microwave
Infrared

Communications Carriers 90

Data Communications Hardware 90

Network Topologies 91

Network Protocols 95

LANs and WANs 96

Intranet and Extranet Communications 98

Distributed Systems 98

Strategic Network Issues 99

Communications Infrastructure 100

Ubiquitous Networks 101

Summary 101

Questions for Review and Discussion 103

Selected References 103

Chapter 4 Key Terms 104

Online Activities 107

PART III: SOFTWARE AND HARDWARE STRATEGIES AND USES

Chapter 5 - Applications Software for Businesses 111
    Learning Objectives

The Concept of Office Automation 111

Office Applications Software 113
    Word Processing Software
    Spreadsheet Software
    Database Software
    Graphics Software
    Other Office Applications Software

Management Decision-Support Software 122
    Project Management Software
    Decision Support System Software
    Group Decision Support System Software
    Executive Information System Software
    Artificial Intelligence Software
        Expert Systems Software
        Neural Networks

Evaluation of Applications Software 135

Summary 137

Questions for Review and Discussion 139

Selected References 139

Chapter 5 Key Terms 140

Online Activities 144

Chapter 6 - System Software Considerations 145
    Learning Objectives

Purposes of System Software 145

Control Programs 146

Processing Programs 147
    Concurrent Processing
    Simultaneous Processing

Language Translators 151
Utilities and Other System Programs 152
Specific Operating Systems 153
    Operating Systems for Large Computer Systems
    Operating Systems for Midrange Computers
    Operating Systems for Small Computers
        PC-DOS and MS-DOS
        Microsoft Windows
        UNIX and LINUX
        Mac OS

System Software Compatibility 160
Summary 160
Questions for Review and Discussion 162
Selected References 162
Chapter 6 Key Terms 163
Online Activities 165

Chapter 7 - Computer Components and Options 167
    Learning Objectives

Overview 167
Input and Output 168
    Input
        Keyboard
        Pointing Devices
        Scanners
        Speech/Voice Recognition
        Other Forms of Input
    Output
        Screen Displays
        Printers
        Audio Output
Secondary Storage 177
    Encoding Systems
    Tape Storage Media
        Reel-to-Reel Magnetic Tapes
        Magnetic Cartridges
    Magnetic Disk Storage Media
        Floppy Disks
        Hard Disks
    Optical Disk Storage Media
        Write-Once Disks
        Rewritable Disks
    Additional Storage Options

Smart Cards
Holographic Storage

Processing 187
Primary Memory
ROM
RAM
Central Processing Unit
Arithmetic-Logic Unit
Control Unit
Interpretation and Execution of Instructions
Large System Processors
Microprocessors
Chip Technology
Memory Chips
Microprocessor Chips

Summary 197

Questions for Review and Discussion 199

Selected References 199

Chapter 7 Key Terms 201

Online Activities 208

PART IV: DEVELOPMENT AND MANAGEMENT OF INFORMATION SYSTEMS

Chapter 8 - Programming Languages 211
Learning Objectives

General Programming Concepts 211

First-Generation Programming Languages 214

Second-Generation Programming Languages 215

Third-Generation Programming Languages 215
FORTRAN
COBOL
BASIC
C

Fourth-Generation Programming Languages 218

Programming Language Trends 219
3GL Tools
Object-Oriented Programming Languages
Visual Programming Tools
Scripting Languages
5GLs

Summary 225

Questions for Review and Discussion 226

Selected References 226

Chapter 8 Key Terms 227

Online Activities 228

Chapter 9 - Database Development and Management 231
    Learning Objectives

Database Development Overview 231

General Concepts and Terms 232

File Organization 233

File Access 234

Data Models 235
    Hierarchical Structure
    Network Structure
    Relational Structure
    Object-Oriented Structure

Database Management Systems 240

Distributed Databases 242

Data Warehouses and Data Mining 243
    Data Warehouses
    Data Mining

Knowledge Management 245

Summary 246

Questions for Review and Discussion 247

Selected References 247

Chapter 9 Key Terms 248

Online Activities 250

Chapter 10 - Systems Development Procedures 251
    Learning Objectives

Systems Development Overview 251

Felt or Identified Need 253

Initial Investigation 254
    Problem Definition
    Feasibility Study

Requirements Determination 256
    Study of Existing System

User Requirements and Constraints

System Design 261
    Logical Design
    Physical Design

System Implementation 264
    Acquisition of Hardware and Software
        Hardware Acquisition Considerations
    Sources of Hardware
        Software Acquisition Considerations
    Custom Software versus Packaged Software
        Internal versus External Development
    System Installation
        Site Preparation
        Hardware and Software Preparation
        Data Preparation
        Preparation of System Users
        Conversion
        Testing

System Maintenance 273
    System Review
    System Alterations

Trends in Systems Development 275
    Rapid Application Development
    Internet/Intranet Development
    Business Process Reengineering and Other Management Strategies

Summary 277

Questions for Review and Discussion 278

Selected References 278

Chapter 10 Key Terms 279

Online Activities 280

**Chapter 11 - Information Resource Management
Strategies** 283
    Learning Objectives

Information Resource Management Overview 283
    Organization of Information Resource Management
    Overview of Information Resource Management Decisions

Management of Hardware and Software 285
    Asset Management
    Performance Monitoring
    Configuration Management
    Hardware and Software Security

Management of Data. 289
    Data Consistency
    Data Security
        Access and Control
        Virus Protection
        Transmission Protection
        General Procedures
    Routine Backup and Recovery
    Disaster Recovery

Management of Human Resources. 296
    End-User Application Development
    Support Systems for End-User Computing
        Training
    Help Desks and Related Assistance
    Control Systems for End-User Computing
        Control of Application Development
        Hardware and Software Controls
        Data Controls

Management of Procedures 305
    Quality Assessment
    Cost Allocations
    Usage Logs

Summary 307

Questions for Review and Discussion. 308

Selected References 308

Chapter 11 Key Terms 310

Online Activities. 311

Index. 313

Part I

OVERVIEW OF INFORMATION SYSTEMS

Part I provides an introduction to the world of information systems, with descriptions of ways in which technology has influenced us personally and professionally. It includes descriptions of the basic components of information systems and also describes global, ethical, and social issues that have arisen. Each chapter in this and all remaining parts of the text concludes with a set of online activities.

Chapter 1   Information Systems Overview
Chapter 2   Information Systems in Organizations

CHAPTER 1

Information Systems Overview

LEARNING OBJECTIVES

After studying the contents of this chapter, you should be able to

1. Describe the general progression of developments that have led to today's uses of computers.
2. Discuss effects of information technology on personal and professional activities.
3. Identify and describe the components of an information system.
4. Identify and contrast the traditional categories of digital computers.
5. Describe the process involved in the flow of data through a system.

DEVELOPMENTS LEADING TO TODAY'S TECHNOLOGY

The use of computers has become an integral part of our business and personal lives and has had a significant impact on our society. The technology involved has become so extensive that you might think computers have been used in businesses for hundreds of years. But a brief review of the evolution of computers will show that the significant developments in business and personal uses of this technology have occurred only in the last few decades.

Some of the initial technological basis for computers was developed in previous centuries, but business uses of computers did not begin to evolve until the middle of the twentieth century. By considering how quickly and extensively our professional and personal lives have been changed by this technology in recent years, we can better prepare ourselves for the inevitable changes yet to come. Figure 1.1 is a step-by-step overview of the developments that are the basis for our current computer technology.

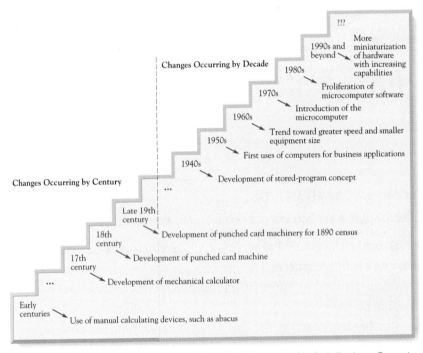

Figure 1.1 Steps Leading to Development of Today's Business Computers

EFFECTS OF INFORMATION TECHNOLOGY ON OUR LIVES

Information technology and the resulting information systems that are developed to use the technology effectively have caused significant differences in the way businesses operate and in the way some of our personal business is transacted. Many of these developments have improved our lives, although some changes have caused new problems.

One primary advantage of using information technology in businesses is that it is a labor-saving device. An investment in new technology may pay for itself rather quickly, partly because it does not require employee benefits such as insurance, vacations, sick leave, and coffee breaks. Information systems can be developed to use the technology to perform many operations much faster than humans. Further, the system can repeat the same activity with identical accuracy 1,000 times or more without getting bored or developing a headache. Information systems do not have the resistance to change that humans might demonstrate when the needs of a job change. Information systems can be used for tasks that would be impossible or unsafe for humans to perform. For example, robotic systems were used to clean up radioactive debris from the Three Mile Island nuclear accident in the 1970s and are used today to assist physically disabled persons in performing a wide range of tasks.

One result of using information systems in businesses involves the changes that have occurred in job activities. A number of jobs have disappeared, especially those requiring unskilled labor, because machines can perform some tasks more competently than humans. Robots are used for spot-welding on automobile assembly lines and for placing very small parts on circuit boards. Robots have taken over some jobs that are not suited for the human hand or eye, or that are too strenuous for most humans. Nonetheless, while some jobs have disappeared, many new jobs have emerged that are directly related to information technology.

Changes in Business and Professional Activities

Many business and professional activities are now possible or have changed because of the extensive availability and increased capability of information systems. (These changes affect personal activities, as well.) Immediate access to a great deal of data is one of the obvious changes, such as making airline ticket purchases in a very few minutes because people at locations worldwide can access the database and obtain the needed information. Some changes are a direct result of advances made in computer microprocessor chip technology, which allow more and more instructions to be placed in a very small space. Today these chips are found in many devices in addition to computers.

Automobile Manufacturing

Fierce competition among automobile manufacturers, along with U.S. government standards related to emissions and fuel economy, have influenced the development of continually smarter cars. A large part of the growth in the use of microprocessor chips for cars is occurring in the engine controls, drive-train controls, instrumentation systems, safety and security systems, and entertainment systems. These engine controls can analyze the mixture of fuel and air and adjust the amount of fuel going to the engine. They can also monitor the engine-coolant temperature to keep the engine from overheating. This new technology has also resulted in increased and more efficient air bag deployment, cleaner exhaust gas, better antilock braking, and improved antitheft systems. Increased use of microprocessor chips is expected to cause an increase in demand for automotive engineers.

Today's Indy race cars are equipped with systems that record and chart all aspects of car behavior. Among the factors measured and recorded are engine revolutions per minute, exhaust pipe temperature, shock absorber loadings, and degrees of steering applied to the front wheels. Results are used to tune and improve the setup of cars and also to make adjustments to a driver's style and technique. Previously, drivers had to guess about the changes needed.

Medical Diagnoses

New information systems are being used in medical training as a method for medical students and physicians to cope with an explosion of medical information that would otherwise be impossible to keep up with. These systems allow instant access to much more information than a human can remember, and they provide simulations for hands-on experiences. One example is a system for monitoring heartbeats. An amplifier and speaker are used to reproduce a variety of heart sounds, many of which most medical students might not have an opportunity to encounter during their training. Another example is a program for practicing split-second decisions without actually risking a patient's life. Treatment of a trauma patient is simulated, allowing the medical student to make treatment decisions. Another program can diagnose diseases by asking questions about symptoms, observations, and test results. This program can be used for assistance with difficult or unusual cases and is not limited to student simulations.

Aircraft Manufacturing and Use

Airplanes have become highly automated. Manufacturers (as well as passengers) hope that information systems on new aircraft will reduce the chance of human error, which is a factor in about two-thirds of commercial air accidents. New planes fly with a pilot and copilot. The flight engineer has been largely replaced by microprocessor chips in the navigation and monitoring systems. Some sophisticated systems tell the pilot how to fly the plane; for example, the system does not let the pilot bank the plane too far to the left or right. Another program prevents the plane from falling below a minimum authorized speed. Flight management systems (FMSs) on airplanes do many of the routine tasks. After the pilot enters into the on-board system the route, wind forecast, altitude, and plane weight without fuel, the FMS calculates whether the fuel load will let the plane fly at a certain altitude, and it regulates the engine throttles for the most efficient use of fuel. After the pilot enters a destination into the system, the FMS determines the most direct route, indicates the distance and arrival time, and feeds navigation data to the automatic pilot to direct the plane to its destination.

Many airlines use an information system for load control functions. Load controllers determine the appropriate mix of passengers and cargo so the aircraft is balanced correctly for safe and efficient operation. After the plane is loaded, data is transmitted automatically to the cockpit, indicating to the pilot how to set the aircraft's stabilizer for takeoff. The load-control process was previously done manually and required the work of many employees, with more chance for error and slower results.

New systems being developed for air traffic control can suggest avoidance maneuvers if two planes are heading toward each other. Aircraft that are not close to air traffic controllers can be monitored by satellite. Flight plans and rescheduling are updated automatically. Microwave radio-guidance systems can be used so that pilots can land the aircraft even if bad weather keeps them from being able to see the runway.

Disabled Workers

Numerous information systems have been developed for workers with various types of disabilities. As a need has arisen, someone has developed a solution using information technology. Many of these ideas are later adapted for use by the general public. One example of a development for disabled workers involves speech synthesizers, which have been used to provide speech for people who have no voice. Someone else's voice is used to store speech sounds into a computer's memory. The computer's keyboard is often used to enter desired statements, which are then spoken by the synthesizer. If the person cannot press keys to indicate the desired statements, various options are available (such as a sensor attached to the eyebrow that uses movements as a basis for entering commands).

Changes in Career Options

Many new careers have become available through the use of information technology in businesses. Other careers now require a knowledge of information technology concepts and applications because of their widespread use in handling part of the workload.

Additional career information is available at the Web site.

Some careers are direct developments of the information technology industry, and continued changes will cause new jobs to emerge along with changes to current jobs. Here are a few of the types of jobs that have evolved:

▼ Data entry operators, who transform original data into a form the system can understand and use

▼ Systems analysts, who review current systems and determine changes needed

▼ Programmers, who develop instructions for desired system activities

▼ System operators, who run large information systems, including mounting and removing tapes and disks containing data and instructions

▼ Training and assistance personnel, who help employees who use computer systems to work more efficiently and effectively with their hardware and software

▼ Multimedia developers, who create on-screen audio and visual materials for use in a variety of business applications, such as sales presentations and employee training

▼ Network managers, who supervise and maintain an often-complicated system of multiple pieces of equipment that are linked within a business

▼ Web site developers, who create business sites on the Internet that may include a variety of items, such as business data, multiple links to related sites, customer-related capabilities for viewing and/or ordering products and services, and many forms of multimedia.

Additional career opportunities are available in sales of computer hardware and software as well as in service areas, such as repairs and consulting assistance.

Jobs in other fields have changed dramatically in recent years and often require more knowledge of information technology. Engineers and architects, for example, are now using computer applications in developing very sophisticated designs. Advertisers and movie producers can create special effects without the need for stunt doubles and the corresponding risks that were sometimes involved in the past. The list of jobs affected by this technology affects people in all fields and at a wide range of levels of skill and knowledge, such as store clerks, restaurant employees, accountants, and attorneys.

COMPONENTS OF INFORMATION SYSTEMS

System is the term used to describe any combination of related elements that work together to achieve a desired goal. A system can have numerous subsystems (and sub-subsystems). These subsystems are complete systems but also are interrelated and must work together with the other subsystems to provide a complete system.

A system is merely a sequence of appropriate steps for completing a task. We all have systems we use to get various tasks completed, and some of our systems are more efficient than others. We have both business (or professional) systems and personal systems, many of which do not require the use of a computer. You have probably developed a system for getting to work or school on time. A system is any series of steps followed to reach some goal or complete a task. The system may include some form of technology. If your method of traveling to work or school includes anything other than walking, you are using technology as part of your system.

An information system is defined as components that work together to provide desired information in the proper format at an appropriate time. A single business organization may have many types of information systems and subsystems. Since the main focus of this text is on information technology and its use in business, our definition of information system assumes the use of computers as a part of the system. Of course, businesses may have many manual systems as well as information systems. An information system, then, involves the use of information technology for some business purpose. Information technology refers to the computer equipment itself and whatever is stored in it—programs and data. An information system is developed to use this technology effectively to meet a business need.

The general purpose of an information system in a business is to supply something that adds value. Information system activities may include collecting and storing data, performing various types of data processing, and developing reports based on the data so that better decisions can be made. Information systems can be used to improve services that in turn benefit customers, such as faster responses to questions or quicker processing of orders. These services help the company to be more competitive, especially if other organizations offer a similar product or service.

Information systems have become essential for many businesses in their efforts to make the best decisions possible while striving to maintain a competitive advantage. Competitive advantage refers to an organization's ability to provide a product or service more quickly or of higher quality than its competitors. Every organization needs to offer something that causes customers to choose that organization's products or services instead of another's. Manufacturing companies began using assembly-line systems many years ago in an attempt to improve the speed and quality of their production process and hopefully to provide a product or service that was better than the competition's. Information systems today contribute significantly toward creating and maintaining a competitive advantage. Highly efficient and dependable systems of processing, storing, reporting, and transmitting data are often essential for organizations to remain competitive.

Information technology today is helping companies to reduce their operating costs while improving their ability to meet the needs of their customers. Business strategists often recommend that organizations avoid putting too much emphasis on the technology itself. Instead, companies should focus on satisfying their customers' needs. Then when they use the technology appropriately to develop information systems to meet their goals, they are more likely to be successful.

The primary components necessary to have a working information system include the following:

▼ people to operate or use the system

▼ procedures (instructions for the people)

▼ information technology, including

> hardware (the computer equipment)
>
> software (instructions for the hardware)
>
> data that is to be processed through the system

Figure 1.2 depicts the concept of an information system. Within the information technology subcircle, programs or instructions are being provided to the computer hardware, along with data. Within the overall information system, procedures (another form of instructions) are provided to people, who provide the data being sent to the hardware. The final result is the information being provided to the people. Each of the components is described further in the following sections.

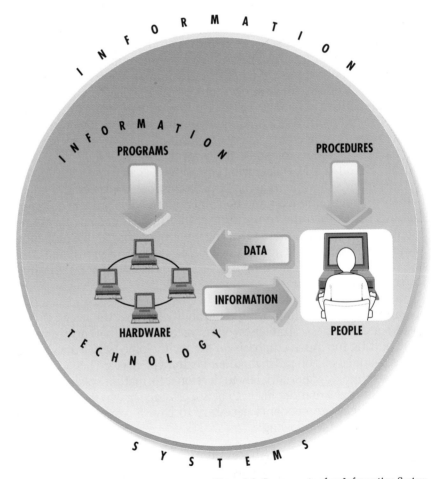

Figure 1.2 Components of an Information System

People

Information systems cannot work without human assistance. The hardware cannot be manufactured, sold, or repaired without people. The software programs do not write themselves; all software involves creations by people.

Once the hardware is in place and the software is developed or purchased and installed, human interaction is still required. Hardware and software are operated and maintained by people. The data must be entered into the system in some form that requires human assistance. And the results of the system are typically designed for use by people who need that output for successful completion of their work.

People are primarily responsible for ensuring the accuracy of the system. The system hardware itself is very reliable. When electric current passes through a circuit, the result is the same the thousandth time as it was the first time. The main problems with accuracy generally come from human error and have resulted in the term GIGO (Garbage In, Garbage Out). In other words, if the data or programs put into the system are inaccurate, the results will also be inaccurate. This concept is very important because some people seem to assume that everything produced by a computer system is automatically correct. The result can be correct only if what was entered initially was correct, and if the programs (instructions) were appropriate.

Procedures

People need instructions indicating how to perform work in the desired manner, in the same way that hardware needs instructions (software). These instructions for the humans are called procedures. Procedures must be developed and clearly stated for every information systems activity that is to be performed by the people. Development of well-written procedures is a very difficult task. One reason for the difficulty is that the people doing the writing are often those who already know how to do the task quite well. They therefore find it hard to explain the steps from the point of view of someone who has no prior knowledge of the activity.

Businesses often have different procedures manuals for each major task to be performed. A great deal of time and money is invested in developing these manuals. Unfortunately, sometimes not enough time and money are spent ensuring that the employees read and follow these manuals and in being sure that the manuals remain up-to-date and accurate.

Hardware

Hardware is the physical equipment—including the computer itself—that handles the processing, the keyboard, mouse, display screen or monitor, and other peripheral (or attached) devices such as printers and storage media.

Computers used for a majority of business applications are digital computers. They use the digits 0 and 1 (the binary numbering system) to represent data. Analog computers are less widely used in business activities because they are typically used for measurements, such as temperature, length, and volume. Analog computers are found in some manufacturing and other business applications, but are most widely used for scientific applications. Table 1.1 gives a brief description of some of the digital events that have led to today's digital systems.

Year	Digital Event
1863	Numbered home and business addresses began to be used.
1879	Phone numbers were assigned.
1936	Social Security numbers began to be issued.
1951	Telephone area codes were assigned.
1953	ZIP codes were assigned to mailing addresses.
1998	Transmission of digital television signals began.

Table 1.1 Examples of the Digital Revolution

The traditional subcategories of digital computers are microcomputers, minicomputers, mainframe computers, and supercomputers. This list proceeds from smallest to largest. However, with the continuing increase in capabilities of all types of computers, no clear-cut dividing lines exist. Some persons are now defining a mainframe as a computer in which all the primary or main capabilities reside within one unit or frame, which avoids the problem of overlapping capabilities between some minicomputers and mainframes. A trend among some vendors is to use the terms small, midrange, and large to refer to categories of computers.

Microcomputers (also referred to by other terms, including personal computers (PCs), desktop computers, laptops, or notebooks) are widely used. They can sit on a desktop or a laptop, depending on physical size. Many desktops in offices today are equipped with "docking stations," which are units where the small portable models can be inserted and linked to standard desktop screens, keyboards, and other hardware. With a docking station, a portable model can be used in the office as well as at other sites. Some computers can be carried around in one hand.

Microcomputers are generally considered to be single-user systems; one system can provide all that is needed for one person to perform certain tasks. In addition, individual microcomputers are now being linked into a network so that the single user of one microcomputer can also access data from other computers, including minicomputers and mainframes.

In some ways today's microcomputers are as powerful as the mainframes of just a few years ago. The most popular type of microcomputer is the "IBM compatible," which is not necessarily the IBM brand but uses the same internal processor design, and is estimated to have a significant majority of the world market. These microcomputers can use all the same types of software and can retrieve stored data regardless of the specific brand of microcomputer used.

Portable microcomputers that can run on batteries, such as notebook computers, have become very popular because they are mobile and are therefore not limited to one location. Some experts predict that in the near future more portables than desktop models will be sold for standard number crunching and word processing. The main drawbacks of the current portables are that their batteries need recharging, the viewable screen and the keyboard are both smaller, and they may lack some of the capabilities of desktop computers for producing sound, graphics, and video (multimedia).

The term workstation is used today to refer to a "high-end" (highest capability) desktop computer. Vendors and many information systems technologists now use "workstation" to represent a separate level of single-user computer, typically containing greater capabilities than a standard desktop computer but fewer capabilities than the computers described in the next few paragraphs.

Minicomputers were designed for multiuser applications, but with less capability, smaller size, and lower cost than mainframes. Because of the recent popularity of microcomputers and workstations and the increase in their capabilities, the demand for minicomputers may be decreasing. Microcomputers can now be linked to each other in an office or linked to mainframes to create multiuser systems. Some sophisticated minicomputers are replacing mainframe computers as the link with microcomputers.

Mainframe computers, like minicomputers, were designed for multiple users. Mainframes are capable of handling large sets of data and can process the data at higher speeds than most microcomputers and minicomputers. As with microcomputers and minicomputers, a range of capabilities exists among mainframe equipment. Mainframe computers are usually found in businesses that have very large sets of data, extensive processing needs, or both. Mainframe computers require considerably more work to install, while a microcomputer involves simply plugging in the parts. Mainframes require special personnel (such as full-time system operators) as well as special facilities, including more sophisticated wiring, flooring, air conditioning, and fire and water detection devices. Mainframes were the first type of computer available for business use.

Not too many years ago, most information needed by corporate executives was stored in mainframe computers. But with the innovations in recent years in microcomputers, software, electronic mail, and networks, more of the information is available at the desktop where people need it. Companies can now have closer strategic relationships with two important groups, their customers and their suppliers. However, mainframes continue to be used when greater capabilities are needed than can be provided through the use of multiple smaller computers.

Supercomputers are a category of computers that have the highest level of capabilities and are also the most expensive. They can handle very complex calculations at much higher processing speeds than is true of other computers, partly because they contain more processors. Supercomputers are used most often for large research projects and other situations in which very high-level processing needs exist.

Seymour Cray was considered a pioneer in the development of supercomputers to run large business and government operations. His organization created multimillion-dollar computers that were used for sophisticated tasks such as weather forecasting and military experiments. In recent years, the demand for supercomputers has decreased, as these machines with massive capabilities are not needed by as many organizations. This result is due to several factors, one of which involves the increasing processing capabilities of smaller computers. However, the U.S. Energy Department announced in 1998 that they had awarded a large contract to IBM to build a supercomputer capable of making 10 trillion calculations per second by the year 2000, with continuing increases in calculation capabilities in succeeding years.

Software

Software is the term used for the step-by-step instructions provided to the hardware that tell it what to do. These instructions are also called programs. Software includes operating system programs and application programs.

Operating system programs include software that directs the hardware's activities. Operating system software is generally provided with the purchase of hardware, although upgrades to newer versions or different systems can be made. Some operating systems now available can be used with more than one type of hardware.

Application programs are software applications written for specific purposes. Some of the most widely used applications include word processing, spreadsheets, graphics, and database programs. Many other application programs continue to be developed. In addition, specific applications have been written for more narrow purposes, such as law office accounting and other applications that are unique for a particular organization or industry.

Data

Data is a term referring to the raw facts about some topic. The data is converted into meaningful information during processing. The next section discusses data further, and an entire chapter describes methods of managing data. Traditionally, "data" was used as a plural form of the word "datum." However, in recent years it has become used as a singular reference to items stored in computers, and the current usage was chosen in this text.

The data about a topic is typically organized into fields, records, and files. An individual file is made up of related items of interest. As shown in Figure 1.3, the fields are the vertical columns identifying the items of interest, and the horizontal rows contain the individual records of those items.

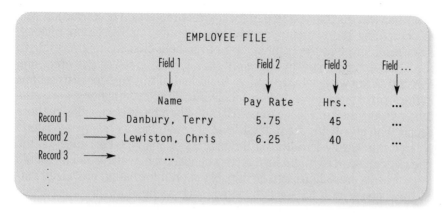

Figure 1.3 Fields and Records in a File

Multiple files of related facts may be developed, such as a customer credit information file, a customer name and address file, and a customer account activity file. These files can be linked as needed to provide reports or other information on demand. Several related files are referred to as a database. Management and use of an organization's data are very important and often very complex.

ADDITIONAL TERMS AND RELATED CONCEPTS

A few additional basic information systems terms and concepts are introduced in this section. Comparisons are made among the terms data, information, and knowledge, followed by a description of the concept of data/information flow.

Data, Information, and Knowledge

The terms data, information, and knowledge are sometimes used interchangeably. But data, as mentioned above, refers to the raw facts that are collected. Data might include such raw facts as customer names, addresses, ages, purchases, and other items of interest. For student files, data might include name, social security number, courses completed, credit hours of each course, and grade for each course. Data continues to accumulate, with some data changed or updated daily.

Information is the term used for the result after data is processed into something meaningful. Information might include a list of the customers who are between the ages of 21 and 30 that a sales representative is interested in contacting about a new product intended for that age group. Information about students could include a report of those students whose grade point averages meet the minimum requirements for a particular honorary organization.

Knowledge is the next step in the logical progression of converting data to something more useful for strategic planning and decision making. Knowledge involves the combination of methods that make it possible to use and perhaps share information after having created, gathered, and stored it. A knowledge-based system includes built-in rules or instructions in the form of procedures that are followed in different situations. For a customer group, the knowledge imparted might be a recommendation of those people who qualify for the highest level of credit, based on varying criteria entered into the system during the process of analysis. For students, the knowledge imparted might be a recommendation of which student should be awarded a prestigious scholarship, based on information provided related to whatever criteria are designated, such as financial need, academic record, extracurricular activities, and college major. Knowledge bases are used most often in businesses when (1) a large set of data must be compared and considered, (2) time is a factor, and (3) the decision is important enough to warrant the expense of the system. And we now have employees who may be referred to as "knowledge workers," a term sometimes used for those people who are involved in the development of knowledge for an organization. These people might be engineers, accountants, etc., i.e., people from a wide variety of fields who are contributing to an organization's knowledge.

Data/Information Flow

Data flow is a term used to describe the overall process involving the flow of data from the time it enters an information system until it leaves the system. As shown in Figure1.4, the main elements are input, processing, and output. A related element is feedback. The term information flow is also used for this process; individual preference of terms appears to depend on whether you want to refer to what you have at the beginning of the process (data) or at the end (information).

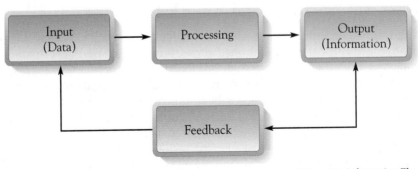

Figure 1.4 Information Flow

Input refers to the process of collecting raw data and entering it into the information system in some manner.

Processing involves converting the data into a meaningful form, such as classifying it, sorting it, performing calculations, creating summaries or reports, and storing the results.

Output refers to providing the information in a form that can be viewed, either on the computer screen (monitor) or in a printed form.

Feedback is considered essential to information flow because it involves reviewing the input, processing, and output activities to determine if changes should be made and then communicating those recommendations. It provides information to management about the performance of the system, so it has a direct effect on future input, processing, and output.

In designing systems, the output desired is identified first. Then the items needed to obtain that desired output are identified. During this process, the data needed is indicated (the input), as well as the processing activities that will be required.

As you can tell, this text begins with a study of some of the major concepts of information systems and their use in organizations, to provide a basis for the remaining topics. We then proceed in a logical fashion from this worldwide view of information systems to more specific uses of information systems (applications). Next we review the technology that is needed for organizations to perform the applications that have been described, followed by a section describing the design and development of information systems to use the technology to perform the applications. The text ends with a discussion of management concerns related to the important information systems resources that organizations have acquired.

Summary

Technological developments in previous centuries served as a basis for today's computers. But the most significant changes to date have occurred in the second half of the twentieth century.

Computers and their underlying technology have had a major impact on our society, in our business as well as personal lives.

Numerous careers and products are now available that were nonexistent before information systems and related technology reached their current capabilities. New careers are also available because of the computer hardware and software industries. Changes have occurred in all types of careers because of technological advancements.

A system is a group of elements working together to achieve a goal. An information system applies the system concept by combining all the components in the system appropriately so that desired information is available when it is needed and in the way it is needed.

The term information system is generally used to refer to the use of information technology in the performance of business and professional activities. Information systems come in all types and sizes, with one orga-

nization often having multiple information systems. The term information technology refers to the computer hardware and software, along with
data, that are used for some desired purpose.

The main components of an information system that must work
together are the people, the procedures, and the information technology
(the hardware, software, and data).

Computers used for business applications are primarily digital computers that use 0s and 1s to represent data and instructions. Analog
computers are more widely used for scientific applications than for business applications.

Categories of hardware in use today include microcomputers (and
workstations), minicomputers, mainframe computers, and supercomputers. It has become difficult to identify clearly the line that separates each
of these categories. Some vendors are now referring to the categories as
small, medium, and large.

Software provides the hardware with step-by-step instructions that
are sometimes referred to as programs. Software includes operating system programs that direct the activities of the hardware and application
programs, such as word processing and spreadsheet programs.

Data refers to raw facts, and information refers to results after the
data has been processed or manipulated into something that is meaningful. Knowledge is an accumulation of information that is ready to be used
and shared.

The flow of data through a system into something meaningful
includes procedures involving input, processing, and output, along
with feedback.

Questions for Review and Discussion

1. Describe major advantages and disadvantages of the increased use
of technology for (a) health care, (b) airline operations, and (c) college
course registration.

2. Identify situations in which a mainframe computer would be more
likely to be used than a microcomputer.

3. Explain the relationship between the terms "information system"
and "information technology."

4. Assuming that a desired college student outcome is a diploma or
degree, describe the input and processing that would probably be
needed for the school to be able to produce the desired outcome. What
subsystems are probably involved?

5. Identify ways in which information technology has had an effect on your life.

Selected References

Haimerl, Duncan. "While Car Computers Are Costly, They Clearly Earn Their Keep." *Minneapolis Star Tribune*, August 6, 1994.

Hamilton, Jon. "High-Tech Clipboard Aids Nurses." *The Commercial Appeal*, November 22, 1992.

Holusha, John. "Robots, Workers Toil in Tandem." *The Commercial Appeal*, September 11, 1994.

Hoversten, Paul. "Supercomputer to Dethrone Deep Blue," *USA Today*, February 13, 1998.

Mears, Jennifer. "Computer Innovator Seymour Cray Dies at 71," *The Commercial Appeal*, October 6, 1996.

Naisbitt, John, and Patricia Aburdene. *Megatrends 2000*. New York: William Morrow and Company, Inc., 1990.

Chapter 1 Key Terms

System
related elements working together to achieve a goal.

Information system
components including information technology, people, and procedures that work together to provide appropriate information in the proper format whenever needed; one business can have multiple information systems.

Information technology
the combination of hardware, software, and data needed by an information system.

Competitive advantage
an organization"s unique qualities that allow it to compete successfully with other organizations offering similar projects or services.

GIGO
acronym for "garbage in, garbage out," meaning that the computer is no more accurate than the data provided to it by humans.

Procedures
the information system component that provides instructions to the people involved in the system.

Hardware
equipment in a computer system, such as the processor and external (peripheral) items such as a keyboard, display screen, and printer.

Digital computer
hardware widely used for business activities and designed to use the digits 0 and 1 to store data and instructions.

Analog computer
hardware designed primarily for scientific uses, such as measurements.

Microcomputer
also called in other ways, e.g., as a desktop computer, or personal computer (PC), laptop, or notebook; designed as a single-user system, although groups of microcomputers can be linked to share resources.

Multimedia
use of special forms of input or output, such as sound and animation.

Workstation
high-end (highest capability) microcomputer, sometimes considered as a separate category of computer.

Minicomputer
multiple-user system designed with fewer capabilities and at lower cost than a mainframe computer.

Mainframe computer
large, high-capability computer designed for multiple users and requiring special personnel to operate and maintain it.

Supercomputer
very high-capability, high-cost computer, used primarily for complex calculations such as those in research projects.

Software
instructions or programs for computer hardware.

Operating system program
instructions for hardware operations or activities.

Application program
instructions for specific purposes or business uses, such as letter writing or mathematical calculations.

Field
an individual category or item of interest in a file.

Record
an individual row in a file containing data about one person, place, or thing based on designated items of interest (fields).

File
a collection of fields and records.

Database
a group of related files.

Data
raw facts that are collected.

Information
result after data is converted into something meaningful.

Knowledge
productive use of information.

Data/information flow
overall process of movement of data through an information system.

Input
process of collecting data and entering it into the information system.

Processing
conversion of data into a meaningful form (information).

Output
results of processing that can be viewed by humans.

Feedback
appropriate communication related to performance of data/information flow process.

Online Activities

Refer to the companion Web site at www.wiley.com/college/simon for a variety of online activities: additional chapter content, *Wall Street Journal Interactive Edition* access, review materials, student assignments, and relevant links.

GO TO   http://www.wiley.com/college/simon

 THE WALL STREET JOURNAL.

Your four-month access to the Interactive Journal allows you to research articles published within the last 30 days in the Interactive Journal, Barron's Online, and Dow Jones Interactive. A Help feature is available if you need assistance in specifying your search topic.

For career and company information, take advantage of careers.wsj.com. Use the Keyword search in Job Seek and search "information technology." Look over the types of positions available in this field. "Who's Hiring" offers links to company websites.

Research each topic in the Interactive Journal and analyze the results of your search.

1.   Careers in information technology. Which careers will probably exist 10 years from now? Which ones did not exist 10 years ago?

2.   Business uses of computer technology. What trends do you see emerging?

3.   Use of computer technology by disabled employees. How do you think technology has affected the employment of persons with disabilities?

CHAPTER 2

Information Systems in Organizations

LEARNING OBJECTIVES

After studying the contents of this chapter, you should be able to

1. Provide descriptions and examples of the common types of information systems.
2. Describe ways in which information technology and information systems are used by different organizational functions and at different management levels.
3. Identify global, ethical, and social concerns that have resulted from development and use of information technology.

COMMON TYPES OF INFORMATION SYSTEMS

Within a business or other organization, information systems are usually classified in specific ways, often according to the type of work performed or the result desired. Information systems generally serve two main purposes in providing a useful product or service:

1. To assist in the actual operations within a business.
2. To supply information for management of the business.

As technology began to be used in operating businesses, systems were developed to make the most efficient use of the technology. Once data could be collected from operations, business people also realized that reports could be created based on that data to assist managers in decision making.

Many types of information systems can be found in businesses. One of the most widely known systems used for actual operations is called a transaction processing system. The system commonly used for creating reports for managers is referred to as an information reporting system. These systems have been in use for many years and are described below, followed by brief descriptions of a few of the many other types of systems that have been developed.

Transaction Processing Systems

Transactions occur throughout our lives, both personally and as part of our business or professional lives. Each time you purchase something, a transaction occurs. If you purchased a pair of shoes today, a transaction would occur. You would decrease your supply of cash and increase your supply of shoes, and the reverse would be true for the business from which you purchased your shoes. If you used a credit card instead of paying cash, you would cause an increase in the amount of money you owe to the credit card company, and the credit card company's records would also change.

Businesses must keep records of each transaction (thus, a transaction processing system). Thousands of transactions occur daily in some businesses, while others may have very few transactions daily, depending on the type and size of the organization. Typical business transactions might include selling an item of merchandise, purchasing office supplies, paying an invoice, purchasing new items of merchandise, or a customer returning merchandise—the possibilities are practically endless. Transactions are not limited to businesses that provide a product; businesses providing services, such as a medical office or a credit card company, also have numerous transactions daily.

A transaction processing system was one of the first types of information systems developed for business applications. As the volume of transactions increased in growing businesses, it was easy for managers to recognize the benefits of using information systems to keep up with the variety of records involved. Transaction processing systems maintain records of such things as sales, purchases, customer records, creditor records, and bank records. One transaction affects multiple aspects of a business, even when it is a small operation.

Instead of being the customer, suppose that you are the owner of a shoe store that employs three sales clerks and a few other personnel. What changes would need to be made in your records when a customer comes in and purchases a pair of shoes by paying cash? Your list of changes to the records might include the following:

▼ an indication that you have reduced the total number of available pairs of shoes for sale, as well as availability of a particular style and shoe size

▼ an indication that you have increased your cash receipts by the amount of the sale

▼ an indication that a particular sales clerk has increased the total sales for the time period, especially if commissions based on sales are paid

▼ an update of the customer's name and address records or confirmation that the stored records are accurate, if individual customer records are maintained

Some retail stores (especially those that are independently owned) may offer in-store credit, by which the store allows customers to charge purchases without needing a credit card, and the store maintains its own records. If this shoe transaction had been charged to a store account, the transaction processing procedures would change somewhat. Instead of an increase in cash, an increase would occur in amounts owed by customers (accounts receivable). An invoice, possibly generated automatically by the system, would be sent to the customer at the appropriate time, often at the end of the month. Additional processing would occur when the customer pays the invoice (another transaction). If the customer does not pay on time and the balance becomes overdue, additional processing may occur, such as the calculation of interest on the unpaid balance and a report of those customers with unpaid bills. This one shoe sale will also affect the end-of-year income tax records of both the business and the person who earned a commission based on the sale.

Let's consider another possibility with the customer's purchase of a pair of shoes—the customer might have used a major credit card that your business accepts. Because credit cards have become so widely used by persons who do not want to carry cash or write checks, many businesses accept credit cards to avoid the risk of losing customers. Businesses have also been able to save money by using credit card systems; for example, they may be able to reduce the number of employees needed because they maintain fewer customer records in-house. They get their money very quickly from the credit card company, usually more quickly than if they maintained their own accounts.

Credit card transactions today can be processed very quickly. When a customer purchases an item using a credit card, the card can be "swiped" through the appropriate equipment and the price entered. The data is transmitted immediately to a system at a company that handles credit card purchases, such as American Express. The submitted transaction is automatically compared with the cardholder's available balance, and a message or code is then sent to the store clerk authorizing or denying the transaction. Some of these systems also send funds automatically to the store's account for transactions that are approved.

Systems of this type are called online (or real-time) transaction processing (OLTP) systems because the store is sending data to the system for processing at the time of the sale, with the credit card sale approved as part of the transaction. If a customer were purchasing an item through a mail-order catalog, the sale would not need to be processed immediately. The mail-order company may choose to use a batch processing system, for which the credit card company typically charges a lower fee than it charges for online access. With a batch processing system, the credit cards can all be checked in one processing run, often at night, with the transactions then completed by the retail company the next day.

Continuing with the example of the retail shoe store, other businesses are involved in supplying these stores with their stock of shoes. Stride Rite, for example, is a shoe manufacturer that had a goal of improving its competitive position by having orders delivered to retailers more quickly. To improve its position, management analyzed procedures and determined that too much time elapsed between the time a transaction began (the order was received) and the time it was completed (the order was shipped). Management had to decide what type of information system would result in the greatest benefit for the cost. The outcome was the development of an information system that receives orders from retailers electronically. The orders go through the internal Stride Rite processing system more quickly, so that the items desired are sent to the retail customer in less time. In addition, the information system produces an invoice that is sent electronically to the retailer as soon as the order is completed.

To summarize the Stride Rite example, information technology was no doubt involved when the strategic decisions were made regarding efforts to improve the company's competitive decision. Then an information system (including interrelated subsystems) for processing transactions was developed based on the need that was identified.

As you have been thinking about the effects of one transaction on a business, you may have realized that a transaction between two businesses affects transaction processing systems of both businesses. While the Stride Rite system is changing its records for a transaction, the retail business has its own transaction processing system that is changing its records as well.

One recent trend in the retailing industry involves retailers forming information systems partnerships with their suppliers. Manufacturers who have information system links to retailers can monitor the retailers' sales data so that they can supply needed products at the right time. The manufacturer provides a needed service to the retailer, and the retailer decreases storage costs by retaining fewer items in inventory. This concept is referred to as just-in-time inventory, because the products arrive just as the organization needs them. The technology has been referred to as electronic data interchange (EDI). EDI and other forms of electronic transactions are described further in Chapter 3, Electronic Commerce and Related Technologies.

Transaction processing systems are an essential part of the operation of a business. With the increasing pressures of competition, businesses continually look for ways to improve these and their other systems.

Information Reporting Systems

Once businesses developed transaction processing systems, they needed to produce reports based on the data that was stored as part of the process. Separate systems had to be developed to create the desired reports. Information reporting systems provide routine reports that are known to be needed by managers and therefore can be specified within the procedures developed as part of the system. These reports can summarize performance based on data accumulated during operations. In a manufacturing operation, for example, the system could obtain results indicating the amount of materials used to produce an item during a period of a day, week, or month, and check to see if the results meet with expectations.

Thus, an information reporting system was the first type of management information system (MIS) that was developed as an outgrowth of the computerization of transaction processing systems. Managers realized that they needed reports of the results of transactions and that their computers could be used to access the data already collected, analyze and summarize it, and provide whatever information was of interest. One type of report that became quite useful is an "exception report," in which a range of acceptable values has been stored that can be compared with actual values from operations or business transactions. The exception report provides an indication of those areas that were outside the acceptable values, pinpointing quickly for the manager the items that might need immediate attention.

The term management information system, or MIS, was used initially to refer to the rather structured (predesigned) reports known to be needed by management. MIS is now used more widely to refer to the overall concept of providing information for managers, not limited to the predesigned reports but also including systems of gathering information that are not entirely structured (either unstructured or semistructured, depending on the portion predesigned). The level of "structure" is usually defined by the amount of human intervention or participation involved. A structured report can be defined ahead of time and specified as part of a system, thus requiring little or no human participation. An example of a structured report without human input would be one that uses sales data to compare the supply of products on hand with the minimum amount desired and indicates a need to reorder, when appropriate. At the other extreme would be a report based on a variety of factors, both internal and external, that might be used to consider the purchase of a new plant facility. The report would not be of a routine nature, and the factors considered would need to be indicated by the persons involved. Of course, the final recommendation would require extensive human participation. Any system that is used by managers or that provides information for managers may be considered a type (or a part) of an MIS.

Other Types of Information Systems

As business people have become more knowledgeable about information systems and as computer software and hardware have increased in capabilities compared with cost, information systems have become widely used for many purposes. Here are two general categories based on types of use:

1. Information systems used for typical activities or applications in a business office.

2. Information systems used for managerial decision-making activities.

Office applications systems provide efficient, computer-based methods of doing typical office activities, such as data collection or letter and report writing, with documents saved for later editing and re-use as appropriate. Software packages are readily available for many other automated office activities.

Decision-support software has been added to offices to assist managers and others in their work when decisions are needed. Many such software packages have been developed, some of which are quite sophisticated. As is true of many of the topics in this chapter, these types of systems are described further in later chapters.

STRATEGIC AND OTHER MANAGERIAL USES OF INFORMATION SYSTEMS

Additional information regarding strategic decisions is available on the Web site.

Information systems of varying types and sizes can be found in business and professional organizations (and in some personal activities, too). A single business organization usually has several information systems; each system can be designed specifically for that operation or function. Some systems are used to meet high-level (strategic) needs; others meet middle-level (tactical) needs and lower-level (operational or supervisory) needs. One way information systems are used is to provide managers at different levels with appropriate information for decision making. Listed below are examples of ways in which information is provided to assist managers at different levels.

Top Management: Strategic decisions, such as new directions to consider; based on external information such as market conditions and competition, as well as internal reports (usually in summary form). Much of the external information can be obtained by accessing data stored on numerous computerized databases that are available worldwide. The uses of information systems in several paragraphs below provide examples of strategic decisions. The term "strategic" can be found often to make it easier for you to notice these examples that are intended to demonstrate the importance of these systems in top-level decision making.

Middle Management: Tactical decisions, such as how to transform top management desires into an appropriate plan of action; based on information from top management and reports of current operations. These reports of current operations may be provided automatically and sent directly to a manager's desktop system.

Lower Management: Operational decisions, such as which employees should change to a new procedure to meet goals of management; based on information provided by middle management and detailed operations reports. These operations reports may be provided automatically by information systems created for that purpose.

Figure 2.1 combines these management levels with the flow of data and instructions. Data usually flows from the operational level to higher levels as needed, while instructions or directives start at the top and flow downward.

Additional information on management decision-making activities is available on the Web site.

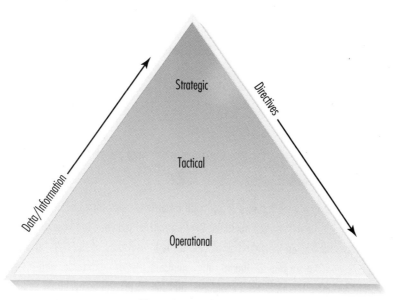

Figure 2.1 Levels of Management vs. Data/Information Flow

The decisions at different management levels may involve structured, semistructured, or unstructured information systems. In situations where the data is available from processing activities, the decisions typically are more structured. At the strategic level, for example, the decisions might be related to financial decisions based on reports that are readily available. At the tactical or middle-management level, reports might be used for a review of the budget. And at the operational level, reports might indicate which raw materials need to be ordered.

On the other end of the scale are the unstructured decisions, which do not occur on a regular basis so are not likely to have reports designed for those situations. Activities that are considered unstructured in some businesses may be considered semistructured in others, depending on the level of data available. Strategic decisions that are unstructured could be wide ranging, such as environmental or social responsibilities described later in this chapter. At the tactical level, an example of an unstructured decision might be an effort to hire new employees, since that may not be a regular activity that can be developed into an information system. At the operational level, an unstructured decision might be related to the selection of new software. Such a decision would be dependent on current needs and current software capabilities and might not have an information system available designed for this activity, since it does not occur daily and may be different each time it occurs.

Decisions related to all aspects of information systems are being made by managers today, which requires these people to have a greater knowledge of various information systems components than has been true in the past. Each remaining chapter in this text contains a "Management Perspective" to provide an introduction to some of the types of decisions that managers can expect to face. Also, the online activities for each chapter contain business cases that provide additional decision-making examples.

Management Perspective

Sometimes a workstation is linked with lower-level microcomputers to form a network in which the workstation maintains the large sets of data and can be accessed by the microcomputers as an individual employee needs to use some of the data. In addition, multiple workstations may be linked with a minicomputer or mainframe, with the workstation becoming the lower-level equipment that can be used to access larger equipment as needed. Management decisions must be made to determine accurately the level of capabilities needed before large numbers of computers are purchased. A trend has developed in some businesses toward using multiple smaller computers in a network, where possible, rather than one large computer; managers must weigh the information system needs of the organization against other concerns, such as cost and security issues, before making a decision. Consideration also should be given to the difficulties encountered in managing multiple computers in a network arrangement.

STRATEGIC DECISIONS RELATED TO INFORMATION SYSTEMS

Information systems are used to assist executives in making strategic decisions and may also be the focus of the decisions, e.g., when major investments in information technology or in an entirely new system are being considered. Information systems decisions must be in line with or supportive of the organization's strategy. Strategies should be developed for information technology and related information systems that fit with the strategies of the overall organization.

Information technology can be (and often is) a critical component in supply chain activities (described further in another section of this chapter). Much of the success of these systems is dependent on information systems strategies that can continue to change or adjust to meet the organization's needs. These strategies should be designed to provide up-to-date and appropriate information as needed in the organization while also handling the on-time development and deployment of new systems.

The information systems strategy should be expected to include plans for continually improving business operations as well as services to employees and to customers or clients. These improvements should add value to the organization, such as better service at a lower cost than if this system were not used. In other words, information systems strategies are important for operational activities, and investments in these operational activities and the use of information technology are important strategic decisions for an organization.

FUNCTIONAL USES OF INFORMATION SYSTEMS

Within different areas or functions of an organization, individual information systems are developed to assist in performing business operations and to assist in decision making. Several of the typical functional areas of a business that have their own information systems and subsystems are described below. These functions and others are likely to be found in all types of organizations, regardless of the specific purpose of the organization. In addition, cross-functional relationships must exist. Decisions often must be made based on information from several functional areas, and success or failure in one area also directly affects another area. The human resources needs of an organization, for example, are affected by the organization's success in marketing a product or service; marketing efforts are affected by the efficiency of the production/operations function; and all these functions affect the organization's finances.

Human Resources Information System

Human resource management is an organizational function that handles recruitment of employees and placement within the organization, followed by activities during their employment such as salary decisions, work evaluations, and training and development. Human resources information systems provide support for this management function. Records about employees include such items as personal data, pay records, insurance records, and accumulated vacation and sick leave time. Employee records can be compared with records of job requirements to determine which employees have the appropriate skills for a job, or which of them would benefit from a particular type of training. The management decisions made based on these information systems are often at the operational or tactical level. Strategic decisions may also occur, for example, if consideration were being given to expanding to a new location, including a review of personnel availability compared with needs.

Human resources information systems are found in all types of industries, whether the primary function involves a product or a service—or both. As an example, think about the human resources information systems likely to be found in hospitals. Included in this area would be all the people who work in hospitals—doctors, nurses, managers, secretaries, pharmacists, researchers, trainers, food preparers, and many others. Decisions must be made as to the number of workers of each type that will be needed, along with where and when each person will work. Salaries must be determined and numerous records must be kept, including job skills, pay rates, benefits programs, vacation days allotted versus days used—the list could be quite extensive. Decisions are based on the analyses provided through information systems. Hospitals must justify all the staff positions and salaries compared with the use of their services (costs versus benefits).

Human resources information systems are available that can assist with many aspects of this functional area. Some systems include online analytical processing (OLAP) tools, such as those that can track overall human resource costs at all times. OLAP tools allow analysis of large sets of data in a real-time (online) environment to provide up-to-date information.

Accounting/Financial Information System

Accounting/financial information systems provide an organization with data that identifies amounts of money earned and spent, along with tax information. Accounting systems maintain records of all types of transactions that occur in the business, as well as results of those transactions. For example, the data stored can be used to indicate how much money is owed to the organization by its customers (accounts receivable) and how much the organization owes to others (accounts payable). Various reports may be created that can be used at all levels of management, such as payroll records by department, costs of a manufacturing process, and reports of the organization's financial status. Financial systems are generally concerned with activities such as managing the organization's cash and investments, as well as budgeting considerations and financial planning. Managers at all levels use this information to develop budgets. This information would also be reviewed by top management before strategic decisions are made that might affect the financial stability of the organization. For example, when a major purchase or new procedure is being contemplated, information can be provided to help determine the effect of the change on income and expenses of the organization and its ability to pay its bills and make a reasonable profit over the next five years.

Let's continue our discussion of hospital information systems. Hospitals must have very accurate and detailed accounting and financial information systems. In addition to handling the payroll of all the employees, hospitals must maintain extensive records related to charges for each patient as well as payments received. As with other organizations, they must pay for a variety of products and services they receive from outside sources. Their information systems give them a means of analyzing their financial records and determining areas where changes should be made.

Marketing/Sales Information System

Marketing/sales information systems can be used for many purposes related to efforts to sell an organization's products and services. For example, it is often desirable to study appropriate methods of advertising, analyze potential products, manage sales orders, and maintain a customer database to track buying trends. Marketing and sales information systems are widely used at the operational and tactical levels as a part of the effort to meet needs of current customers and to attract new customers. Summary data is reviewed at the strategic level when long-term decisions are being considered, such as a major change in the marketing approach. Hospitals, as an example, must remain competitive to stay in business and must convince patients to come to their facilities rather than to others (in those situations where patients have the opportunity to make a choice). For example, many hospitals have increased their newspaper and television advertising. This advertising strategy is not developed haphazardly. A great deal of study of information systems reports forms the basis for this decision. Follow-up analyses are often performed to study the success of a particular marketing campaign.

Information technology, primarily computers and electronic communications capabilities, is being used widely for "sales force automation." Strategic decisions have been made in many organizations to invest extensively in this technology so that salespeople could provide better service to their customers by having access to online data at all times. This strategy has provided some organizations with a competitive advantage when this immediate access was valuable enough to customers to result in an improvement in the organization's market position.

Production/Operations Information System

The term production generally refers to the creation of goods (products), services, or both. Every business organization creates something of value to someone else; otherwise, the business will have a very short life. This item of value may be something physical that is created, such as manufacturing an automobile; or it may be a service, such as performing automobile repairs. The various activities that occur in organizations to provide their products or services are called operations. Automobile manufacturing company operations could include design activities, parts manufacturing, and assembly-line activities, as well as many others.

Production/operations information systems attempt to assist an organization in determining the best methods of performing its primary activities. Many reports can be produced that assist at the operational and tactical levels of management, such as those that indicate quantity and quality of work completed. Strategic decisions, such as a change to a new product or service, would be based partially on internal production/operations information systems data, although external factors, such as trends or competition, are sometimes even more important factors.

A major concern of production/operations information systems in hospitals involves patient care. One decision many hospitals are making is related to improving the nursing services for their patients, such as through the use of handheld computers. The benefits of these systems must be compared with the very large costs involved. In traditional systems, nurses make notes about each patient (blood pressure, body temperature, etc.) and manually transfer these notes to a chart sometime later—sometimes several hours later. Some new systems involve the use of touch screens on handheld computers. Data about the patient can be entered into the system immediately. In addition, the nurse or physician can retrieve information from the system about the patient at any time. The nurse's time has been saved in entering new data, and patients' records are more likely to be up-to-date when treatment and other decisions are being made. Some of these systems allow physicians to access the patients' records from locations away from the hospital. Individual systems are linked so that data about a patient can be accessed for other purposes, such as meal planning, insurance records, billing, and room assignments. Hospitals have many information systems working at the same time, and management at all levels must continually monitor these systems and make strategic decisions that will retain or improve their competitive position.

Some information systems may seem pretty ordinary—just keeping records. But the real power of an information system lies in its ability to link different sets of data for a variety of purposes, so that the organization can obtain whatever information it needs to make decisions at the time needed. These decisions could involve changing to a different product, adding new employees in an area where a need is forecast to occur, changing the price of a product, or thousands of other potential decisions that are strategic to the company's success. The use of information systems has enabled businesses to make changes more quickly. Customers are attracted to firms that can provide a high-quality product or service and can provide it quickly. As competition intensifies, companies continue to look for ways to improve their operations, and information systems are updated and altered to refine the process.

Cross-Functional Relationships

Many cross-functional relationships are part of the total information systems strategic design today, especially with the capabilities we have for linking computers of different types and in different locations to share data.

The supply chain has to do with the sequence of processes and business partners that deliver products and services to a customer. Many organizations today have agreements to operate as working partners with their customers and suppliers, and information systems are developed to provide all parties with accurate and timely information for use in making decisions. Related to the supply chain is the demand chain, which refers to the process of creating, planning, and committing to customer demands for products and services. The supply chain and demand chain together become the value chain, which represents the set of value-adding activities for an organization, progressing from the initial generation of a demand through the fulfillment of that demand. In making decisions about the use of information systems, the value chain may be reviewed to determine the points at which the addition of information systems could provide the greatest benefit or competitive advantage.

Information systems are critical to the processes of developing and managing various stages and activities that occur. Different areas (and multiple businesses) are often involved, such as sales and marketing, engineering, manufacturing, finance, and others. Order fulfillment is a key part of the chain, using information systems that integrate inventory management, demand forecasting, delivery, and billing. These systems must be designed to have materials on hand at the appropriate time and all aspects of the process planned and coordinated to provide good service, which then retains customers and improves profitability.

In the area of patient care, for example, the supply chain can involve a variety of service activities, including health-care claims that should flow in, be processed, and flow out without delay. Patients should be able to go through various stages of the chain without having to answer the same questions each time they get to a different stage. The key to success in these systems is development of appropriate information systems.

Software has now been developed that supports the processes involved in the supply chain and generally helps to organize the overall business activities of an organization. This software is widely referred to as enterprise resource planning (ERP) software. Vendors of this type of software include SAP, PeopleSoft, and Oracle. Instead of separate software for individual functions, this software is designed to manage processes across the functions for the entire organization (the enterprise), such as sales, production/operations, human resources, and finance. Software of this type provides more coordination and the capability of sharing data among various functions. However, it is typically very expensive to install to fit the organization's specific needs, as well as to maintain. Top-level, strategic decisions are involved in making a change to this type of system.

An article in *Fortune* indicated that over half of the Fortune 500 companies now have ERP systems. The article also identified problems encountered that included systems that were difficult to implement or to maintain. A possible future direction suggested for businesses is to consider the use of an application service provider (ASP), which is an organization that could provide ERP systems for customers over the Internet. Additional developments related to ERP are expected to emerge.

New Concerns Because Of Information Technology

In addition to the typical concerns about operating a business, the use of information technology and related systems has caused new issues to arise. Concerns related to global, ethical, and social issues are described below.

Global Concerns

You may have heard references to a global village, a concept suggesting that our technological advancements are making it easier for us to communicate with people in other countries worldwide as if they were nearby—as if everyone were in one village. Physical distance is no longer a significant detriment to conducting business, because technological advancements continue to move us toward systems in which we can communicate and conduct business regardless of location. Organizations have determined that they have to treat the world as their workplace, and this has become a primary part of their strategy. They have to expect that work and trade will be occurring around the world around the clock; they must plan and make strategic decisions accordingly.

Types of Organizations

Some confusion exists about the terms used to refer to types of organizations involved in today's global society. Many organizations that refer to themselves as having global operations might not be considered global by other organizations, depending on how strictly the term is defined. Although there are variations in the terminology used, one set of rather general definitions is provided here. Keep in mind that some people do not distinguish between different levels of global operations and simply refer to every operation that is not domestic as global. The other terms listed should help you, though, to recognize that distinctions are sometimes made in regard to the level of nondomestic business—regardless of the label attached to it.

A domestic organization produces and sells its products and services only in its own country.

An international organization has a headquarters office in its home country, along with foreign subsidiaries that are dependent on the headquarters in the home country for major decisions, such as new products and new technology.

A multinational organization has one or more foreign affiliates or production facilities. The organization typically operates as a self-contained unit in each country, often having separate managers in each country.

A global organization operates as one worldwide organization rather than as a group of independent geographic entities or as a primarily domestic operation with foreign subsidiaries. A global organization may have either one central headquarters or multiple headquarters. The actual location of the "home office" does not affect the business decisions, which are implemented consistently worldwide. A global organization looks for what it needs—such as the highest-quality product at the lowest cost or the best combination of facilities, materials, technology, and people—without regard to physical location. An organization with a global vision thinks in terms of a borderless world.

Some people add another designation, transnational organization, to refer to a firm that combines interdependent global needs with local needs, along with appropriate technological capabilities. The goal is to combine the economies of scale of a large organization with the advantages of flexibility and market knowledge of a local country. Regardless of the definitions of the terms, businesses are still trying to determine what arrangement works best for them.

Need for Global Awareness

As we move toward a global marketplace, we are also moving toward a worldwide information network. Through this network we can communicate with anyone at any location at any time, in a variety of ways and in different languages—including voice, data, text, and images. Businesses today must be knowledgeable about telecommunications and related information systems applications, and they must use these capabilities appropriately to compete in the global marketplace. Competition is expected to increase in every aspect of business operations, including production and sales of goods and services. Businesses will have more options regarding the locations of their facilities and the locations of materials they purchase, as well as the locations of their employees. Companies that take advantage of the power of information technology worldwide will have a competitive advantage, and other businesses will have to try to catch up.

Global Strategies

Businesses must have a strategic global plan to ensure that they are developing and maintaining the technological knowledge and skills needed for global competition. Businesses must be able to provide products and services that are not only priced competitively in the world market but also are of world-class quality. Products and services must be able to be measured against a world standard.

Businesses also need to emphasize the value of their own employees in competing successfully in a global marketplace. The key employees of the organization must have a global mindset, meaning that they need to be able to see the "big picture" rather than looking at everything from one limited viewpoint. Stephen H. Rhinesmith, author of *A Manager's Guide to Globalization,* suggested several procedures that can help employees to develop this global mindset:

▼ Study the importance of teamwork and how to be successful at interpersonal relations.

▼ Think about cultural differences and why and how people in different cultural backgrounds think and act the way they do.

▼ Read about world events from viewpoints other than your own; for example, read *The Economist* or *The Financial Times* to obtain a European perspective.

Businesses must conduct extensive research before pursuing global activities. Many newspapers and journals publish information related to global operations. Another source of assistance for businesses interested in becoming more knowledgeable about the global marketplace is the U.S. and Foreign Commercial Service of the U.S. Department of Commerce. They have an electronic database that is continually being updated and that contains information on a wide variety of topics, such as tariff rates, potential opportunities for foreign sales, and market research reports for specific industries in particular countries. Some of this information is available to the public through subscription.

Because of the increasing importance of global business operations, each remaining chapter of this text contains a "Global Perspective" to provide some examples of global concerns prevalent in businesses today.

Global Perspective

Competition among business organizations has become more complicated with the trend toward a global society and freer communication. Companies must decide on the best locations for manufacturing and other facilities as well as systems for communicating worldwide with suppliers, employees, and customers. One advantage of the use of information technology is that it has become easier to keep up with what other organizations are doing. But companies may experience many legal and technological problems when trying to build communication networks in other countries. For example, standards used for uniformity of equipment in one country may conflict with standards in another country, and there is wide variety in governmental regulations and guidelines related to data security.

Organizations must consider many more options today before deciding to compete globally. They may have to develop systems that vary depending on the location. Coca-Cola™ became involved with financial investments in bottling plants in locations such as China, Germany, Norway, and Russia. By taking a more active role in bottling plant systems instead of using independent bottlers, Coca-Cola had more influence in controlling product quality and in managing the operations, which led to significant increases in revenue.

Ethical Issues

Ethical issues are very important to businesses, and the use of information systems has caused new issues to arise. Ethics is generally defined as having to do with right and wrong behavior, and it is not limited to topics governed by laws. Business ethics is concerned with professional standards of conduct—behavior related to work in various business professions. Not everyone agrees on what constitutes ethical conduct, but businesses are interested in using methods of developing and maintaining a successful organization while also being fair, just, and trustworthy. Ethical behavior in business includes personal integrity, honesty, fairness, and respect for the rights of others. Many businesses try to screen potential employees based on these characteristics, but it is very difficult to identify a person who might become an unethical employee. In addition, it is much more difficult to train people in ethical behavior than to train them to perform job tasks. Problems with ethical behavior are also related to our increasingly global operations. Procedures that are considered unethical in one country might be considered ethical or even mandatory in another country.

Even though ethical behavior is difficult to define, a trend has developed toward more inclusion of these topics in educational preparation for jobs. A recent research project studied the relationship between academic dishonesty and employee dishonesty. Results indicated that people in the study who engaged in activities in college that were considered to be severely dishonest were more likely to engage in activities at work that were considered severely dishonest. Correspondingly, respondents who participated in little or no dishonest behavior in their college careers were likely to engage in little or no dishonest behavior at work, indicating that a relationship exists between academic dishonesty and unethical business practices. One recommendation from the research was that universities assist their students by strongly enforcing behavioral guidelines and insisting that students take responsibility for their own behaviors and moral obligations.

Another study involving surveys of more than 3,000 high school students and 3,000 college students found that 31 percent of each group indicated they would be willing to lie on a résumé, on a job application, or during a job interview to get what they wanted. The study also found that only 39 percent of high school students and 68 percent of college students indicated that they had never cheated on an exam or quiz. Other studies have shown that very high percentages, up to 91 percent, of college students admitted to some form of academic dishonesty.

A survey reported in *USA Today* indicated that about one-third of undergraduate students at four-year colleges who have their own computers also have unlicensed copies of software. However, over half indicated that they do not think it is appropriate to have this "pirated" software.

Businesses sometimes provide written policies for their employees indicating that unethical behavior will be treated as justification for dismissal. Organizations may have Codes of Ethics for their employees; however, such codes often are fairly general and may not provide specific guidelines for some situations, such as proper uses of information technology. Another problem is that there is a wide range of ethical abuses, from the very serious, such as sabotage of the company's data, to a simple prank that causes a momentary disturbance on a few desktop computers.

Numerous ethical issues have developed in recent years that are specifically concerned with the use of information technology. A few of the major issues are described in this section; new issues continue to arise.

Privacy

Privacy includes keeping confidential information confidential. For example, credit reports and school records cannot be released to others without the person's consent. Social security numbers and credit card numbers could be used in unintended ways if not protected. Employees must be aware of regulations and must be trained in proper procedures to ensure confidentiality. The privacy of electronic mail messages has become an issue in recent years. Electronic mail concerns are described extensively in Chapter 3.

Security

Security issues involve several topics, including data, hardware (e.g., computers and printers), and software (e.g., programs developed or packages purchased). Security of data is somewhat related to privacy to the extent that increased protection of data reduces the likelihood of private information becoming public. But much of a company's data security is concerned with controlling who has access to the data and who has the authority to make changes. The "need-to-know" concept is often used so that only those people who have a specific need have access to certain data, and some of those people may have a "read-only" access so that they cannot alter the data. Security of hardware, of course, involves making sure that all equipment remains in the desired locations in an undamaged condition. Security of software is a special concern of businesses, because the business is responsible for ensuring that employees do not make unauthorized copies of copyrighted software. Internet access worldwide has caused additional security issues to arise. Additional discussion of security concerns can be found in Chapter 11.

Accuracy

Accuracy of data is related to security in the sense that businesses must prevent unauthorized people from accessing and changing data inappropriately. But inaccuracies can occur in other ways, such as when authorized people make errors in entering data or do not follow appropriate procedures when manipulating data. Businesses must develop systems that include safeguards for checking the accuracy of data, and employees must be trained properly. Some accountability for accurate work is helpful in encouraging employees to follow appropriate procedures. The chances of inaccurate data are great enough that many people regularly check the credit records that have been gathered about themselves to be sure all data stored is up-to-date and correct.

Ownership

Questions sometimes arise in a business as to the ownership of data, especially when employees quit their jobs with their current employers and want to take their work or specific knowledge to the next job. For example, a programmer who has developed an extensive applications program could be hired by another company to develop a similar system. The company that paid the salary of the programmer usually feels they own the work, while the person who performed the work may claim ownership of the knowledge. Clearly stated organizational policies can alleviate some of these potential problems. Some businesses require their employees to sign documents at least once a year that clarify any questions about ownership of their work. These documents may include a stipulation that a departing employee may not take a job with a competitor for some period of time, such as two years, or may not develop similar programs for some specified length of time.

This topic in general is referred to as intellectual property. Computer programs represent a relatively new type of intellectual property. In addition to the problems of employees going to work for other companies and possibly taking their work with them (or at least their knowledge), businesses have problems with legal protection for their programs worldwide. Development of programs is a very expensive endeavor, and businesses are attempting to reduce potential losses through copyrights and patents. However, the effectiveness of current options is questionable, especially in dealing with other countries.

Other Issues

Many other ethical issues exist. Interestingly, information technology can be involved as either the target of some activity or as the method of performing some unethical activity. For example, people could attempt to change or delete data stored about themselves, or they could perform unauthorized searches within sets of data to obtain confidential information about other people.

Social Issues

Social issues related to information technology are topics related to maintaining or improving the quality of human life. Information technology can be of assistance in studying potential solutions for a wide array of topics, such as working conditions, education, environmental protection, health care, and public transportation systems.

In the process of being used to solve other social issues, information technology has caused new social issues. For example, working conditions of data entry operators have become an issue because these workers are subject to headaches, backaches, and other discomforts. Questions have arisen about health risks from sitting in front of a computer for long periods. Another social issue related to information systems has to do with considering the impact of decisions. If a decision is made to change the procedures for performing a task so that an information system can be used, what will be the effect on the employees who were previously doing the work? Will the improvements made by a particular decision justify any hardships or discomforts that are also caused by the decision?

Many social issues, as well as ethical issues, are related to global concerns because so much of what we do has an effect worldwide, whether we realize it or not. Pollution and waste are two simple examples of social practices that have an impact on the rest of the world. Also, privacy and security procedures used in the United States are not widely accepted in some other parts of the world.

Ethical and social issues continue to be a major concern in businesses today, as described above. Each remaining chapter in this text contains an "Ethical Perspective" or "Social Perspective."

Ethical Perspective

Hospitals have many transaction processing and information reporting systems. They maintain files containing considerable personal data about their patients, such as family history, insurance records, medical history, treatments, medications, and diagnoses of current ailments. Because many of these patient file systems have become computerized in recent years, security for the files is an additional information systems concern. In the past, there have been cases of clerical employees who were bribed by the media or by insurance investigators to look at records of certain patients. With a computerized system containing enough passwords and checking mechanisms, it might be possible to do a better job of maintaining the privacy of this data than has been true with paper file systems of the past. The downside is that break-ins to a computerized system could result in a much broader breach of security than ever before.

Summary

Two widely used general types of information systems are transaction processing systems and information reporting systems. An information reporting system was the first type of management information system. Information systems are now relied upon for many strategic decisions.

Information systems are used at all levels of management—top (strategic), middle (tactical), and lower (operational)—to help organizations provide a better product or service than that of similar organizations, thus gaining a competitive advantage.

Management decisions may involve structured, semistructured, or unstructured information systems.

Information systems are developed for various functional areas within organizations. Many cross-functional relationships also exist.

New ethical and social issues have arisen because of the use of information technology in our business and personal lives, including concerns about confidentiality of data and working conditions. New global issues have also surfaced, primarily because of the capabilities of transmitting data and messages worldwide.

Questions for Review and Discussion

1. Describe a transaction processing system that might be used by a college bookstore selling texts and school supplies to students.

2. If you were the manager of a college bookstore, what types of reports would you need for making decisions regarding expanding some sections of the bookstore while reducing other sections?

3. If you were the manager of a college bookstore, what would be an example of a possible (a) strategic decision, (b) tactical decision, and (c) operational decision?

4. Could EDI be used in a bookstore operation? Discuss reasons for your answer.

5. What global, ethical, and social issues might arise in managing a college bookstore? Provide one example for each type of issue.

Selected References

Campbell, Laurel. "Computer Links Create 'Seamless' Patient Data," *The Commercial Appeal*, April 26, 1998.

Chizzo, Scott A. "Supply Chain Strategies: Solutions for the Customer-Driven Enterprise," *Supplement to Software Magazine*, January 1998.

Frye, Colleen. "The Supply Chain's Missing Link," *Software Magazine*, October 1997.

Gillin, Paul. "Shoe Retailer Makes Strides with EDI." *Computerworld*, June 1, 1992.

Gurley, J. William. "The New Market for 'Rentalware," *Fortune*, May 10, 1999.

Hold, Stannie, and Lynda Radosevich. "PeopleSoft Finally Gets International Feel," *InfoWorld*, April 6, 1998.

Jones, Del. "Companies Grapple with Limiting Employee Abuse," *USA Today*, April 27, 1998.

Maney, Kevin. "Technology is 'Demolishing' Time, Distance," *USA Today*, April 24, 1997.

Marklein, Mary Beth, "High-Tech Way to an Easy 'A'," *USA Today*, May 19, 1993.

Rhinesmith, Stephen H. *A Manager's Guide to Globalization.* Homewood, IL: Richard D. Irwin, Inc., 1993.

Sims, Randi L. "The Relationship Between Academic Dishonesty and Unethical Business Practices." *Journal of Education for Business,* March/April 1993.

"Supply Chain Prep," *Software Magazine,* May 1998.

USA Today, (USA Snapshots graphic), April 6, 1998.

Chapter 2 Terms

Transaction
any business activity, such as a purchase of office supplies or the sale of a product to a customer.

Transaction processing system
a system that keeps records of all aspects of an organization's primary business operations.

Information reporting system
form of management information system in which predesigned reports are prepared regularly about business operations, primarily for planning and control purposes.

Online (real-time) transaction processing system (OLTP)
processing of data occurs immediately upon entry into the system.

Batch processing system
processing of a group (batch) of data at one time rather than as each item is entered into the system.

Just-in-time (JIT) inventory
system of monitoring inventory levels so that products or materials arrive as they are needed.

Electronic data interchange (EDI)
technology used for just-in-time inventory monitoring.

Management information system (MIS)
general reference to a system that provides some type of business information to managers for use in making decisions.

Structured report
a type of report that contains standard business information and can be designed in advance.

Unstructured report
a type of report that is not routine in nature and therefore cannot be designed in advance.

Semistructured report
a type of report in which only a part of the needed information can be predicted and designed in advance.

Strategic decisions
upper-management decisions that involve long-range planning and consideration of external as well as internal factors.

Tactical decisions
middle-management decisions that involve conversion of top management's long-range desires into near-term (such as monthly) action plans to be provided to operational management.

Operational decisions
lower-management decisions related to day-to-day operations.

Human resources information system
an organization's employee information, including personal data and job records.

Online analytical processing tools (OLAP)
systems designed to analyze specified online or "real-time" data.

Accounting/financial information system
ways in which money is received and spent by an organization.

Marketing/sales information system
an organization's methods and results related to selling its products and services.

Production/operations information system
an organization's main business activities, such as the types of products or services created during a specific time.

Cross-functional relationship
system that links data from multiple business functions to provide better information.

Supply chain
sequence of activities and groups involved in the overall process of delivering products and services to a customer.

Enterprise resource planning (ERP)
software that helps to manage and coordinate the cross-functional operations of a business.

Demand chain
process of responding to customer demands for products and services.

Value chain
the overall value-adding activities from the demand chain through the supply chain (handling all aspects of supply of and demand for a product or service).

Global village
a reference to the ease with which people in one country can communicate with people in other countries worldwide, as if they all resided in the same village.

Domestic organization
business activities occur only within the organization's home country.

International organization
business organizational design in which major decisions are made in the home country, although some operations occur in other countries.

Multinational organization
business organizational design in which operations occur in more than one country, with separate, independent management in each country.

Global organization
business organizational design in which the whole world is considered equally when decisions are made, without preferential regard to the location of the home office.

Transnational organization
business organizational design in which global needs are combined with local needs to take advantage of some aspects of global as well as local operations.

Ethics
appropriate behavior, such as professional standards of conduct in business professions.

Social issues
concerns about the quality of human life.

Online Activities

Refer to the companion Web site at www.wiley.com/college/simon for a variety of online activities: additional chapter content, *Wall Street Journal Interactive Edition* access, review materials, student assignments, and relevant links.

GO TO http://www.wiley.com/college/simon

THE WALL STREET JOURNAL.

Your four-month access to the Interactive Journal allows you to research articles published within the last 30 days in the Interactive Journal, Barron's Online, and Dow Jones Interactive. A Help feature is available if you need assistance in specifying your search topic.

For information on human resources, take advantage of the "HR Issues" link in careers.wsj.com. Management issues are often topics in "Today's Features."

Research each topic in the Interactive Journal and analyze the results of your search.

1. Ethical or social issues as discussed in this chapter. What decisions or policies have businesses faced that are related to these issues?

2. Supply chain or value chain management. How has technology been used to enhance these activities?

3. Human resource management systems and/or transaction processing systems. How important is information technology to these systems?

Introduction to
Information Systems

Part II

ELECTRONIC COMMERCE AND RELATED TECHNOLOGIES

Part II describes ways in which electronic commerce has become an important facet of business information systems. First the ways in which electronic communications and business transactions occur are discussed. Then the technology that makes electronic commerce possible is described.

Chapter 3   Electronic Commerce and Internet Technologies

Chapter 4   Data Communications and Networking Considerations

CHAPTER 3

Electronic Commerce and Internet Technologies

LEARNING OBJECTIVES

After studying the contents of this chapter, you should be able to

1. Indicate general ways in which electronic communications are used for business activities.
2. Describe sources and features of communications software.
3. Identify benefits and concerns related to electronic commerce.
4. Discuss advantages and disadvantages to businesses of using specific electronic capabilities available through use of the Internet.
5. Discuss business uses of intranets and extranets.

OVERVIEW

The technology for communicating electronically has expanded rapidly in recent years, with a corresponding increase in uses of electronic communications for business activities. Businesses can use their computer systems to communicate directly with suppliers and customers worldwide, in addition to communicating internally from one desktop computer to another. Both internally and externally, data can be exchanged, messages can be sent, research can be conducted—the list of business uses of electronic communications continues to grow.

Electronic commerce (also referred to as "e-commerce" or "e-business") generally refers to commercial transactions taking place in electronic form. This terminology became widely used with the emergence of the

Internet as a business tool. However, electronic commerce has actually been in use by businesses for decades, using technology such as electronic data interchange. These technologies are the focus of this chapter, preceded by a brief description of software required for basic electronic communications.

Basic Communications Software Requirements and Features

In addition to special hardware (described in Chapter 4), computers that are to communicate with each other must have appropriate communications software. Communications software manages the transmission of data between computers by providing instructions to the hardware so that it can perform its communications operations appropriately.

Many businesses want to be able to send and receive data or messages from one computer to any or all of the other computers in the organization. Sometimes the situation requires communications across short distances, such as between computers in one building; other situations require communications around the globe. All the computers involved must have the appropriate communications software (and hardware) before messages and data can be sent and received successfully.

Most communications software packages are easy to set up and use, because they contain menus or prompts. Many communications packages have facilities for automatically dialing any numbers that are used frequently. Also available is an option that redials after a short length of time if the number was busy.

In addition to transferring data files, communications software is used widely for sending messages to other computer users (electronic mail). Computers can be set up so that receivers of messages are notified that they have messages as soon as they log on to their computers each day. The receivers can either print the messages or simply view them on the screen. Messages can be saved, deleted, or sent to someone else. Additional capabilities of communications software packages may include

▼ Error checking features, to ensure that data is transmitted correctly.

▼ Security, such as data encryption (coding) and passwords that must be correct before the system can be accessed.

▼ Controls, such as managing the activity so that two devices do not attempt to use the same communications line at the same time or checking to be sure that copyrighted software programs are not downloaded where they might be illegally copied or altered.

Sources of Communications Software

Some operating systems include communications software within the system. With early operating systems for PCs, such as MS-DOS, software for communicating with other equipment had to be purchased separately. These and other operating systems are described further in Chapter 6. Numerous software packages were (and still are) available to provide communications capabilities. And many new microcomputers now come equipped with all the hardware and software you need for communicating electronically. If you need to purchase a modem, which is the hardware often used to send computer data over telephone lines, a communications package is frequently included as part of the purchase. Cable modems are also a hardware option and are available from cable television providers.

ELECTRONIC DATA INTERCHANGE

Electronic data interchange (EDI) is a term that refers to the process used by many businesses for sending transaction data over communication lines (electronically sending data back and forth). This transaction data is sent over secure, direct links between the organizations. The banking industry is one of many extensive users of the capabilities of electronic transfer of data. Credit card transactions and automatic teller machine (ATM) transactions are two examples of the use of electronic communications for financial activities. Some retailing businesses are connected electronically with their suppliers so data about inventories can be monitored, orders placed, and invoices sent electronically. The retailers do not have to wait for paper forms to be processed, and suppliers are paid more quickly for their products. Ordering, billing, and paying for parts and other supplies take place over private electronic networks. EDI capabilities have been used widely to improve the efficiency of an organization's supply chain.

The Federal National Mortgage Association (Fannie Mae) developed software programs to help mortgage lenders transfer data electronically, thus reducing the time and expense involved. Previously, home loan application data had been entered on paper, sometimes as many as eighteen times. With this software, however, required data can be entered one time, with EDI used to transmit files electronically.

Electronic data interchange has been used for many years by businesses and continues to be used, although Internet-based electronic commerce activities have had phenomenal growth in recent years.

INTRODUCTION TO THE INTERNET

Internet usage by businesses is one of the biggest communication changes in recent years. As its name suggests, the Internet is an international network of networks. One of the earliest developments leading to today's Internet was ARPANet (Advanced Research Projects Agency Network). ARPANet was developed by the U.S. government in 1969 for people doing research for the Defense Department, including contractors, the military, and some universities. In 1986, NSFNet (National Science Foundation Network) was created, linking supercomputer centers across the United States and eventually expanding to universities and research consortiums around the country. At the same time, networks in other countries (including European countries, Australia, Japan, Korea, New Zealand, and Hong Kong) began expanding and connecting to each other as well as to NSFNet. The result is the Internet we have today, which has connections on all continents and in many countries.

Although the Internet has the potential to be a worldwide network of networks, many parts of the world do not have the level of technology needed to participate. The economy of a country is usually a major factor, as businesses need to be operating successfully and identify a need for the Internet capability before an interest develops in obtaining the technology. In many countries, you would not find computers, modems, an Internet connection, or even a telephone line in individual homes.

Global Perspective

The Global Schoolhouse Project (GSH) was developed to connect kindergarten through grade 12 classrooms from around the world by using the Internet. In addition to schools in several U.S. cities, other school participants are located in countries such as Australia, Canada, England, France, Finland, Germany, and New Zealand. The project is sponsored by the National Science Foundation, with support from several corporations, universities, and other organizations. The primary objectives of GSH are:

To demonstrate how Internet information resources can be used as a classroom tool for research as well as a method for interactive, collaborative learning.

To teach students methods of becoming more active learners and managers of information.

To develop online training and support for teachers for using the Internet effectively in classrooms.

To demonstrate current technologies in classroom settings.

To encourage collaborative partnerships among business, government, school, higher education, and local communities in integrating technology into classrooms.

This project provided one of the first good educational opportunities to emphasize the global nature of the Internet.

The Internet allows entirely different types of computers to communicate with each other, regardless of how far apart they may be located. Rules (called protocols) were developed related to methods of transferring data without regard to the type of hardware. TCP/IP (Transmission Control Protocol/Internet Protocol) is an abbreviation for two of the fundamental protocols used for many Internet activities. Internet "host" computers handle exchanges of data, and individual computers that are linked to a host computer can then send or receive data.

With the discovery by businesses of many uses for the Internet's World Wide Web, the concept of EDI has been expanded to include capabilities for more types of business transactions to occur electronically. Many of these Internet capabilities are described below, after discussions of general advantages and disadvantages, as well as methods of obtaining Internet access.

Advantages and Disadvantages Of Commercial Internet Use

Table 3.1 identifies some advantages and disadvantages of using the Internet that businesses must consider.

Advantages	Disadvantages
▼ A large variety of software assistance is available for people involved in engineering, government, or computing activities. ▼ Internet has a very wide reach worldwide, affording a way to contact an extensive array of organizations and people. ▼ Overall cost is considered low; several hundred dollars may be charged for monthly access, but most messages are free.	▼ There is a lack of security of messages and data, because no one person or group really "runs" this mixture of networks, although individual networks may have their own controls. ▼ Interruptions in service sometimes occur, primarily because the Internet is a federation; no one company is responsible.

Table 3.1 Advantages and Disadvantages of Internet Usage

Problems involving copyright laws have also occurred with Internet usage. A report in *The Wall Street Journal* described someone browsing the Internet and locating many copyrighted drawings of Disney characters, as well as full-color scenes from Disney movies. Companies who own

Additional information regarding the Internet is available at the Web site.

copyrights to various works lose a lot of money to this type of desktop piracy. Some companies offering services through the Internet are working on contracts that system users must sign, promising not to violate libel, copyright, or obscenity laws. Others have legal warnings that regularly appear on the screen.

Although using the Internet involves security and control problems, businesses typically have determined that the problems are outweighed by the wide range of Internet capabilities.

Ethical Perspective

Some copyrighted works in software and on the Internet have no copyright protection and are intended to be copied. For example, "clip art" programs are developed and sold for the purpose of being copied into individual documents by consumers. It is not permissible, however, to copy clip art for purposes of developing competing programs. Many concerns today about copyrighted material are related to Web sites on the Internet. Many sites now have copyright notices that clearly state what uses of their material are permissible. Responsible Internet users should always read these notices and use only those materials they are granted permission to use. Businesses must be very careful not to allow employees to place copyrighted materials on the organization's Web site without appropriate permission.

Internet Access

Many colleges and universities have host computers with direct connections to the Internet. Faculty, staff, and students at these institutions may have individual "accounts" so that they can access the Internet through the school's host system. Other organizations also have host computers with direct access to the Internet and may give their employees access to some, if not all, Internet features. Commercial online services (such as America Online) also offer Internet access to any of their customers who pay the required fee for that service. These commercial organizations provide services in addition to Internet access, such as access to data that is available only to subscribers to the service. ISPs (Internet service providers) are another method of obtaining Internet access. Basic ISPs do not provide any additional services and typically have lower fees than commercial online services, because they provide only Internet access.

The procedure for accessing the Internet through your computer is usually quite simple, and instructions are provided by your Internet access provider. When you are given an account, you receive a username (also called a user ID) and an initial password (a password that you typically change to something else that you specify the first time you access the system). You need a password so that others who do not know your password cannot access your account. Your username is the name you use as the first part of your email address. For example, your address would follow this pattern:

username@hostname.domain

The "domain" is the type of organization providing access. If your address is "username@AOL.com," AOL is the host and in this case is a commercial business. If a university provides your access, the address ends with .edu. There is a domain name system (DNS) that makes sure no duplicate names occur.

You access the host computer by whatever method has been set up for your system (many variations occur with different systems, but a menu option, screen picture, or icon is usually involved). Once you gain initial access, you typically enter your username and a password at a system prompt. In some systems, the series of on-screen prompts and responses for your first use of the system is similar to those shown in Figure 3.1.

System Prompt	Your Response
Login:	<USERNAME>
Password:	<INITIAL PASSWORD>
New password:	<SECOND PASSWORD>
Verification:	<SECOND PASSWORD>

Figure 3.1 Sample Prompts for Setting Up User Account Name and Password

In addition to a requirement that you change to a new password of your own design when you set up your user account, many systems also require that you change your password at designated time intervals, such as monthly. You will see messages on the screen indicating that your password is expiring, at which time you will probably be provided with a similar set of system prompts to indicate a new password. This procedure ensures a little extra security for your account.

After completing these initial procedures of setting up an account, you are ready to use whatever Internet resources your system supports. You can determine your options by looking at the menu choices or icons that appear on your screen. For example, you may have an initial menu choice of accessing the Internet that, when selected, displays a list of specific Internet features available to you as submenu options. Many Internet features are described in other sections of this chapter.

World Wide Web (WWW)

The World Wide Web (WWW, or "Web") was designed in 1989 in an effort to help an international group use online technologies in collaborating on their research efforts. In 1993, it had about 100 Web "sites," and that number quickly grew to tens of thousands as many businesses and individuals began to take advantage of its capabilities.

The Web provides a method of searching through databases using hypertext and hypermedia. Hypertext uses pointers or links (sometimes called hyperlinks) from one item of text to another so that you can continue searching through multiple layers of related data. Hypermedia adds other forms to the text, such as sound, images, or animation. The Web is public domain software that is considered a global information system with access to a huge volume of information on the Internet. For the Web user or "client," the Web uses a simple hypertext language called HTML (Hypertext Markup Language), making it easy to link applications written in many programming languages. Another component is a Web "server," a system that uses a process called HTTP (hypertext transfer protocol), which is a simplified version of FTP for transferring files. The server is needed for distributing information through the WWW. More information regarding the client/server model can be found in Chapter 4.

The Web includes all the Web servers on the Internet. Each server has a unique name, and each document or other resource on a Web server has a URL (uniform resource locator) designation. The URL is similar to a file name, but includes the type of resource (such as HTTP), the address of the resource, and a path name. If someone asks you for the URL of your business, the person wants to know the Web address, such as "www.ibm.com." This address is actually preceded by the protocol, e.g., http://www.ibm.com. If you wanted to use the Web for file transfer protocol purposes (described later in this chapter), the protocol to use at the beginning would be ftp:// instead of http://.

The Web contains thousands of documents or pages that can be displayed, with connections on one page to information on other pages that may be located elsewhere. To obtain information stored in the Web, you need software called a browser. A browser retrieves HTML documents using the HTTP protocol and formats them for appropriate screen display. The browser is also capable of interpreting hyperlinks in a document and moving from one document to another, regardless of where the documents are actually stored. A browser is designed specifically to be used with the Web.

Two browsers used widely are Netscape® Communicator and Microsoft's Internet Explorer. Netscape's original browser was based on Mosaic, which was developed by the National Center for Supercomputing Applications (NCSA) at the University of Illinois and sometimes referred to as NCSA Mosaic. Mosaic became popular quickly because it was designed as a graphical user interface (GUI) browser to make it easy to navigate the Internet by looking at pictorial screens and menus, clicking a mouse or using a keyboard to make selections. It also used highlighted or underlined items to provide links to data at other locations or on other pages, allowing easy touring through a "web" of information for which the computer user defines the path. Previous access to Internet materials used text-based options, such as lists of titles from which to choose an item of interest. These earlier systems did not contain links within a document to go directly to documents or pages at other locations.

Netscape Communications, a company formed by some of the original team that developed Mosaic, revised the browser and the HTTP server now available as Netscape Communicator. New features continue to be developed. For example, these browsers now contain Web page creation software. You may have created your own Web page(s). Many schools allow their students to place Web pages on the school's Web servers (the computers which are set up to work with browsers and individuals to provide appropriate services). After you use some type of Web page creation software or a text editor to create a Web page, you save that file on your computer disk. Then you can use FTP software to transfer (upload) your file to the Web server.

Web home pages are something like storefronts, which a potential customer can use to get an introduction to what is inside. Thousands of businesses of all types and sizes have developed Web pages. Many of these pages are designed to promote the businesses and to provide information quickly to potential customers. Web use has been increasing at an even greater rate than the overall growth rate for the Internet, and Web site design and use have become major strategic decisions for many organizations. Web pages are relatively easy to design; very little expense is involved in getting a few pages up and running. The expense occurs later in keeping the pages current and appropriate.

Because of the web concept of linking data, an introductory page can have multiple subsets of pages that users can view, with the succeeding pages that appear dependent upon selections the user makes on a previous page. In addition, the contents of home pages can be updated regularly. A group of pages for a particular organization or purpose is referred to as a Web site.

Table 3.2 is a brief reference list of some basic Internet terminology. Anyone who spends a little time "surfing the Internet" (looking around at various options) will be able to add other terms to this list.

BUSINESS EXAMPLES
OF INTERNET ELECTRONIC COMMERCE

Federal Express was one of the first to provide additional business uses of the Internet when it began to provide a system where customers could

Term	Description
host	Computer with two-way access to other computers on the Internet.
user ID	Account name for individual user; precedes @ symbol in Email address.
hypertext	Link between one document and related documents located elsewhere
WWW	World Wide Web; system for organizing information available on the Internet, using hypertext; each Web server has a DNS host name
DNS	Domain Name System; system for assigning unique names to Internet hosts
Web server	Handles requests from Web browsers
Web browser	Retrieves documents for user, formats them, and handles navigation from document to document, depending on user requests

Table 3.2 Basic Internet Terminology

track their packages. Their Web site for package delivery is much more extensive today and allows customers to complete shipping forms (air-bills) online, with the package information immediately registered in the FedEx® system. Regular customers have their own identifying data already stored in the FedEx system, as well as addresses of their own customers, so this data can be provided automatically on the form, thus providing a time-saving reason for using the online system.

Other business uses of electronic commerce that have been most successful so far in terms of usage have included sites for selling products such as books, computer hardware and software, CDs and cassettes, and sites for making travel arrangements. Amazon.com has been considered one of the pioneers in electronic commerce, providing books, music, and videos. The online site opened in mid-1995 and has served millions of customers. The site has several features that are considered important for continued success, such as:

▼ ease of use by regular customers, whose billing data have been recorded and do not need to be entered each time,

▼ a personalized approach, in which customer interests are stored so that they can receive information about additional products they might like, and

▼ an efficiently designed site, one whose performance was measured and reported as faster and more accessible than most other sites at the time of the test.

SECURITY ISSUES
OF INTERNET ELECTRONIC COMMERCE

One of the primary ⟨...⟩ transactions over the
Internet has been th⟨...⟩ ⟨...⟩s
have spent consider⟨...⟩ ⟨...⟩rs
would be willing to ⟨...⟩ ⟨...⟩g
used. These certific⟨...⟩ ⟨...⟩u
can exchange certi⟨...⟩

Private and pu⟨...⟩ ⟨...⟩tes
may be used for a⟨...⟩ ⟨...⟩ey
claim to be. These⟨...⟩ ⟨...⟩ in
cases where the m⟨...⟩ ⟨...⟩ate
certificates can als⟨...⟩ ⟨...⟩loy-
ees are accessing ⟨...⟩ ⟨...⟩em
by their employer⟨...⟩

Public certifi⟨...⟩ ⟨...⟩ss is
who they say the⟨...⟩ ⟨...⟩mer.
With a credit card⟨...⟩ ⟨...⟩heck
the certificates in⟨...⟩

Persons cons⟨...⟩ ⟨...⟩some
sites anonymous⟨...⟩

▼ Check the pr⟨...⟩ ⟨...⟩ite,
before entering ⟨...⟩

▼ If options are ⟨...⟩ ⟨...⟩l
information; for example, some sites allow you to obtain travel information anonymously.

▼ Consider using privacy software that allows you to surf the Web
anonymously or to send an anonymous email message.

▼ Delete the contents of the memory cache on your computer regularly, since it contains a record of your Web travels and thus provides
information about your interests.

EXPECTED GROWTH
OF INTERNET ELECTRONIC COMMERCE

Online shopping is not expected to eliminate the need for the traditional
retail stores, but online shopping is expected to increase. Online shopping
reportedly represented about $2.4 billion in sales in 1997, and some have
projected sales to be about $25 billion in 2002.

One of the large growth areas is expected to be business-to-business
sales, with some estimates indicating that it may represent at least

three-fourths of electronic commerce in a few years. One major reason is the integration now possible of organizations' supply chains with those of their partners, creating very efficient value chains.

In addition, companies are forming online partnerships in which data is linked to provide greater value to customers. For example, Priceline.com℠ provides an opportunity for consumers to bid for plane tickets and other items. The bids are forwarded to those sellers of the products or services who have agreed to participate in the online system.

Electronic commerce provides an excellent opportunity for growth for many businesses. Its capabilities and uses are expected to continue to grow. However, having a Web site doesn't automatically guarantee success. Many people have tried to start businesses on the Internet without

Management Perspective

The potential for electronic commerce is prompting many businesses to develop Web sites, especially given the low initial cost and the fact that competitors may have pages that could attract customers. It will take time to determine whether this will become the technology of choice for a majority of future business transactions, partly because not all businesses know whether their primary customers have the capability or desire to use the Internet. Some businesses that based too much of their operations on their Web site have already failed.

In addition to the overall advantages and disadvantages of the Internet, several advantages and disadvantages specifically related to the Web must be considered before investing considerable time (and other resources) on the system.

Advantages of business Web use include:

    Ease of creation of home pages

    Ease of navigation of the Internet

    Low installation costs

    Possible increase in customers

    Ease of acquiring software

    Lack of new hardware needed

    Low communication costs with customers worldwide

Disadvantages of business Web use include:

    Need for Internet access

    Uncertainty regarding security of some activities

    Possible loss of clients who do not use the Internet

    Lack of face-to-face interaction

    Possible high maintenance costs for updates to site

success. The competition will continue to increase, and there must be a reason for people to want to do business at a particular site. Anyone operating a business online must have the resources to keep the site up to date and operating efficiently. While the basic Internet technology itself is not expensive, the cost of developing and maintaining the Web site may be greater than expected.

One additional deterrent to electronic commerce growth is related to global operations. Although it is possible to conduct electronic business transactions worldwide, at least wherever the Internet is available, differences in cultures and in technology have caused some difficulties. Also, trade barriers that exist for other transactions also exist for online activities. Businesses should not assume that having a Web presence on a global network will automatically increase their business activities globally.

Additional electronic commerce information is available at the Web site.

ADDITIONAL INTERNET TECHNOLOGIES

The Internet is used for a wide variety of activities. Some of the most widely used technologies are described in this section.

Electronic Mail and Telecommuting

Electronic mail (email) refers to the process of sending and receiving messages by computer system. Software designed for this purpose is required. The email message is sent to a "mailbox," which is a file whose address is based on a specified number of the system and the number of the mailbox (similar in concept to your home address). The message can be retrieved only by someone who knows the appropriate access code or password—someone who is approved to open the mailbox. Email messages can be sent to people at the next desk, in the next office, in the next building, or in any location worldwide where the person has an email address.

Every day, large organizations send and receive thousands of messages as part of their work with their own employees all over the world. They also use email for external communications, e.g., to get technical specifications quickly from vendors and to get product updates. This capability has become essential, partly because quick access to information is often a key aspect of obtaining a competitive advantage.

Electronic mail is used extensively in businesses and homes, and the number of electronic mail messages continues to increase. Surveys have indicated that about half of all computer users are more likely to send an email message to an out-of-town recipient than they are to make a long-distance telephone call. In addition, about a third are more likely to use an email message to an in-town recipient rather than making a local telephone call. One reason for the use of email, of course, is that you do not have to deal with telephone busy signals or persons who are out of the office or unavailable at the time of the call.

One problem with the increasing use of electronic mail is sometimes referred to as electronic eavesdropping, which refers to reading (and sometimes saving or recording on disk) messages or data being sent over communication media to someone else. Reading messages intended for someone else without permission is generally considered to be unethical (if not illegal), even if no printed copies are made of the information, although a few exceptions exist, such as an employer who may have a legal right to review the workday activities of an employee.

Here are some things to consider when selecting electronic mail software packages:

▼ Ease of learning and use
▼ Versatility
▼ Performance

Examples of ease of learning and use include installation and set-up procedures, online help, functions, features, and documentation (explanations, step-by-step procedures, etc.). Examples of versatility include connection options and remote dial-in capability (ability to access your messages from other computer sites). Examples of performance include how long it takes for a message to be sent and how long the computer is tied up during this process.

Every business organization should develop specific policies related to employee use of electronic mail. Here are a few suggested usage policies:

▼ Change your password at least once a month.

▼ Do not use a password that would be easy for someone else to guess, such as your name.

▼ Do not send confidential, highly sensitive, or embarrassing information through electronic mail.

▼ Do not send copies of messages to people who do not really need them.

Exit from your electronic mail when you leave your desk, or change to a password-protected screen saver so that no one else can view or use your email system.

One method for indicating intended feelings in an electronic message is the use of emoticons (emotional icons), which are also sometimes called smileys, and are created by using standard keyboard symbols. For example, if you wanted to indicate that humor was intended, you could create this emoticon at the end of a sentence: :-)

Tilt your head to the left to see the smiling face. Frowns and many other facial expressions are possible. See Table 3.3 for a few of the many emoticons that have been created in the past few years.

Symbols	Description
:-)	Smile
:-D	Laugh
:-(	Frown
:-0	Shock
:-I	Apathy
%-(	Confusion
#:(	Bad hair day

Table 3.3 Emoticons

As with all other aspects of electronic mail, be careful in using these symbols. They could also cause a message to be misinterpreted. Also, using too many emoticons can be irritating to recipients.

A development made possible by the availability of communications software for microcomputers is telecommuting, by which business employees may work at home and use communications software to send and receive data and messages between home and office. This concept has been encouraged in large cities as a method of decreasing traffic congestion and air pollution from automobiles, and some employees like it because of the time savings. In situations where a person needs to be in the office part of the time, businesses can still save considerable office space (and thus operating costs) by having employees work at home part of the week on alternating days so that offices can be shared.

Not every type of work is appropriate for telecommuting. You can probably think of many examples in which the person must be physically present at the work site to perform the jobs. For example, haircuts are a bit difficult to provide electronically. Some problems that have been reported with telecommuting include:

1. difficulties in supervision by management

2. the employees' desire for social interaction with other employees.

A form of telecommuting sometimes called teleworking refers to persons who work away from the office but not necessarily at home. They could be sending data from a branch office, from a client's office, from a hotel room, or from any other place where they have the capability of communicating electronically with the home office. This method also has the advantages of using less office space and reducing time and transportation costs if the employee does not need to physically make a trip to the office to deliver data.

The term virtual office has been used to refer to this recent capability of being able to conduct business from any location, of seeming to be in the office without really being there.

File Transfer Protocol (FTP)

As its name suggests file transfer protocol (FTP) is a method of transferring files from one computer to another. For example, if you wanted a copy of a file on another computer, you would first access that computer and then retrieve the file. FTP is sometimes called anonymous FTP, because you can often enter anonymous as a username when requesting files. Any host computer that has the anonymous FTP service will allow any person who has access to use FTP capabilities by entering anonymous as a name. The person's email address is then used as the password.

Several software products are available that have made FTP easier to use. These products allow you to use keyboard arrow keys or a computer mouse to select desired options from an on-screen graphical display. If you do not have one of these products, you can use FTP over the Internet using the method discussed earlier in this chapter.

Sources of FTP addresses are widely available. Many FTP sites are heavily involved in research and development activities during business hours and often request that other FTP users avoid busy times of the day, especially if large files are to be transferred. During business hours, you may experience particularly slow speeds in downloading files, although slow speeds occur at other times, too, depending on the data transfer capabilities.

Another important consideration about using FTP to obtain a file is that some of the sites do not regularly check their files for viruses. You should run a virus check on any file you obtain before using the file.

FTP can be used for "uploading" files, too. With this software, you can transfer files from your current storage location to another location, such as to a Web site, as discussed above.

Newsgroups and Mailing Lists

Usenet began around 1980 (before the Internet became well known) and has expanded to include thousands of computer sites and millions of participants. Its discussion areas, called newsgroups, are interactive computer discussions on a wide and continually expanding range of topics that you can simply read or add information to. These discussions are text-based and are separate from email, although the same technology is used.

Usenet does not have a controlling person or group to determine which newsgroups can be included, but a Usenet computer site does have a news administrator who manages that site, cooperates with other news administrators, and exchanges articles. A news administrator can determine an expiration date for articles and remove them after the expiration date.

Data in a newsgroup is organized by topics or general areas of interest. A newsgroup name contains a designation of the main category, followed by other sections that give more details about the type of newsgroup (each part of the name is separated by a period). Table 3.4 shows seven major categories of Usenet newsgroups, including an example of a specific newsgroup that might be available for specific interests within that category.

Category	Description
comp	computer hardware, software, and related topics Example: comp.edu
misc	topics that fit no other categories or fit multiple categories Example: misc.jobs.offered
news	Usenet information, news software, helpful hints for new users Example: news.newusers.questions
rec	recreational activities, sports, hobbies, arts Example: rec.boats
sci	research in specific scientific disciplines Example: sci.astro
soc	social issues, political discussions Example: soc.politics
talk	open-ended discussions of controversial topics, such as politics, religion Example: talk.environment

Table 3.4 Usenet Newsgroup Categories and Descriptions

Many other categories exist, such as those for specific geographic regions or types of organizations. Anyone with Internet access can "subscribe" to a Usenet newsgroup. After selecting Newsgroups from your menu options, you can use your arrow keys to tour the list of available newsgroups. You highlight the desired newsgroup and press <Enter> to begin reviewing its contents.

You can also "post" or send material to a newsgroup. Those who decide to contribute to a newsgroup should follow some basic guidelines (sometimes referred to as netiquette). Here are some suggestions:

▼ Look for any FAQs (frequently asked questions, pronounced "fax") postings, and read them before posting your article so that you don't ask something that has an answer readily available.

▼ Read articles in the newsgroup of interest for a reasonable period before contributing so that you know that group's general procedures and typical topics and so you don't repeat information already given.

▼ Be careful about your wording and content; if you would not want your comments printed on the front page of your local newspaper, don't send them to a newsgroup, whose readers can be anywhere in the world.

▼ Avoid humor or sarcasm, since it is difficult to be sure that all readers will understand your intended tone.

Electronic mailing lists, sometimes referred to as "LISTSERVs," have been available since the mid-1970s and are now used more extensively because of the increasing number of Internet users. Unlike newsgroups, mailing lists use email as the means for topic discussions. As is true of newsgroups, mailing lists are available on an extremely wide range of topics.

Mailing lists may be moderated or unmoderated. With a moderated system, the moderator or "list owner" reviews all the mail received and decides which messages will be sent by email to those on the mailing list. Unmoderated systems have no one to screen the messages before they travel to each email address on the mailing list.

One problem that has occurred with mailing lists in recent years has involved situations in which people improperly used a mailing list as a means to send advertisements to large numbers of email addresses. The use of mailing lists to send undesired materials has been referred to sometimes as "spamming."

Intranets and Extranets

After businesses obtained the technology that allowed Internet access throughout their operations, they discovered that this same technology could be used for effective communications within their organizations, referred to as an intranet. Businesses now provide many types of Web pages that are available only for their own employees. Web pages make it very easy for persons at all levels to obtain information, using links and instructions that are provided on the pages. Some types of information found on intranets include

▼ news of interest to employees,

▼ corporate policies,

▼ job opportunities, including opportunities to schedule appointments,

▼ training opportunities, including electronic forms to register for sessions of interest, and

▼ forms for submitting travel expense claims electronically.

Intranets have several advantages for businesses. The Web pages are not difficult to develop, and they can be changed more quickly and perhaps less expensively than printed materials. Messages and materials can be available for employees worldwide as soon as the related Web page is placed on the system.

One primary concern of intranets involves security. Since Internet technology is being used, some protection must be developed to prevent outsiders from accessing internal systems, while still allowing them to access the organization's Web site on the Internet. A major part of this security is typically referred to as a firewall, designed specifically to prevent unauthorized visitors from accessing resources inside the organization. The firewall typically consists of a combination of hardware and software that controls access. Any traffic that tries to pass by this firewall is examined thoroughly before being authorized to enter. Firewalls are not limited to operations between the intranet and the Internet. For example, some systems have firewalls within their intranet that are used to check requests for access to certain areas containing sensitive data within the intranet. A variety of firewall types have been developed, with developments continuing to occur.

An extranet also uses Internet technology. However, its emphasis is on providing connections between separate organizations much like EDI systems described above, except that Internet technology is used. With an extranet, parts of two different organizations' intranets can communicate with each other. Businesses that wanted to have the capabilities of EDI but could not afford it are finding the use of Internet technology to be the solution. For security, "tunnels" are used, which are secure data pathways that include encryption (coding) systems to protect sensitive information.

Intranets and extranets are being used for automating many types of business communications, including

▼ business to business,
▼ business to suppliers,
▼ business to customers/clients,
▼ business to payment system.

Intranets and extranets, like EDI, can improve the speed of data flow along the supply chain.

Trends

Additional uses of the Internet for business-related activities continue to emerge and expand. For example, electronic conferencing tools are available to allow business partners to meet electronically rather than in the same physical location. Several options are available, such as voice conferencing (voice output only), data conferencing (data output only), and videoconferencing (audio and video output). Discussion forums and chat rooms are also available for business activities that aid in gathering information or input or in reaching decisions.

Current predictions indicate a continuing increase in the use of the Internet for all types of business-to-business activities, and new and improved technologies will continue to be developed.

Summary

Business uses of electronic communications continue to expand.

Communications software is a part of the computer system needed for one computer to communicate with another. This software typically relays instructions to a modem (hardware widely used for communications) so that the transmissions can occur.

Communications software may be included with the purchase of a modem. It may also be included as part of an operating system, or it may be purchased separately.

In addition to generally making it possible for one person to send messages to another by computer, communications software may have other capabilities, such as ways of checking the accuracy of the transmission and encrypting the data.

Electronic data interchange is used for transmissions of various types of data from one business location to another. This capability can be used for many business transmissions, both internally and externally.

The Internet is an international network of networks. The Internet was designed initially for purposes of research but now has many other services. The World Wide Web is used extensively by businesses and individuals, partly because of its linking capabilities (similar to a web) that allow a person to select an item of interest and branch to further information on that topic.

Electronic commerce is continuing to expand in capabilities and usage. It involves the use of the World Wide Web to conduct business. A large growth area is expected to occur in business-to-business sales.

Electronic mail (email) is messages sent and received through use of the computer system. Messages are delivered to specific mailboxes, and access to a mailbox requires entry of the appropriate access code or password. One problem with email is that other people sometimes learn the password and gain access to mail not intended for them.

Telecommuting refers to working at home and sending the results to the company's offices electronically. A similar term is teleworking, referring to working at any other location and transmitting data electronically. A teleworker could be transmitting work results from any part of the world.

File transfer protocol is used to transfer files from one location to another.

Newsgroups and mailing lists are available for exchanging information on a variety of topics.

Intranets and extranets use Internet technology to provide similar communications capabilities within an organization with customers or vendors.

Questions for Review and Discussion

1. Why is communications software needed by most businesses today?

2. Describe at least three major problems that businesses have encountered regarding the use of electronic mail by their employees.

3. From the point of view of business management, what are the advantages and disadvantages to the business of the use of employee telecommuting?

4. Compare and contrast EDI and extranets.

5. Discuss major reasons why numerous online businesses have not been profitable.

Selected References

Allbritton, Chris. "E-Mail a Big Stand-in for Phone Usage." *The Commercial Appeal*, August 12, 1998.

Duncan, Ray. "Electronic Publishing on the World-Wide Web." *PC Magazine*, April 11, 1995.

"International Vendors Back DNS," *InfoWorld*, May 12, 1997.

McKenzie, Kevin. "FedEx Monitors Fast-Changing Internet for New Opportunities." *The Commercial Appeal*, February 12, 1995.

Miller, Leslie. "Now Appearing on the Internet: People Like You." *USA Today*, February 7, 1995.

Reichard, Kevin. "Netscape Seizes the Extranet Opportunity." *Internet World*, June 1997.

Semich, J. William. "The World Wide Web: Internet Boomtown?" *Datamation*, January 15, 1995.

Smith, Ben. "Internet with Style." *Byte*, January 1995.

Vacca, John R. "Mosaic: Beyond Net Surfing." *Byte*, January 1995.

Woo, Junda, and Jared Sandberg. "Copyright Law Is Easy to Break on the Internet, Hard to Enforce." *Wall Street Journal*, October 10, 1994.

Chapter 3 Key Terms

Electronic commerce
use of Internet technology and Web pages for conducting business.

Communications software
provides instructions to hardware for transmission of data from one computer to another.

Electronic data interchange (EDI)
use of computers with communications capabilities to exchange data between businesses.

Internet
an international network of networks.

Protocol
set of rules for transferring data.

Transmission Control Protocol/Internet Protocol (TCP/IP)
protocols used for Internet activities as well as intranet and extranet activities.

Host
a computer with two-way access to other computers in a network.

Commercial online service
an organization that provides various electronic communication capabilities or services for a fee.

Internet service provider (ISP)
organization that provides access to the Internet but does not provide other special services to subscribers.

Username (user ID)
the identifying name of a computer user, which serves as part of the person's email address.

Domain name system (DNS)
system that manages the Internet host names so that no duplicates occur.

World Wide Web (WWW, or "Web")
software that simulates a web by using hypertext, which involves links to data that can be stored at many other locations worldwide; it also uses hypermedia, such as sound, images, and/or animation.

Hypertext Markup Language (HTML)
coding method used to provide links from one location to another on
the World Wide Web.

Hypertext Transfer Protocol (HTTP)
protocol used for transferring from one location to another while
using the World Wide Web.

Uniform Resource Locator (URL)
address of an Internet location, such as a specific Web page.

Browser
software used with World Wide Web to locate desired information.

Home page
initial or introductory page for a particular type of World Wide Web
information, with options that are linked to further information on
the chosen topic.

Web site
group of pages for one overall purpose or organization.

Electronic mail (email)
messages sent from one computer to one or more other computers,
with each recipient and sender having a separate mailing address
(mailbox).

Electronic eavesdropping
accessing email messages intended for someone else, without
authorization.

Emoticon
keyboard-constructed icon used in email to indicate the writer's
intended feelings.

Telecommuting
using a home computer with communications capabilities so that the
work results travel to the office while the employee stays at home.

Teleworking
similar to telecommuting; sometimes used to refer to situations in
which employees may be working at a variety of locations other than
their homes and sending their work to the office electronically.

Virtual office
capability of conducting business and appearing to be working in an office without actually being there.

File Transfer Protocol (FTP)
a method of transferring files from one computer to another.

Newsgroup
an interactive computer discussion group on any of a very wide range of topics.

Netiquette
guidelines for appropriate procedures to use when contributing to a newsgroup.

FAQs
frequently asked questions; widely used with Usenet newsgroups.

Mailing list
a form of discussion possible by sending messages to email addresses of people who have put their addresses on the electronic list.

Intranet
use of Internet technology for communications within an organization.

Firewall
security method for preventing unauthorized access into an organization's intranet.

Extranet
use of Internet technology for communications with organizations in which data must access internal intranets.

Online Activities

Refer to the companion Web site at www.wiley.com/college/simon for a variety of online activities: additional chapter content, *Wall Street Journal Interactive Edition* access, review materials, student assignments, and relevant links.

THE WALL STREET JOURNAL.

Your four-month access to the Interactive Journal allows you to research articles published within the last 30 days in the Interactive Journal, Barron's Online, and Dow Jones Interactive. A Help feature is available if you need assistance in specifying your search topic.

Much of your research will lead you to the Tech Center. Monitor the "Tech Briefs" and "What's News in Technology" daily.

Research each topic in the Interactive Journal and analyze the results of your search.

1.   Telecommuting. What issues do businesses face when telecommuting is used extensively?

2.   Electronic Data Interchange (EDI). What technology is being used? What can we expect regarding the use of EDI five years from now?

3.   Business uses of the Internet for electronic commerce. What concerns do businesses have related to the use of this technology? Do you see any specific trends emerging related to business-to-business transactions versus business-to-consumer transactions?

CHAPTER 4

Data Communications and Networking Considerations

LEARNING OBJECTIVES

After studying the contents of this chapter, you should be able to

1. Explain what is meant by the term data communications.
2. Describe the important characteristics of communication channels.
3. Identify and contrast various data communications media.
4. Discuss options available related to communications carriers.
5. Identify types of communications hardware.
6. Explain and describe network topologies and protocols.
7. Discuss various aspects of local area networks and wide area networks, compared with intranets and extranets.

GENERAL CONCEPTS

Businesspeople now have to be more knowledgeable about data communications and networks. Many of an organization's strategic (and other) decisions are directly related to the topics discussed in this chapter. A general understanding of data communications and networking terminology will help you to prepare for the expected continuation of this trend.

Data communications refers to computer-based electronic transmission of data. It is generally recognized that many businesses in existence today could not function without the use of data communications networks. A network is a collection of computers and other types of hardware connected through communications media, along with the programs that allow these computers to share information.

Organizations establish networks to share resources. The most common type of resource shared in a communications network is data. Other types of resources shared in communications networks are discussed later in this chapter.

Computer communications networks have changed the way that many companies do business. Automated teller machines (ATMs) connected to bank computers changed the geographic areas in which banks do business. Banks may now have a presence in more locations with increased convenience to customers than was possible through branch offices. ATMs also changed the times of availability of banking services. Customers may make deposits to or withdrawals from the accounts at any time of day or night rather than being restricted to traditional bankers' hours. These ATMs also changed the relationships between customers and banks. Some bank customers may go for years without talking in person with bank personnel. While not all customers may like interacting in this way, many appreciate the flexibility of time, location, and relationships made possible by communications networks. Some banks now provide some of their services over the Internet, too.

Computer communications networks may also affect the strategic or competitive relationships among companies. American Hospital Supply Corporation (AHS) installed terminals in the purchasing offices of its customer hospitals. These terminals were connected to the computers at AHS. When purchasing agents in the hospitals noticed that they were getting low on some supplies, they would simply enter order information directly into the terminals; these orders would be transmitted electronically almost instantly to the computers at AHS. AHS could then pull and ship the orders without the typical delay of receiving and opening the mail; keying, verifying, and editing the orders on the computer system; and then transmitting the orders to the shipping group. Thus, the time between recognizing the need for and receiving supplies could be greatly reduced. When the competitors of AHS realized that this system was causing them to lose sales, they offered to install their terminals (connected to their computers) in the hospitals' purchasing offices. But many of the hospitals rejected the offer because they were satisfied with the service they were receiving, did not want more terminals taking up space in their offices, and did not want to learn how to enter orders into another system. In this case, AHS's computer communications network changed the nature of competition in the hospital supply market.

Communications technology is also significantly affecting the flexibility of work itself. Telecommuters (also called teleworkers) are able to work from their homes (or at any of a number of alternative locations away from the traditional job site) as a result of a variety of communications technologies. We may well be moving to virtual organizations made up of asynchronous, distributed, collaborative work groups; i.e., teams of people working together (collaborating) on projects but working at different places (distributed) and even at different times (asynchronous timing), interacting through communications technology.

Computer communications networks have made many organizations more efficient, effective, and competitive. They have changed the time and location of product and service delivery and the relationships between customers and suppliers and within organizational decision-making groups. In the future, companies must consider the impact of communications networks in order to survive.

Global Perspective

Standards related to technology are not the same from country to country. Linking a company's computers in several countries is often unreliable, because data has to be transmitted over a mixture of national telephone networks that follow different technical standards. Efforts are intensifying to develop global standards for electronic data transmission and for international data security, but this process is expected to take several more years. Global transmission problems, as well as security issues, have become more extensive now that we have the capability to connect to an organization's local area network (LAN) from anywhere in the world and can continue to communicate and to work on projects regardless of our physical location.

Telecommunications (from the Greek *tele*, meaning far off or at a distance, and the Latin *comminicare*, meaning to make common or known) refers to any communications over a long distance. This term includes the use of telephones and telegraph, as well as data communications. This chapter focuses on the data communications part of telecommunications, which is the part most closely tied to the use of computers.

Data communications, like human communications, consist of the following four components, as shown in Figure 4.1:

a sender

a receiver

a medium

a message

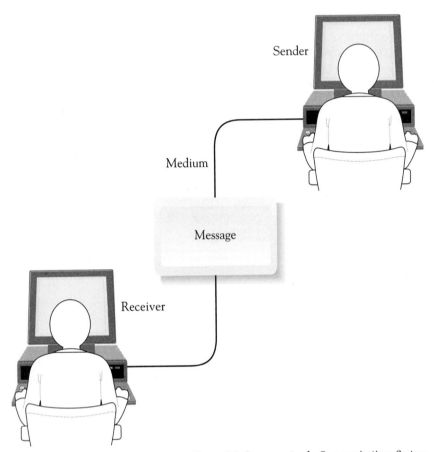

Figure 4.1 Components of a Communications System

The message is what is to be transmitted between the sender and the receiver. Typically, in the data communications context, the message is represented by a group of bits. The sender, also called the transmitter, is the originator of the message. The receiver is the intended ultimate recipient of the message. The medium is the thing that the message is transmitted over or carried on. The medium is also referred to as the channel in data communications. As with human communications, true communications in the computer context occurs only when the receiver understands the message from the sender.

Several types of data may be transmitted over communications networks. These include voice, text, images or graphics, and video. While these types of data may appear to be very different, they may all be represented as groups or strings of bits for transmission over communications channels.

Characteristics Of Communications Channels

Communications channels include several characteristics that must be considered when determining the best arrangement for a particular situation. Important characteristics described in this section include the following:

type of service

direction of communication

number of data paths

number of connections

type of signal

speed of transmission

mode of transmission

Type of Service

The types of services provided by networks may vary greatly. The highest possible level of service is through dedicated communications facilities. When you connect a personal computer to a printer with a cable, you have a dedicated communications channel, meaning that it is dedicated to or assigned exclusively to that particular service. This connection is relatively permanent and for the exclusive use of the devices connected to it. Any message sent over a dedicated communications channel will arrive at all the other devices promptly, in the same order in which it was sent, and with the same time intervals between the parts of the message.

The type of service that we are all probably most familiar with is circuit switched. When we use our telephones to call a friend or family member, the communications circuit is established only for the duration of the call. Then this circuit is released by the telephone system to be available for someone else's call. Although circuit-switched service has many of the advantages of a dedicated circuit, there may be some initial delay in establishing the call (dialing time and the possibility of a busy signal). But the cost of circuit-switched service is typically less than for a dedicated channel since the facilities are shared and thus paid for by all the users.

A common type of service over data communications networks is packet switched (also called store-and-forward). With packet-switched service, several computers may be interconnected through a network, and it may be necessary to relay a message through one or more intermediate computers in the network to get a message from the originating computer to the intended destination. Long messages are separated into smaller packets (typically of no more than 128 or 256 characters) for transmission through the network.

Direction of Communication

A communications channel over which data may be transmitted in only one direction is called simplex. Broadcast television and radio are examples of simplex communications.

A communications channel over which data may be transmitted in one direction or the other, but not in both directions simultaneously, is called half duplex. Examples of half-duplex communications include citizens band (CB) radio and many home intercom systems. With these systems, you generally have to push a button to talk and release the button to listen. While the button is pressed you cannot listen for incoming messages, and while the button is released you cannot send outgoing messages.

A communications channel over which data may be transmitted in both directions at the same time is called duplex or full duplex. Standard telephone channels are full duplex. It is possible for you to be carrying on a conversation with another person over the telephone with both of you talking at once, although typically this is not a good method of communicating successfully. While computers may talk and listen at the same time, people do not appear to do this very well. Figure 4.2 illustrates the various communications channels and directions.

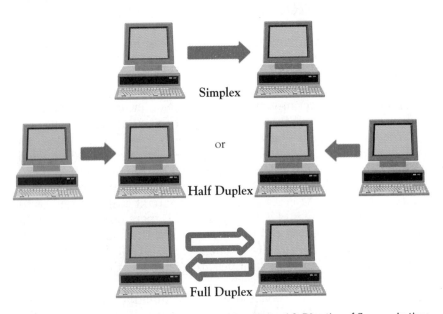

Figure 4.2 Direction of Communications

Number of Data Paths

A communications channel may have only a single data-carrying path, or it may have more than one. If a communications channel has only one path to carry data, each bit follows the preceding one over the channel, one after another. This is called serial communications. If there are several data paths in a communications channel, the bits that make up a character may travel over the different paths at the same time. This is called parallel communications. If you send two 8-bit characters of data over a serial communications channel, each of the 16 bits of data is sent one at a time, one after the other, over the single data-carrying path. If you send two 8-bit characters of data over a parallel communications channel with eight data-carrying paths, each of the eight bits of the first character is sent over separate data paths simultaneously. Then the eight bits of the second character are sent over these eight data paths (see Figure 4.3). (A "bit" is a binary digit, either a 0 or 1; see Chapter 7 for more on this topic.)

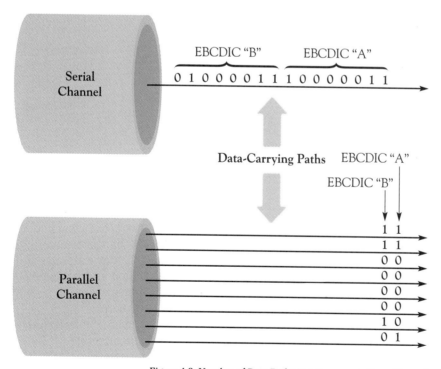

Figure 4.3 Number of Data Paths in a Communications Channel

Communications between your computer and your printer provide a basic example of the "need to know" about data paths. Some printers have a serial interface or connection to the computer, while others have a parallel interface. It is critical that you purchase the right type of printer to connect to your particular computer.

Number of Connections

A point-to-point communications channel is one that has only two devices (such as two computers or one computer and one printer) connected to it. A multipoint communications channel has more than two devices connected to it (see Figure 4.4).

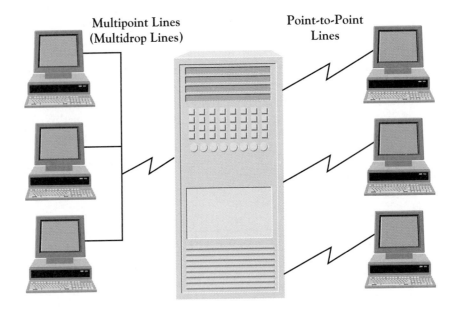

Figure 4.4 Point-to-Point vs. Multipoint Channels

Type of Signal

Two basic types of signals may be transmitted over a communications channel: digital and analog (see Figure 4.5). Digital signals are discrete, and analog signals are continuous. For example, digital watches jump from one second (or minute) to the next, while analog watches indicate time in a continuous fashion. ("Real" analog watches have "sweep" second hands—thus they are a true model, or analogy, of time.)

Information to be sent over a communications channel may be inherently digital, or it may be inherently analog. The transmission facilities—the communications channels and other equipment for carrying signals—may also be either digital or analog. To transmit computer data (digital) over regular telephone lines (analog), it is necessary to use an analog signal to represent the digital data. This is accomplished by starting with an analog signal (called a carrier signal) and altering it to represent the 1s and 0s generated by the computer. The process of altering one

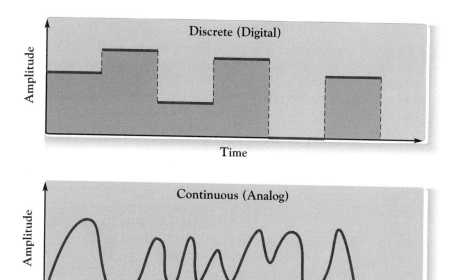

Figure 4.5 Digital and Analog Signals

or more of the characteristics of a carrier signal to represent the value of the data to be transmitted is called modulation. The device that we connect to our home computer to communicate over telephone lines with the computer at the school or office has to modulate the analog signal on the telephone line to represent the digital data from the computer and has to demodulate the analog signal coming back into a digital signal so that it can be understood by the computer. The device that performs this modulation/demodulation process is referred to as a modem.

A device that converts analog video and audio data into digital signals so that they may be sent over digital transmission facilities is called a codec (from coder/decoder). It performs a process called pulse code modulation, which is essentially the same process that allows voice and music (analog data) to be stored on compact disks (CDs) (digital representation).

Advancements in modem technology continue to occur. For example, telephone companies now offer high-speed digital subscriber lines (DSLs), and cable companies can provide a high-speed cable modem. The increasing multimedia capabilities of the Internet's World Wide Web have contributed to the need for higher-speed transmission.

Additional information about modems is available at the Web site.

Speed of Transmission

Speed of data transmission over communications channels is typically measured in bits per second. This term is frequently confused with the term baud. While bits per second (bps) refers to how fast data may be sent over a communications channel, baud rate refers to how fast signals may be sent over a communications channel. These may appear to be the same, but they are very different. If you have only two signal states (for example, 0 volts and +1 volt), then one of these signal states may be used to represent the 0 bit and the other to represent the 1 bit. If you send ten of these signals each second, you are sending 10 bits per second, since each signal represents one bit. But if you have four possible signal states (for example, 0 volts, +1 volt, +2 volts, and +3 volts), each signal state may represent two bits. With a single bit there are only two possible values: 0 and 1, but with two bits there are four possible values: 00, 01, 10, and 11. With four signal states you can represent each of these four possibilities, so each signal that you send may represent 2 bits. If you send ten of these signals each second, your signal transmission rate is 10 baud but your data transmission rate is 20 bits per second (10 signals per second x 2 bits per signal).

The speed of signal transmission and consequently the speed of data transmission is limited by the bandwidth of a communications channel. The bandwidth of a communications channel is the difference between the highest and lowest frequencies that may be transmitted over the channel.

Mode of Transmission

Communications may be synchronous or asynchronous. The word synchronous literally means "same time." Asynchronous means "not-synchronous," or "not same time." If both you and your instructor have watches, it is very unlikely that they will keep identical time, so some disagreement may arise about when your class is supposed to end. But if there were only one official clock, used by both you and your instructor, there should be no disagreement about the time. In the same way, two computers—each with its own "clock"—transmitting data over a communications channel may disagree about how long a second is (since the clock of one will invariably run at a different speed than the clock of the other). And at data transmission speeds of several thousand bits per second, this disagreement could result in a serious misunderstanding and lost data. Consequently, after sending each character, the two clocks are reset or resynchronized to reduce the likelihood that they will begin to vary so much that data is lost. Thus, asynchronous communications—meaning each of the communicating computers provides its own clock or timing signal—is also referred to as character-at-a-time transmission.

If both devices used a single clock, there would be no disagreement about how long a second is, and very long strings of bits (whole messages) could be sent without data loss or misinterpretation due to different timing signals. In synchronous communications the sending computer transmits not only a data signal but also a clocking or timing signal. (The clock signal is actually "embedded" in the data signal.) This is somewhat like an electronic metronome sent over the communications channel. Thus the sending computer uses the timing signal to determine how long a second is for sending the data, and the receiving computer uses the same timing signal to determine how long a second is for receiving and interpreting the data. Since with synchronous communications we can transmit a complete message without fear of losing or misinterpreting data due to timing problems, it is frequently referred to as block-at-a-time transmission.

In asynchronous communications, the bits that make up each character are sent over the channel at fixed intervals with no idle time between the bits. But there typically is idle time between the characters that make up a message. In synchronous communications, blocks of characters are sent over the channel with no idle time between the bits of the characters or between the characters themselves. Start and stop bits identify the beginning and ending of each byte (or character) in asynchronous communications but are not needed or used in synchronous communications.

DATA COMMUNICATIONS MEDIA

Data communications media refers to the channel or means of transmitting data. Commonly used media described in this section include wire pairs, coaxial cables, optical fiber, broadcast radio, microwave, and infrared media.

Wire Pairs

The most common communications medium is wire pairs. Wires must be used in pairs to allow for an electrical circuit. Today we generally find wire pairs used in communications in the form of twisted-pair wires. Twisting each of the wires in the pair around the other cancels noise and interference from electrical signals traveling through the other wire and from external sources. The twisted pairs may be wrapped in a metal sheathing to further reduce interference from external power sources. The resultant media are called shielded twisted pairs. Twisted-pair wires without this shielding are called unshielded twisted pairs. Local telephone companies use twisted-pair wires (consequently called telephone twisted pairs or TTP) to connect your home and office phones to the equipment in their central offices. Twisted-pair wires are relatively cheap and relatively low speed.

Coaxial Cable

Coaxial cables are also widely used communications media. They are used over long-distance connections between telephone central offices and in local area networks. They consist of a central copper wire surrounded by insulating and spacing material, all of which is surrounded by an outer conductor. The outer conductor completes the electrical circuit but also shields the channel from external electrical interference. Coaxial cables typically provide for a greater bandwidth than do wire pairs and consequently allow for faster data transmission.

Optical Fiber

The development of optical fiber has been a significant event in the history of data communications. In this technology, glass fibers with a diameter much smaller than that of a human hair are used to carry a light signal generated by a laser (light amplification by stimulated emission of radiation) or LED (light-emitting diode). As far as we currently know, this type of communications is the most secure that there is. While it is fairly simple to tap into signals over other types of media in order to listen without permission, this is not easily done with optical fiber. But this characteristic of optical fiber also makes it more difficult to add new computers and terminals to a communications network, since the ease of tapping into the media is related to adding new devices to a network. Another important property of optical fiber is that the light signals traveling over it are immune to electrical and magnetic interference. While running copper wires or coaxial cables near an electrical transformer or other types of electrical signals or electronic devices can result in considerable noise and corrupted data, optical fibers can be used without these problems. Thus, optical fiber media are particularly useful in environments (such as hospital operating rooms) where a lot of electrical equipment is in use and it is imperative that the data not be distorted.

Broadcast Radio

We are all probably familiar with broadcast radio media. Most of us listen to AM and FM radio stations. These same media can be used to send computer data as well as music and talk. Although traditional broadcast radio is simplex, we are now using the same type of media for full-duplex transmission in our cellular telephone systems.

Many of us now carry personal digital assistants (PDAs) or personal communications systems (PCSs)—handheld computers built into devices no larger than current models of calculators, with sophisticated input and output capabilities for use anywhere at any time—and these can be connected with databases and other users throughout the world through cellular communications facilities.

Laptop computers have been under development recently that use radio transceivers (combination of transmitter and receiver) for communication with office computer networks without the need to use wires of any type.

Microwave

Both terrestrial microwave and satellite microwave systems use the same type of energy to transmit signals. We can recognize these systems by the large parabolic antenna or dishes that are used to transmit and receive signals. Microwave signals are line-of-sight signals; the transmitter and receiver must be in a straight line with no barriers between them. To accomplish this with terrestrial microwave systems, repeaters are placed at intervals between the transmitter and receiver in order to go over mountains or other types of barriers and to accommodate the curvature of the earth. In satellite microwave systems, earth stations on the surface of the earth transmit signals through their dishes to a transponder on a satellite orbiting above the earth. Then the transponder retransmits the signal to another earth station. Because the typical satellite is so far above the earth (over 22,000 miles above the equator), it has a line-of-sight view to a very large area. These satellites are typically in geosynchronous orbit (GEO) with the earth, which means that the satellites are circling the earth at the equator at the same speed as the earth is rotating on its axis, so that the satellite is over the same place on the earth all the time. This allows us to aim the dishes and leave them pointed in the same direction at all times.

In addition to GEO technology, we now have low- and medium-orbit satellite systems. More satellites are needed to cover the entire earth when they are not positioned as far away, but the latency is lower. Latency refers to the amount of time it takes for data to get from one point to another. It has been estimated that a round trip of data to a satellite in geosynchronous orbit has a latency of about 0.24 seconds. In comparison, estimated latency is 0.14 seconds round trip involving a medium-orbit satellite and about 0.03 seconds round trip involving a low-orbit satellite.

Several companies have been developing satellite systems in recent years. For example, Teledesic is developing a system using low-orbit satellites. Its original plan was to use over 800 satellites, but the number was later reduced to less than 300. By about the year 2002, they may be offering high-speed Internet connections through this system.

Microwave signals are subject to distortion by the weather. Rainfall—or even heavy fog—can cause interference. If you subscribe to community antenna television (CATV, also called cable TV), you may have experienced poor television reception during rainstorms. Also, heavy winds or icing can distort the parabolic shape of microwave antenna and impair reception. Another serious signal distortion (noise) problem occurs when the sun, the communications satellite, and the earth station are aligned. The sun radiates a tremendous amount of energy; when the sun is behind the communications satellite, the noise of the sun overpowers the data signal arriving at the earth station. This condition is known as sun transit.

Infrared

Additional information on wireless services is available at the Web site.

Infrared media may seem very sophisticated, but in fact it is very common. Most remote controls for television sets, VCRs, and stereo systems use infrared communications. Infrared signals are also line-of-sight signals. They are beginning to be used in "wireless" local area networks. Reflectors on the ceilings of open offices bounce signals transmitted from one computer around the room to receivers connected to other computers. Some companies like these wireless systems because of the increased flexibility due to not having to install wires or cables between computers. Some concerns have been expressed about security, though, because it is difficult to control who picks up a signal unless you encrypt (or scramble) the data.

COMMUNICATIONS CARRIERS

Organizations like "the telephone company" that provide a common type of communications service to virtually all customers are known as common carriers. This service is sometimes referred to as POTS (plain old telephone service). Businesses can build communications using this type of service from companies such as MCI®, Sprint®, the Bell Operating Companies, and AT&T®. But the businesses must then add the capabilities they need for modern, sophisticated, high-speed communications to these basic facilities. In response to a demand for enhanced communications services and facilities, some organizations have become value-added carriers. These are typically companies that lease or rent POTS-type services from common carriers, enhance them in some way, and resell the use of these enhanced communications facilities to a third party.

DATA COMMUNICATIONS HARDWARE

Communications networks can use many types of hardware. Perhaps the two most commonly recognized are computers and terminals. Computers serve as repositories of data and programs in communications networks and generally share these data and programs with users at other computers and terminals. Terminals began as input/output devices for large central computers. Initially, these terminals had few capabilities other than entering information that was then transmitted to the central computer for processing and printing or displaying information that was sent back from this computer. Today, there are many different types of terminals with a wide range of capabilities and applications. It is very common now to find computers, particularly microcomputers, used as terminals to other computers.

Large companies typically construct many networks to accommodate a variety of users and needs. It then frequently becomes useful or even necessary to share information among these different networks. A bridge is a device (typically a computer) that is used to connect two networks that use the same architectures (protocols and topologies, which are described in the next two sections). These similar networks are referred to as homogeneous. Gateways connect heterogeneous networks—that is, networks that use different architectures.

A router is a device that does exactly what its name indicates. As described earlier in relation to packet-switched networks, when a computer receives a message that is intended to be sent on to some other computer, it might have a choice of channels over which to send the message. The purpose of the router is to make the appropriate choice of what channel (or route) the message is to take on its way to its destination.

As mentioned earlier, a modem is a device that allows users to send digital information over analog communications facilities.

Multiplexers and concentrators are types of line-sharing devices— that is, they allow multiple computer conversations to be conducted over shared communications channels simultaneously. There are many different kinds of multiplexers and concentrators, and the distinctions between these two types of devices have begun to blur. One vendor of communications equipment refers to a particular type of multiplexer that it markets (a statistical time division multiplexer) as a concentrator.

NETWORK TOPOLOGIES

The topology of a network—its structure or architecture—refers to the interconnection of devices and channels. There are an almost limitless number of ways of connecting computers (and terminals) in a network. As mentioned earlier, each microcomputer could be connected directly (point-to-point connection) to a central computer, or several computers or microcomputers could be linked together with a single channel (see Figure 4.4).

Some of the more widely known topologies for connecting computers are discussed here.

A fully interconnected (or plex) topology is one in which each of the computers in the network is connected via point-to-point communications channels to each of the other computers in the network (Figure 4.6). If the network has only two computers, only one link is required to fully interconnect them. If a third computer is added to the network, two more links must be added for the network to be fully interconnected. When a fourth computer is added, three new links must be added, and so on.

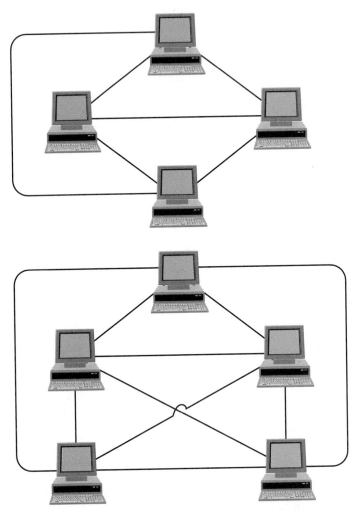

Figure 4.6 Fully Interconnected Topologies

The number of required links in this type of network increases very rapidly. A network of just 10 computers requires 45 links to be fully interconnected. The number of required links in a fully interconnected network can be calculated as $(N(N-1))/2$, where N is the number of computers in the network. This type of topology provides excellent backup in the event of a failure of one or more of the links but can be very expensive.

A chain topology is one in which the first computer has a point-to-point link to the second, the second is linked to the third, and so on, for each of the computers in the network. This is a fairly simple and inexpensive network topology, but the failure of a single link can split the network and cease communications.

A loop is like a chain, but the last computer on the network is linked through a point-to-point channel back to the first computer on the network. A loop topology is sometimes confused with a ring topology, but they have very different characteristics. The cost is slightly higher for a loop than with the chain (one additional link), but the failure of a single link will not stop the network from operating (Figure 4.7).

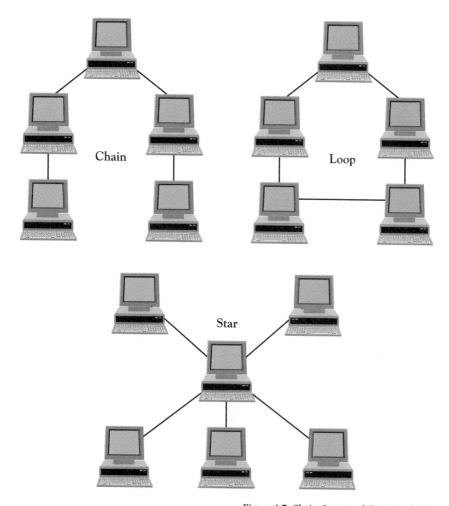

Figure 4.7 Chain, Loop, and Star Topologies

A network topology in which one central computer is connected by a point-to-point communications channel to each of the other computers in the network is a star. The failure of a single link affects communications to and from only one computer in the network, but a failure of the central computer brings down the entire network. Many organizations that use this topology install a backup computer for the central computer to ensure that this one failure does not have a disastrous impact on their communications.

One of the most widely discussed and least understood topologies is the ring. In a ring, point-to-point channels connect a set of hardware devices (called ring repeaters) together in a configuration similar to a loop. Computers may be connected to (or plugged into) these ring repeaters.

A bus topology is one in which all the computers in the network are connected to a common communications channel. Figure 4.8 illustrates ring and bus topologies. (This is actually a multipoint channel, as described earlier, but it is referred to as a bus when all the computers connected to it are peer devices. That is, there are no super/subordinate relationships among the devices on the channel.)

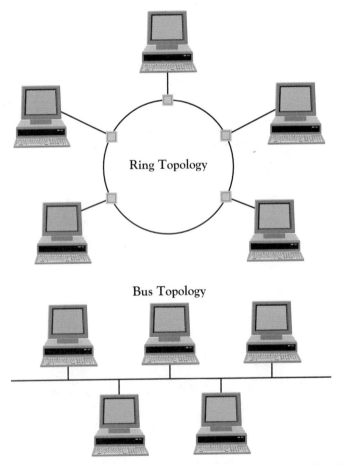

Figure 4.8 Ring and Bus Topologies

Bus and ring topologies are very common in local area networks (LANs), but virtually nonexistent in wide area networks (WANs).

NETWORK PROTOCOLS

A network protocol is the set of rules for communications in a network. As in human communications, when everyone talks at once without listening, very little can be understood. We need rules that allow us to determine who "has the floor" in conducting a meeting or in other types of interaction.

The International Standards Organization (ISO), a voluntary, non-government organization comprised of representatives of standards-setting bodies from many nations, has developed the International Standards Organization Reference Model for Open Systems Interconnection (OSI). This reference model is not a protocol but is a guideline for the development of protocols that are intended to allow computers and software from many vendors to work together in a network. In developing this model, the ISO separated the functions to be performed in communicating through a network into seven categories or layers. Thus the ISO-OSI reference model is the basis for development of layered communications protocols.

A main purpose of the ISO-OSI reference model (and other layered communications protocol models) is to allow many vendors to develop the various components of communications protocols and have these components work together easily. Having high levels of interoperability or connectivity among the systems or system components provided by a variety of sources is the true meaning of open systems—systems that interact well with many other systems in a network.

One function of a protocol is to determine when each computer connected to a communications channel can be sending information over the channel. One of the earliest protocols to address this issue was called contention. Each of the computers on a communications channel using this protocol contends for control of the channel by sending a string of characters to the other computers on the channel asking permission to transmit data. This type of protocol is typically used only on point-to-point channels. An early popular protocol to address the issue of control of the shared communications channel in multipoint channels was called polling, because one device was in charge of the channel (the master computer) and would ask each of the other computers (the subordinate computers) one at a time if they had anything to send. The subordinate computers would speak (transmit) only when spoken to by the master computer.

Perhaps the best-known protocol for connecting computers to public and private networks with packet-switching services is X.25. This standard, developed by the Consultative Committee on International Telephone and Telegraph (CCITT), has been used widely in Europe and Asia as well as in North America.

Integrated Services Digital Network (ISDN) is a protocol standard describing how a communications channel can be shared to provide a variety of services simultaneously over a single communications channel.

With this service, you could use the telephone line coming into your home to connect your computer to a database, talk to a friend in another city, have your electric meter read by the utility company, and have your house monitored by a security company—all at the same time.

The most widely used protocol in local area networks (LANs) is carrier-sensed multiple-access with collision detection (CSMA/CD). This protocol usually operates on a bus topology. If one of the computers connected to the bus needs to transmit data, it checks the channel to see if a carrier signal is present (indicating that some other computer on the channel is transmitting). If not, it transmits its message but it continues to listen to the channel just in case some other computer transmits at the same time. If it detects that multiple computers have transmitted at the same time, it detects this collision and will wait and retransmit later. In CSMA, multiple-access indicates that all devices on the channel have equal authority and access to use the channel.

Another well-known protocol used in LANs is token passing. This protocol is typically used with a ring topology, but there is also a standard for token passing using a bus topology. With token passing, a token (special string of characters) is circulated among the computers on the network. When the token arrives at a computer, it may change the string of characters, indicating that it has control of or "holds" the token. It may then use the channel until it has no more messages to send or until a specified period of time has elapsed. It then releases the token and sends it to the next computer so it may have a chance to hold the token and thus to control the communications channel.

Many other protocols exist. These protocols address a variety of needs for different network issues. For example, TCP/IP (transmission control protocol/Internet protocol) is used to allow computers to exchange information regardless of the operating system or hardware. ATM refers to asynchronous transfer mode (not to automatic teller machines in this instance). This protocol standard allows a single high-speed communications channel to simultaneously carry very diverse types of services such as voice, television, interactive video, computer data, facsimile, security monitoring, and utility meter readings. A proper understanding of the functions and operation of these and other protocols requires an in-depth study in data communications and networking.

LANS AND WANS

Despite the widespread use of local area networks (LANs), there is no universally accepted definition. So, what is a LAN? Perhaps the best way to answer this question is to see how LANs differ from wide area networks (WANs).

The most distinguishing characteristic of a LAN is the geographic area covered. LANs operate within a restricted geographic area—typically within a single room or building—but by some definitions may cover an area up to a few kilometers in diameter. While WANs typically consist of computers and terminals owned by the network user and communications channels owned by another organization (such as the telephone operating company), all parts of a LAN are usually owned by a single organization.

Almost any topology may be used in a LAN, but some topologies may be inappropriate in a WAN. Specifically, ring and bus topologies are not appropriate in WANs (for reasons too technical to address here). In the same vein, some protocols that may be used in LANs would not be appropriate in WANs. Specifically, CSMA/CD and token passing, which are very popular in LANs, would cause intolerable delays if used in WANs. Ethernet and token ring are perhaps two of the most widely recognized types of LANs. Ethernet uses the CSMA/CD protocol with a bus topology. Token ring uses the token-passing protocol with a ring topology.

The speed of transmission of data is typically greater in a LAN than in a WAN. Whereas many WANs are limited to transmitting thousands or tens of thousands of bits per second, LANs generally transmit millions or tens of millions of bits per second. Also, error rates over LANs are typically lower than error rates over WANs. This is a result of the shorter distances that data has to travel and also the more sophisticated error detection and error correction processes that are used in LANs.

Other than the physical area of coverage, the greatest distinction between LANs and WANs is in the types of resources shared. As mentioned earlier, the resource most commonly shared in networks is data. But LANs also share other resources, including peripherals, programs, and processing power. While it would probably not make sense for a computer in Memphis, Tennessee, to use the printer connected to a computer in Seattle, Washington, for a printout needed in Memphis (since the

Social Perspective

Some of the social concerns of the world also exist on computer networks and are sometimes more difficult to monitor because of potential anonymity. For example, many women have reported that high-tech sexual harassment is a problem on computer networks. Examples have included suggestive graphics and electronic stalking.

However, computer-mediated decision making that is possible on networks has eliminated some of the gender, race, and other forms of stereotyping that occur in some face-to-face meetings. Computer-based communications can hide characteristics such as sex, race, age, etc., that are sometimes a basis for discrimination. People who are reluctant, because of shyness or fear, to express opinions in meetings with bosses or even peers tend to lose that reluctance when the interaction is mediated through computer-based communications.

printout would have to be faxed or sent physically to Memphis from Seattle), it is not at all unusual for a group of people in an office to share a single, high-quality laser printer. This would also be true for other input, output, and storage devices.

INTRANET AND EXTRANET COMMUNICATIONS

See Chapter 3 and the Web site for further information on intranets and extranets.

Intranets are similar to LANs in that they provide communications capabilities within an organization. Intranets use the public Internet's technology for private business operations. Businesses can develop and use Web pages to distribute information internally, which provides easier implementation and access than traditional LAN systems. Web applications are often inexpensive, and costs of developing and maintaining the systems are typically less than for LANs.

Some organizations have changed from traditional LANs to intranets because of the lower cost as well as the relative ease of keeping the system working effectively.

Extranets are something like WANs, except that extranets use the public Internet protocols. Extranets actually use a combination of intranets and the Internet. They are designed to allow for sharing of internal information between businesses and thus represent a less expensive alternative to the concept of electronic data interchange. This process is made possible by allowing a business to have access to part of another business' intranet. This collaboration is often between a business and its suppliers and/or its customers, so that needed data can be provided very quickly, as well as inexpensively. Extranets link parts of intranets of different organizations together.

Extranets need security, including firewalls and special access controls. Many large-scale extranets use VPNs (virtual private networks) for communications. A VPN provides dedicated lines and sends data between private networks over the public Internet.

DISTRIBUTED SYSTEMS

A concept that came into vogue in recent years was referred to as the client/server model, now widely referred to as a form of distributed systems, i.e., data and programs spread out among numerous locations. These systems have taken advantage of the increased capabilities of desktop computers to act as servers and to share the workload. A server is any hardware or software that provides some type of service(s) to other hardware or software—the client. A file server or database server would store information that was accessible to client or workstation computers connected to it through a network. File servers typically have more secondary storage and perhaps are faster and have more primary memory than the typical workstation. A print server would likewise provide access to printers, and a communications server could provide access to other networks through modems or direct connection.

A critical issue in implementing a client/server application is in how to "cleave" the application—that is, determining what parts of the application are to take place on the client and which parts on the server. Middleware is software that links the part of the application on the client and the part on the server to provide an apparently seamless application to the computer user (the person using the system is unaware of the locations of various parts of the application). Middleware allows interoperability between systems where data are scattered across various networks, computers, and operating systems that are otherwise not compatible. It takes messages or requests from an application and directs them wherever necessary, along with handling appropriate protocol translations.

Middleware products are now available for large-scale Web applications, which may involve the use of multiple database servers and many client computers that access the database servers through Web servers. The middleware can manage the various interactions among applications as well as security, routing, and overall distribution of transactions within the Web applications.

STRATEGIC NETWORK ISSUES

Several important issues need to be addressed in planning and implementing communications networks:

▼ Throughput. What is the total volume of data that can be sent through the network within a given period of time?

▼ Response time. How long does it take from the time a user sends a request until the response is received?

▼ Consistency. Does the network consistently provide the same speed and quality of service?

▼ Reliability. Can you depend on the network to function properly? Does it break down often?

▼ Availability. Is the network operational when you need it? Some LANs may operate only Monday through Friday from 8 A.M. until 5 P.M. What happens if you need to work on the weekend and some of the data you need is on a file server on the network?

▼ Security. How well is data protected from unauthorized access, modification, or deletion? Security may be ensured by locating computers and media where they cannot be accessed by unauthorized personnel. Data can also be encrypted, or scrambled, so that only the intended recipient can understand what the data means.

▼ Flexibility. How easy or difficult is it to add computers and users to, or remove computers and users from, a network? Can the network design accommodate changes in the organization?

▼ Backup/recovery. What provisions exist to get the network operational again if one or more computers or communications channels break or stop running?

▼ Efficiency. Does the network design accomplish the other objectives with minimal waste of computer and communications resources? The choice of communications protocols can significantly affect the efficiency of a network. Another method of gaining efficiency in a network is data compression—representing the same amount of data with fewer bits.

Management Perspective

Organizations often underestimate the effort needed to keep their communications networks functioning properly. Managing the change, growth, and maintenance of these networks is critical, and is the responsibility of the person who serves as the network administrator. This person must possess both technological and organizational skills to handle a variety of tasks such as:

Getting computer users on the network, by identifying which users will be given network access, installing the required hardware and software for this access, and establishing network accounts.

Making provisions for extensive continuing help for network users, either with an internal staff or with external providers, or through a combination of both methods.

Handling reports of network problems, including documenting and tracking these problems from the initial report through the resolution of the problem.

Many other tasks exist that require extensive knowledge of the technology as well as the capability of working effectively with employees and vendors.

COMMUNICATIONS INFRASTRUCTURE

Many companies today are concerned with developing a communications infrastructure. A communications infrastructure is an underlying base of facilities, equipment, software, and services that supports the communications-dependent applications developed by an organization. The existence of a good infrastructure makes it possible for a company to take advantage of opportunities from new systems without having to build separate communications facilities for each application.

Most of the issues of any systems development project apply to the development of a communications infrastructure, but some things are significantly different. It is common to define the scope of systems to be developed and to perform associated cost and benefit analyses. But a communications network may transcend several applications, some of which are not even envisioned when the network is implemented. It is difficult at best, and frequently impossible, to determine the impact of the development of a communications network when the full future use of the network is unknown. Also, it is important for developers to understand that networks of computers are inherently more complex than stand-alone systems and consequently require more sophistication and training of users as well as better documentation and support services.

Ubiquitous Networks

Data communications networks are everywhere, i.e., ubiquitous. They are a part of our work, leisure, and education. A huge number of today's jobs require the use of computers and attendant networks. The growth of the Internet has helped blur the lines between work, education, and entertainment. And in many schools today, multimedia information kiosks, video conference remote learning facilities, and other communications resources have changed the way that students relate to their schools and teachers. It is almost certainly true that you will interact extensively with networks in the immediate and long-term future.

Summary

Data communications involves transmission of data by computer. The four components are the sender, receiver, medium, and message. A network is a collection of computers and other types of hardware connected through communications media, along with the programs that allow these computers to share information.

Characteristics of communications channels that must be considered include type of service, direction of communications, number of data paths, number of connections, type of signal, speed of transmission, and mode of transmission.

Types of services available include dedicated, circuit switched, and packet switched.

The direction of communications can take one of three forms: simplex, half duplex, or full duplex.

When each data bit follows the preceding one, one after another along the single data path of a channel, you have serial communications. When there are several data paths and the bits of a character travel over different paths at the same time, you have parallel communications.

A modem is a device used to convert digital computer signals to analog form so that they can be sent over telephone lines. Modems also perform the reverse operation, converting the analog signals they receive to digital form for use by a receiving computer.

Bits per second (bps) refers to how fast data may be sent over a communications channel, while baud rate refers to how fast the signals may be sent. The bits per second may be different from the baud rate.

In asynchronous (or character-at-a-time) communications, each of the communicating computers has its own timing signal. In synchronous (or block-at-a-time) communications, the sending computer transmits not only a data signal but also a clocking or timing signal.

Data communications media include wire pairs, coaxial cable, optical fiber, broadcast radio, microwave, and infrared.

Communications carriers include common carriers, value-added carriers, and private networks.

Data communications hardware, in addition to the computers that originate, receive, and process data, includes gateways, routers, modems, multiplexers, and concentrators. The topology of a network is the structure or architecture of the interconnection of devices and channels. Topology options include plex or fully interconnected, chain, loop, star, ring, and bus.

A network protocol refers to the rules for network connection. X.25 is a well-known protocol for connecting computers to public and private packet-switching networks. ISDN is a protocol standard related to the sharing of a communications channel so that a variety of services can be provided at the same time over one channel. CSMA/CD and token passing are two protocols widely used in local area networks (LANs).

LANs operate within a geographically restricted area, and the organization typically owns all the parts of the LAN. In a WAN (wide area network), communications channels are typically owned by a separate organization such as the telephone company. Speed of transmission is usually greater in a LAN than in a WAN.

Intranets use Internet technology to provide internal communications capabilities. Extranets use Internet technology to connect external suppliers or customers with designated parts of a company's intranet.

In a client/server model, the client wants some type of service such as a data file, and the server provides it. Types of servers include file servers, print servers, and communications servers. Client/server systems are widely referred to as distributed systems.

Middleware refers to software that eases some of the problems previously experienced in communicating with different types of computers and software. It can handle protocol translations so that all the communications can be completed appropriately regardless of the hardware and software being connected.

Determining the scope of networks is typically difficult since the networks may support applications that are not envisioned when the network is implemented. Also, for similar reasons, cost and benefit analyses are difficult or perhaps impossible to properly perform.

Questions for Review and Discussion

1.   Identify and describe the important characteristics of communications channels.

2.   Contrast asynchronous transmission with synchronous transmission.

3.   Identify and describe the data communications media options.

4.   Provide an example situation in which the client/server model is (or could be) used.

5.   Describe the ways in which intranets and extranets are being used in businesses.

Selected References

Babcock, Charles. "Attuned to ATM," *Computerworld*, August 16, 1993.

"Communications Q&A." *PC World,* January 1993.

Deck, Stewart. "One Standard Helps Make 56K a Reality." *Computerworld*, May 4, 1998.

Galloway, Jonathan F. "Commercializing Outer Space." *Phi Kappa Phi Journal*, Summer 1992.

Haskin, David. "The Extranet Team Play." *Internet World*, August 1997.

Hickman, Angela. "Get in the Fast Lane." *PC Magazine*, February 10, 1998.

Hickman, Angela. "Surfing by Satellite." *ZDNet*, March 20, 1998.

Howard, Bill. "The Cable Modem Guy." *PC Magazine*, October 7, 1997.

Levy, Doug. "Wireless Technology May Link Laptops, Phones." *USA Today*, May 21, 1998.

Lipschutz, Robert P. "Safety from the Net." *PC Magazine*, November 18, 1997.

Loeb, Larry. "Is Your Network Safe?" *Internet World*, August 1997.

Mace, Scott. "The Extranet Revolution." *Byte*, December 1997.

Machrone, Bill. "Speed Kills: The Dial-Up Internet." *PC Magazine*, October 7, 1997.

Nance, Barry. "Web Middleware Glue Binds Web Apps." *Network Computing*, May 15, 1997.

Orfali, Robert, and Dan Harkey. *Client/Server Survival Guide*. New York: Van Nostrand Reinhold, 1994.

Snyder, Joel. "What Speed? Go Digital." *Internet World*, December 1997.

Stallings, William. *ISDN and Broadband ISDN*, Second Edition, Macmillan, New York, 1992.

Wilkinson, Harvey. "Making the Wireless LAN Connection," *Managing Office Technology*, August 1993.

Chapter 4 Key Terms

Data communications
use of a computer-based system to transmit data electronically.

Network
a group of computers and other hardware that is connected by communications media so that resources can be shared.

Telecommunications
any communications over long distances, including those by telephone or telegraph as well as by computer.

Message
a group of bits being transmitted.

Sender
the originator of a message being communicated.

Receiver
the recipient of data being communicated.

Medium
the means by which a transmission occurs, also referred to as a channel; examples include wire pairs, coaxial cables, optical fiber, and microwave.

Dedicated communications channel
service in which the connection from one piece of hardware to another is used only for that connection.

Circuit-switched service
communications service in which the facilities are shared and are therefore less expensive than a dedicated circuit.

Packet-switched service
a type of communications service in which messages travel in small groupings (packets) and may be relayed through several computers before arriving at the destination.

Simplex
a communications channel over which data transmission travels in one direction only.

Half duplex
a communications channel over which data transmissions can travel in both directions, but not at the same time.

Full duplex
a communications channel over which data transmissions can travel in both directions simultaneously.

Serial communications
use of one path to transmit bits of data.

Parallel communications
use of multiple paths at one time to transmit bits of data.

Digital signal
a discrete or pulse-type signal.

Analog signal
a continuous signal.

Modem
device that converts digital data to analog (modulation) and analog data to digital (demodulation).

Codec
device that converts analog video and audio data into digital signals.

Bits per second (bps)
how fast data can be sent over a communications channel; bps may be greater than the baud rate.

Baud rate
how fast signals can be sent over a communications channel.

Bandwidth
the range (highest minus lowest) of frequencies that can be transmitted.

Synchronous communications
transmission of a block of characters at a time rather than one character at a time.

Asynchronous communications
one-character-at-a-time transmission of data.

Data communications media
means of transmitting data such as wire pairs, coaxial cables, or microwave.

Latency
amount of time required to get data from one point to another.

Common carrier
an organization that provides a common type of communications service to many people, such as telephone service.

Value-added carrier
organization that enhances the services of common carriers (an added value) and sells the use of this capability.

Bridge
hardware that connects two homogeneous (similar) networks.

Gateway
hardware that connects heterogeneous (not similar) networks.

Router
device that selects the channel (route) to use for transmission of a message.

Topology
method of connecting computers in a network; examples include fully interconnected, chain, loop, star, ring, and bus.

Network protocol
rules for network communications; examples include CSMA/CD, token passing, and TCP/IP.

Local area networks (LAN)
computers linked into a network in a small geographic area and widely used for sharing data, software, and hardware.

Wide area network (WAN)
computers linked into a network in a large geographic area and primarily used for sharing data.

Client/server model
a system that includes at least one server—a computer that provides a service to at least one other computer (a client); often referred to as a distributed system.

Middleware
software that links client and server applications in distributed systems.

Online Activities

Refer to the companion Web site at www.wiley.com/college/simon for a variety of online activities: additional chapter content, *Wall Street Journal Interactive Edition* access, review materials, student assignments, and relevant links.

GO TO http://www.wiley.com/college/simon

 THE WALL STREET JOURNAL.

Your four-month access to the Interactive Journal allows you to research articles published within the last 30 days in the Interactive Journal, Barron's Online, and Dow Jones Interactive. A Help feature is available if you need assistance in specifying your search topic.

Much of your research will lead you to the Tech Center. Monitor the "Tech Briefs" and "What's News in Technology" daily.

Research each topic in the Interactive Journal and analyze the results of your search.

1. Business uses of intranets. What special considerations are needed for the use of intranets in a business?

2. Business uses of extranets. How does the technology for extranets differ from that for intranets? What special issues must be considered when adopting the use of that technology?

3. Wireless communications. What do you expect to occur in the use of wireless technology in the next five years?

Part III
SOFTWARE AND HARDWARE STRATEGIES AND USES

Part III describes ways in which software is used for a variety of applications in offices, from general office work to strategic decision making. In addition, the system software that allows the applications to work on the computer is described. Many crucial business decisions are made to ensure that all the software and hardware can work together effectively to meet the information systems needs of the organization.

Chapter 5	Applications Software for Businesses
Chapter 6	System Software Considerations
Chapter 7	Computer Components and Options

CHAPTER 5

Applications Software for Businesses

LEARNING OBJECTIVES

After studying the contents of this chapter, you should be able to:

1. Describe what is meant by office automation.
2. Compare and contrast the features of typical office applications software.
3. Identify features of software used to provide support for decision making.
4. Discuss evaluation criteria for making appropriate selections of applications software.

THE CONCEPT OF OFFICE AUTOMATION

Office automation refers to the use of information technology to automate activities that are typically performed in offices. Regardless of the size of the organization, some office activities occur on a regular basis, such as paying bills, sending messages, keeping financial records, and budgeting for the future. Of course, these activities are also performed at home, too, which is one of the reasons for the popularity of computers for home use.

You can perform these activities manually, but usually much more slowly than you can with technology that has other capabilities as well. Balancing the checkbook, for example, can be done by entering amounts by hand and perhaps using a calculator to determine the current balance. With the use of information technology, however, a new balance is calculated automatically as you enter each payment or receipt of money. You can include many other features as desired, such as subdividing the expenditures by category for tax purposes or preparing reports of monthly income and expenses. You can even automate the creation of the checks themselves. Businesses with large numbers of checks to write can benefit tremendously from automating as much of the process as possible. The monetary investment in a system to handle this work is outweighed by the savings in personnel costs, in improved procedures for making payments at the appropriate time, and in methods of monitoring the accuracy of the operation.

Automating the creation of messages such as letters, memos, and reports began years ago with the use of the typewriter in offices. Early typewriters had no memory capabilities, so the typist had to start again if a document required major revisions. We eventually had typewriters with the capability of storing several pages at a time so that changes could be made to a document before it was in final form. The largest amount of automation of document development has occurred through the capabilities of desktop computers, which have extensive storage capacities as well as methods of combining different types of materials into one document.

As information technology has improved, and as people have recognized and understood the capabilities better, new uses of the technology have been developed for automating office tasks. Many files are stored electronically now, with the data storage and retrieval processes much more efficient and accurate than the previous methods of putting paper files in folders in drawers and hoping to locate them later without too much difficulty. In addition to the storage and retrieval benefits, the electronic storage of data makes it possible to automate other activities, such as making changes to data in a file, rearranging it for different purposes, and sharing it with others as needed.

Software has been developed to assist in automating many office activities. Two general types of software are referred to as:

▼ applications software, which performs many types of desired tasks using (making applications of) computers,

▼ system software, which serves as an intermediary between the applications software and the hardware.

Some of the types of applications software widely used in business offices are described in this chapter. The capabilities for transmitting files and messages electronically are related to the office applications described in this chapter but are so extensive as to warrant additional discussion in Chapters 3 and 4.

OFFICE APPLICATIONS SOFTWARE

Office applications software refers to the programs that are used to assist in performing a wide variety of office activities. These software programs implement the concept of office automation and are used to improve the efficiency or accuracy (or both) of office activities, as well as to provide entirely new capabilities not available manually. Traditional examples of office applications software include word processing, spreadsheet, database, and graphics programs. The proliferation of desktop computers with increasing hardware and software capabilities has resulted in types of office applications that were not possible previously.

Businesses of all kinds are likely to need word processing and spreadsheet software in their offices. Most organizations other than some very small businesses also have uses for database software, with the level of need dependent on the quantity of data stored and how the data is used. Graphics and presentation software are used to assist in emphasizing important aspects of a report or presentation. Other types of software may be purchased to fit specific needs of a business office.

All these choices represent one of the important business decisions that must be made: What software package, or combination of packages, represents the best choice for a particular situation? The answer to this question must be reviewed regularly. Business needs change, and software products and capabilities change even faster. New products must be evaluated continually to see if they would help in the overall operation of the business so that it can remain competitive.

Software packages are evaluated as to their purposes and capabilities, followed by consideration of other factors such as costs, hardware requirements, and vendor support. Typical capabilities of several types of office applications software are described in the following section, along with suggestions for evaluation.

The primary features of some of the most widely used types of office applications software are described below. You should notice that some overlapping of features exists in different types of software. For example, the word processing software described in the following section often contains some basic spreadsheet and graphics capabilities, and spreadsheet software has some graphics and database capabilities. If your needs were primarily for spreadsheets but with some need for graphics, you might be able to buy only one software package. The extent of graphics capabilities desired would be used to determine whether a separate complete package should be purchased.

Word Processing Software

Word processing, one of the first types of applications to be developed for use on microcomputers, is still used extensively. Word processing software packages are used primarily for documents that involve text in the form of sentences and paragraphs, such as memos, letters, and reports.

The on-screen text-editing capabilities that became available with word processing software were a welcome improvement over the typewriter, with which documents could not be changed easily. The text-editing capabilities are possible because the document is retained in the computer's internal memory and can be changed before it is printed, as well as after it is printed if additional changes are desired. These documents can be saved and used again many times.

Most word processing packages contain similar basic features or capabilities, with the more expensive packages usually containing more extensive features. Businesses must compare the differences in cost with the capabilities, while also considering which capabilities are essential for their offices.

Word processing software always has the capability of entering data in paragraph form. Methods of changing the data (editing) are also supplied, as well as options for changing the appearance (formatting).

Editing capabilities generally found in word processing packages include insertion and deletion of data, with the remaining text automatically adjusted as needed, and copying or moving of words, sentences, or paragraphs, with the text automatically adjusted as needed.

Typical formatting options include centering; underlining; indenting; boldfacing; italicizing; double spacing (or other line spacing options); page numbering; margin changes; use of multiple columns; type style and font, and justification, with extra blank spaces added as needed. (Text is typically set automatically for left justification, with all lines starting evenly at the left margin; this setting can be changed so that lines are aligned at the right margin or aligned at both left and right margins, which is sometimes referred to as full justification.)

Additional formatting options are available, but the ones listed here are usually found in even the most basic word processing packages. When a very professional result is needed, a separate desktop publishing package could be used, although word processing software has continued to add formatting features originally available only in separate desktop publishing software.

Features are available in addition to formatting and editing. Depending on the word processing package selected, some variation exists as to the number and exact capabilities of these features, and new features continue to be developed.

Here are some typical features:

▼ Mail merge, which allows a file containing data (e.g., a list of names and addresses) to be combined with another file (e.g., a form letter), thus creating documents that appear to be personalized. (Some packages include automatic envelopes as well, which place the inside address of a letter into an envelope format.)

▼ A spelling checker, which checks to see if the words used in the document are contained in its dictionary. (The number of words in the dictionary, as well as the number of words that can be added to the dictionary, varies with different packages.)

▼ A grammar/punctuation checker, which reviews sentence construction for possible errors and may also measure length, clarity, and simplicity of the writing.

▼ A thesaurus, which indicates words that can be substituted for a specified word in the document, perhaps when you feel you have used a particular word too often.

▼ Find and replace capabilities, which provide for quick editing, such as searching for every time the word *author* was used and replacing it with the word *writer* in a document.

▼ Word processing software (as well as spreadsheets and other software) often has the capability to let you create macros. Macros are used for storing or recording a series of steps (e.g., the keystrokes for using search capabilities to find and perhaps replace items) so that you can automatically perform this series of steps any time you activate the macro.

Another important feature of word processing (and other) software that should be considered is the availability and depth of help screens. These screens provide explanations for completing various tasks, with varying degrees of assistance available for whatever topic or feature you specify. Early forms of help screens were menu-driven as the only option (you select the area of interest from a list of choices), but many now have become context-sensitive (the help screen automatically displays the topic that is related to whatever function is currently in the process of being performed). Some packages offer both forms of help.

Smart icons (also called buttons or simply icons) are available with most packages. These buttons allow you to select an icon (on-screen picture) to perform a function rather than going to a menu and making selections to indicate your choice through a series of commands. These icons are designed to represent the desired activity by using meaningful pictures; for example, a scissors icon may be used to represent the process of cutting or removing data from a document.

The number and extent of features continue to expand, so technology administrators must keep up-to-date with options available, typically by watching advertisements and reading journals, newspaper articles, and other related literature on a regular basis. Upgrading to a new version should be considered when enough new features are added to justify the cost of the change.

Global Perspective

Because the methods of displaying numbers, currency, dates, quantities, symbols, and punctuation marks vary in different parts of the world, businesses that prepare and send documents to other countries should consider the major differences and select word processing software that can accommodate them. Here are a few examples:

The time of day written as 5:30 P.M. in the United States would be 17:30 in Canada and Kl 17.30 in Norway.

The number 1,000,000,000 in the United States would be stated as one billion, but in some other countries it would be referred to as one thousand million.

Instead of the dollar sign used in the United States, currency in other countries requires special characters, such as the symbol for the British pound or the symbol for the Japanese yen.

Most countries other than the United States measure distances in kilometers rather than in miles and temperatures in Celsius rather than in Fahrenheit.

Icons or pictures on documents must be used with special care, because their meanings can be entirely different — perhaps unintentionally offensive — in some other parts of the world.

Many other variations exist in different cultures. To ensure long-term global success, it is very important to avoid using any wording, symbols, etc., that might be misleading, offensive, or misunderstood.

Spreadsheet Software

A spreadsheet is a series of vertical columns and horizontal rows. Spreadsheet software packages are used when the major activity involves numeric data and calculations. While a word processing package is set up for paragraphs of textual data, a spreadsheet is designed somewhat like an accountant's ledger or worksheet, with columns and rows into which data is entered. Although the primary emphasis of a spreadsheet is on numeric data, alphabetic data can also be entered.

Spreadsheet programs are used widely in business for keeping accounting and tax records, sales figures, and data for which calculations and analyses are likely to be desired. Spreadsheets are also used for personal activities, such as budgets, banking records, and income tax data.

Different spreadsheet packages contain varying numbers of available columns and rows, with some packages having hundreds of columns and thousands of rows. Typically, the columns are used to identify a particular item of interest, and each row contains data about that item. For example, a grade file for a class could contain a column for student names, columns for each test grade, columns for any other grades, and at least one column with a formula to calculate the final grade. Businesses should consider the size of spreadsheets needed as well as other capabilities, such as specific types of formulas needed, when comparing various spreadsheet programs.

Spreadsheets have some of the same editing and formatting capabilities as word processors. For example, you can make insertions and deletions to data in one location (an intersection of a column and row, referred to as a cell), copy or move data to another location, and adjust the widths of columns to fit the size of the data being entered. The extent of formatting options varies with different packages, with some providing different type fonts and type sizes, boldfacing, and underlining, as well as other options.

Most of the widely used spreadsheet packages can perform calculations with user-defined formulas as well as with some built-in formulas. In addition to formulas for totals and averages, here are some other types of formula calculations for which spreadsheets are widely used:

▼ Financial formulas, for calculating depreciation, loan payments for specified interest rates, and internal rate of return on an investment.

▼ Statistical formulas, to analyze a set of data for the highest or lowest value, the mean, and so on, as well as to perform many more sophisticated statistical tests to analyze the data for results of interest.

▼ Logical formulas, to make comparisons, such as checking to see if the contents are greater than a specified value, perhaps followed by instructions for procedures to follow for either a Yes or No answer.

▼ Date and time calculations, for purposes such as determining the number of working days available between the current date and some future date.

One popular use of spreadsheets is referred to as what-if analysis, because you can change the value in a certain cell and have any formulas that use that cell automatically recalculate. For example, you could have one cell that contains an interest rate and other cells that refer to that cell in formula calculations. By changing the interest rate entered in the cell, you can determine what would happen if the rate changed to that amount. Each time you change the value entered, the spreadsheet automatically recalculates. Formulas usually refer to cells by their location or address rather than by their actual contents, so that they can automatically recalculate if the contents are changed. What-if analysis is widely used by managers to help them in making decisions.

In addition to the capabilities of developing formulas and doing many types of calculations, other features are available with many spreadsheet packages:

▼ Macros, so that activities that are done the same way repeatedly can be stored as a series of steps that can be performed automatically when desired.

▼ Windows options, providing a split-screen capability with which multiple sets of data can appear in parts of the screen at one time.

▼ Graphics capabilities, allowing numeric data on the spreadsheet to be displayed in a chart or picture form.

▼ Sorting capabilities, so data can be rearranged alphabetically or numerically from highest to lowest or lowest to highest.

▼ Querying options, enabling you to create a list of those records that meet certain criteria, such as all people who earn less than $8.50 an hour and who have worked more than five years.

▼ File-linking capabilities, to automatically update data in one file when changes are made to related data in another file.

As with word processing and other types of applications software, the number of available features varies, with some packages providing more extensive capabilities.

Add-on packages are also available for many packages, including spreadsheets. Add-on packages are just what the name suggests; they can be added to widely used software and are generally designed to provide features not found in the basic package, perhaps at a lower cost than the cost of another comprehensive package if you need only a few added features. Statistical add-on packages, for example, are sometimes used with spreadsheets to provide more statistical analysis capabilities than are usually provided with the spreadsheets. The add-on package usually does not provide as extensive an array of features as would be found in a standard statistical package.

Database Software

Database software packages are computerized files containing records of important data. Many packages include basic calculations capabilities and sometimes limited paragraph data, but the primary focus is to store miscellaneous types of data, usually with capabilities of linking the data in various ways. As is true with other software packages, changes to data can be made very easily. For example, you can insert and delete information, and you can add new items. Options are also available that affect the appearance of the data on a printed page.

The primary purpose of a database software package is to be able to record items of interest about an object or person and to be able to manipulate this data in various ways to provide useful information. More flexibility of manipulation and linking of data is available in a database package than in a spreadsheet package. A spreadsheet's primary purpose is to handle extensive calculations.

With database software, data in one file can be linked with data in other files so that the data is available to be used together when needed, eliminating the need to record duplicate data unnecessarily within each file. For example, different types of employee data are needed by various departments in a large organization; some may keep insurance records while others keep pay records, and both may need current addresses and telephone numbers. This data can be stored in one file and linked to other files as needed rather than having each department keep its own address records. More chances for error occur when the same data is stored in multiple locations, and updating records in multiple departments becomes a nearly impossible task.

Here are some of the most common features of database software programs:

▼ Sorting and indexing, which give you options for rearranging data. (Sorting typically creates a completely new file with the data physically arranged in the designated order; indexing creates a new file that simply contains a record of the desired order and does not include the actual data.)

▼ Querying, which is used to look for data that meets particular criteria.

▼ A report generator, which lets you design your own form, with column headings that can be entirely different from the field names used in your actual file, and also lets you use only parts of the data.

▼ Programming language capabilities, giving you a means of automating some activities and also combining standard features of the software with programming commands to provide numerous customized applications, such as on-screen data-entry forms.

Mainframe and minicomputer packages usually contain much more extensive features than packages designed for use on desktop computers. Larger computer systems are usually accessed by many people, so they have different concerns, too. Security is needed to control who gains access to different sets of data. With multiple users, it is also necessary to have some form of locking, meaning that one person cannot retrieve a file for the purpose of making changes to it while another person currently has access to the file for the same reason. Without a locking mechanism, the second person gaining access to the file would have no knowledge of the first person's changes and might make unnecessary changes. In addition, since the changes would be made separately, the last update to the permanent file would override or erase the previous update rather than combining the two changes. In other words, the changes made first would be lost. With recent developments involving the linking of desktop computers, these concepts have become important with all sizes of computers. When businesses are considering database packages, the possibilities of having multiple users at the same time is a very important factor in making the selection.

The discussion in this chapter focuses on desktop database software used by individuals or small businesses. The development of databases for most organizations is a large, complex, and extremely important task, and is presented in Chapter 9.

Graphics Software

Graphics software is used for creating attractive charts and diagrams. Graphics are pictorial illustrations that are now so easy to create that they are used extensively in business letters, reports, and presentations to add to the understanding of the material. Graphics software packages generally have more options than the graphics that are included as a part of other software (such as the graphics available within some word processing and spreadsheet packages). The level of use of graphics would be a consideration in deciding to purchase a separate graphics package. Another factor would be the quality of finished product desired.

Presentation graphics is a term used in referring to packages with extensive features that can help make documents appear professionally prepared, and thus good enough to use at an important presentation. Presentation graphics software typically provides capabilities for output as 33mm slides, overhead transparencies, or on-screen slides.

Once a decision has been made to use a graphics package, the extent of options available compared with the needs of the business (and compared with the cost) becomes a primary consideration.

Although there are variations in the number and extent of capabilities, graphics packages often include these features:

▼ A clip art library, a collection of pictures or drawings of objects that are available to be inserted wherever desired in a document or within a graphic display.

▼ Freehand drawing, which allows you to use arrow keys or a computer mouse to move the cursor around on the screen as desired and create your own designs, which can then be combined with other built-in features.

▼ Built-in forms, such as organization charts, flow charts, and bar charts.

▼ Multiple chart capabilities, so that you can arrange several charts on one page or screen display.

▼ Symbols, such as boxes, arrows, and circles, that can be sized and arranged to meet your needs, and that can be combined with words.

▼　Three-dimensional options, to give a more life-like appearance to the graphic display.

Several companies (e.g., Corel and Microsoft) provide "office suites," in which they package several types of programs, such as the software described above. New versions of these suites continue to add more features, such as speech recognition software and programs for converting documents to types that can be used on the Internet.

Other Office Applications Software

Many other types of software are available to support or assist the work done in business offices. These types of software are generally more specialized and therefore used only in offices that need such software. The types of software described in this section are widely used in large offices where the number of employees who need to use the software is sufficient to justify the cost. Following are a few examples of the wide variety of software available.

Forms processing software gives you the means to design on-screen forms that can reduce printing costs and increase productivity. Many of these forms are designed so that the user can access related databases, select some information needed to complete the form, and have the information inserted automatically from the databases. For example, employee-information forms could access the person's records and automatically fill in routine data, such as social security number or years of service. Some of this software can also use electronic mail (email) to route a completed form automatically to each person who needs to approve it. For example, travel expense reimbursement and purchase order forms are being transmitted through email, with the forms being processed and the data input into a database automatically. This type of forms processing capability is sometimes referred to as part of a document imaging system, which generally includes a variety of technologies that allow you to create, obtain, process, and store various types of images.

Work flow software may include the routing of forms through an approval process such as those just described. But it may also include the automating of any office application—not just forms processing. Examples of work flow software that have been developed include mortgage loan processing, product design reviews, and claims processing. The procedures for a particular type of work must be clearly defined and are then automated to every extent possible.

Calendaring and scheduling software can be used to schedule meeting times that fit into the calendar of each participant, to update their calendars, and to display reminder messages as appropriate. They can schedule a conference room and request any needed audiovisual equipment. For this software to work appropriately, all people involved must keep their calendars up-to-date so that the software will have accurate calendars to work with.

MANAGEMENT DECISION-SUPPORT SOFTWARE

Decision support tools refer to software used for assisting managers and others in making decisions. Software is available for numerous decision-making activities, such as those that track the status of a set of goals and help in the organization of tasks and priorities.

Features or capabilities of software often used to assist in decision-making activities are described below. These include project management, decision support system, group decision support system, executive information system, and artificial intelligence programs. The primary distinguishing characteristic of this type of software is that it is used to provide assistance in making typical business decisions.

Project Management Software

Project management software is exactly what its name suggests—software used to assist in managing projects. A project is generally defined as some activity that contains several tasks and that must be completed within a specified time period. The project can be large or small, both in terms of the number or extent of tasks and the amount of money involved.

Project management software has been available for use on mainframe computers for a number of years. But many of the programs were too complex to be learned and used easily. Project management software is now easier to use than in the past, especially with packages based on Microsoft Windows and high-end PC versions now available, as well as packages available for Macintosh computers. Project management software can be used for planning, scheduling, and controlling all aspects of a project. The concept of project management involves dividing the overall project into individual activities or work units. For each activity, the following types of data are then recorded:

▼ Requirements for successful completion of the activity.

▼ The earliest time the activity could begin.

▼ The earliest time it could end.

▼ Any "slack time," or time that the activity could be delayed without delaying the entire project.

Information of this type is then used as a basis for making decisions for the entire project. Some uses of project management software include:

▼ Determining work force requirements and assigning people to tasks.

▼ Locating potential problems in the work schedule and recommending solutions.

▼ Maintaining accounting records of the project.

▼ Preparing management reports concerning the project.

Statistical techniques can be used to determine the probability of completing the project within various time periods. Some project management packages require the most optimistic, most pessimistic, and most likely completion times for each activity as a basis for determining probable completion times.

Project management software can be used effectively for planning before the actual project begins. During the completion of the project, the software is useful for displaying progress reports or for indicating changes that need to be made. Most projects include some unexpected occurrences, and one of the biggest advantages of project management software is the ease of making changes to the data to determine what effect any changes would have on the overall results or time schedule. The chances of correctly deciding on appropriate changes are much better if you use project management software, because you can test several options and get a good picture of the overall results of each choice.

As with all software, the types and extent of features and capabilities vary with different packages. Here are the basic features usually found in project management software:

▼ Front-end modeling, for planning and estimating the size, risk, and overall architecture of the project (a model is defined later in this chapter).

▼ Time reporting capability, for analyzing trends against base values and current plans.

▼ Work request system, for tracking and completing requested tasks within an acceptable time.

▼ Project accounting, for linking time reporting to specific projects to be charged for work, and for linking the project changes to the organization's accounting system.

▼ Resource leveling, for efficiently reviewing work request records and comparing that data with other factors that change resource availabilities constantly.

▼ Integration, for coordinating the functions of various aspects of the software, which is important because of the complex mix of projects and other activities occurring.

Proper planning before using project management software is essential. The major tasks to be included in the project must be clearly identified, and all team members must understand what is involved. Then the work is broken down into small, detailed increments that can be easily controlled. The process of using project management software itself must be planned and managed.

Many types of charts and other forms of output can be prepared through project management software. Some of the most commonly used charts created by project management packages are Gantt charts that emphasize time, and CPM and PERT charts that create diagrams of activities. These charts have been in use far longer than microcomputers have been available. They can be developed and used much more quickly and effectively now that microcomputers and software can be used to assist in their creation.

The main purpose of a Gantt chart (named for its developer, Henry Gantt) is to display all project tasks on a time scale so that the user can see how much time is expected to be needed for each task. Once the project is in progress, actual times are plotted, too, so they can be compared with the expected times. Horizontal bars are used for each task, with tasks usually arranged by date. Separate bars can be plotted for expected versus actual times for each task, with the bar for the actual times increasing in length as the activity gets closer to completion. Some software packages use one bar for each activity's projected time, with the bar then filled in progressively to indicate the amount of actual completion by a certain time period.

The PERT (Program Evaluation and Review Technique) chart and the CPM (critical path method) chart emphasize task relationships more than time required. Tasks are placed in boxes, with the boxes connected by lines that show interrelationships and with arrows that show the work flow. PERT charts (as well as CPM) highlight the critical path, which is the series of activities that require the longest time for completion. Activities along the critical path have no slack time, so any delay would cause a delay in the entire project. Most of these software programs automatically create the network of lines based on a task list and related dependencies provided by the computer user.

Some project management packages combine the best features of several types of charts. For example, the PERT task boxes may be used but arranged according to a time scale. Some Gantt charts include a display of the critical path to emphasize the group of tasks that must be completed on time.

Most organizations with multiple projects that are difficult to manage can benefit from using project management software. Project management software is more affordable today, and the number of available options continues to expand. When considering the use of project management software, you must analyze the company's needs as well as the amount of time required to determine what is available on the market, compared with how much you could improve the management of your activities by using this type of software.

Once you have established a need and are evaluating project management software, test the programs you are considering by using them on your equipment, if possible, with some of your existing data. An alternate method is to develop a model containing several typical tasks and to manually calculate scheduling and other results that can be used as a comparison with the software's results.

Here are some things to look for during the software testing phase:

▼ Scheduling of tasks. How does the software handle task scheduling when you include constraints such as one task that must be completed by a certain time? Also check to see if the software scheduled all related tasks before that completion time, as well as how much time will be required and the availability of any spare time on other tasks.

▼ Resource leveling. Does the software schedule people in the best way? Results may vary from one package to another. Some packages will fit your needs better than others, so you need to compare the results with your needs.

▼ Calculation speed. How long does it take to perform some task? The speed often varies from package to package. People who make these comparisons use the same task and see how long it takes with different packages.

▼ Cost management. How does the software handle different costs, and how much variation does it allow? For example, you might want to use different pay rates for different people; some packages can handle only one pay rate.

▼ Report features. Are there several ways of presenting data? Check to see if the reporting facilities include the features you need. Does the program allow you to delete details that some people (such as executives) do not want to see?

Decision Support System Software

Decision support system (DSS) software is designed to be useful for dealing with unstructured or semistructured problems, in which at least part of the information needed is not known in advance, and therefore cannot use a standard program to provide specific results. Unstructured problems are usually fairly complex, sometimes with no clear path from specific data to a result. Semistructured problems have some parts that are clearly defined and can be developed into programs, but with other parts that are not easy to program because they are not clearly defined. A structured problem is one in which all information needed is known in advance, thereby allowing programs to be developed ahead of time to generate specific reports needed by management (the original purpose of a "management information system"). With the capabilities available today, it is not necessary to limit the information used for decision-making purposes to those items that can be identified ahead of time and placed into a standard report.

The basic idea of a DSS is that data can be subdivided and linked in different ways to fit the needs of different decision makers. A DSS usually obtains its data from several sources—from databases developed specifically for the DSS, from other databases within the organization, or from data entry. Data used by a DSS is frequently internal, such as information from a transaction processing system, but may also be external, such as the numerous data banks available worldwide on a variety of topics.

A DSS can be used for one-time, special-purpose (ad hoc) decisions; but it can also be used for relatively complex situations that regularly occur. A DSS is designed to be flexible so that it can meet the needs of different people. The DSS responds differently depending on the data entered by a particular decision maker. The situations involved typically do not have one correct answer. The decision maker often must select trade-offs—giving up some of one item to get more of another item—to arrive at what is perceived as the best solution for that situation.

With a DSS, you can enter "what-if" questions and get results for different alternatives that you can compare and analyze. As mentioned above, what-if analysis refers to a process in which the person using the system makes changes to variables and learns what effect such changes would have on other variables. Although spreadsheets can be used as a tool for basic what-if analyses, a DSS usually contains more extensive capabilities. Goal-seeking analysis is another option; it operates from the opposite direction of what-if analysis. You begin with a known goal and determine what data is required to reach the goal.

A DSS gives the decision maker the opportunity to consider more alternatives than would normally be possible for one person to consider without the use of a computer. In addition, the DSS provides the potential for a better final decision as well as a quicker decision. DSSs do not replace the judgment of the persons involved and do not actually make the decisions, but they support and enhance the decision-making process.

Most DSSs can handle a variety of situations, are easy to use, and provide quick responses. DSSs usually have several other capabilities:

▼ They can search large amounts of data quickly.

▼ They can locate data that is housed in different locations within a microcomputer, on a separate mainframe, or even in an external database.

▼ They have flexibility in the appearance and content of reports, with no previously prescribed format needed.

▼ They can use a modular approach, meaning that activities can be separated into different programs so that only the parts that are needed are accessed at one time, but all parts are accessible whenever needed.

▼ They can perform mathematical or statistical analyses, such as studies of marketing research survey results.

▼ They can use graphical information for screen display or for printed materials, often to show trends and problem areas.

▼ They can use optimization and heuristic approaches (can find the optimum solution or can determine from heuristics a very good solution; heuristics refers to the process of learning or discovery through investigation).

DSSs are interactive, meaning that people using the DSS can communicate back and forth with the computer system. These interactive systems usually are designed so that they can be used without extensive experience with computers.

DSS software must be able to accept input from people using the system, preferably through the use of menus, prompts, icons, or other easy-to-use methods. It must also be able to provide output results, which can be screen responses or graphical displays, or printed copies of responses.

Here are the typical components of a DSS:

▼ A computer (often a microcomputer, but it can be larger), which can be connected to other computers through a network for accessing data or other resources.

▼ A database that can be internal, such as information from a transaction processing system, or external, such as any of the numerous data banks available nationally.

▼ DSS software that can access related databases and develop and use models that are appropriate for the situation.

▼ Models, such as a variety of mathematical models that can be combined or integrated as needed to fit a particular situation.

▼ A method of communicating with the system ("user interface"), to allow people to access the DSS; typically, simple English-like commands can be entered.

A modeling process is used to help in analyzing alternatives and making recommendations. A model is a simplified representation of some real thing, such as a manufacturing process. A model is usually a scaled-down version of whatever it represents. Models have the advantage of allowing you to try out new methods and make all the adjustments on a small system. Changes can be made faster, at lower cost, and without risk to the data or products. You can use DSS models to analyze data quickly without resorting to trial-and-error on the actual business system.

Basic DSS models typically correspond with levels of management— strategic models for top-level managers, emphasizing long-range planning;

tactical models for middle-level managers, for controlling operations and implementing the plans of the top-level managers; and operational models for lower-level managers, for use in day-to-day activities.

DSS capabilities are now being combined with other techniques to obtain useful results from large data warehouses (described further in Chapter 9).

Group Decision Support System Software

Group decision support system (GDSS) software is a specialized form of DSS with the additional capability of handling a group decision-making environment. GDSS software allows two or more persons to work together to reach a decision (a process sometimes called workgroup computing, with the software itself sometimes referred to as groupware).

Workgroup computing tries to simulate face-to-face meetings but without the time and expense of travel to meetings. It uses messaging systems, interactive scheduling, and project tracking. It provides a record of conversations in case questions arise about such things as who agreed to do a particular task. It also reduces paperwork and the number of meetings. Workgroup computing is a concept that can be used effectively for collaborative work on many types of projects when the participants are not in or near the same office, in addition to its use in the decision-making process.

The use of GDSS rather than face-to-face meetings may actually improve the quality of decisions, for several reasons:

▼ Participants may spend more time analyzing the situation before responding.

▼ All members of the group are more likely to contribute to the process.

▼ Decisions are not based on the tactics of group members who might try to dominate the discussion in a face-to-face meeting.

There are some disadvantages of this method, including:

▼ Some synergy or camaraderie may be lost when the computer is being used for communication; you do not get the feeling of "togetherness" or the teamwork atmosphere that often develops during face-to-face meetings.

▼ Some people may contribute less because they are not comfortable using a computer.

The GDSS process creates a record of everything that was said, which can be used later for clarification or for general reference.

A GDSS requires capabilities that are not part of a standard DSS. These include word processing programs that allow several users to access the same documents, in addition to electronic communications capabilities. The definition of a GDSS seems to vary in different organizations, but the primary focus is on teamwork and the sharing of information electronically as part of a group decision-making process.

A GDSS usually includes a method of voting on alternatives. The Delphi technique is often used in these systems. Decision makers located in different parts of the country or world can provide information. With the Delphi technique, several rounds of decision making may occur until a consensus is reached. This method encourages some creativity and original thinking.

In some organizations, a different form of GDSS has been developed. Participants gather at a GDSS meeting room, where each person uses a computer to express ideas, comments, or other messages electronically. Results are projected on a large screen without an indication of the source. Participants can vote on rankings of ideas anonymously through use of computers and software in the room. Individual discussion among group members can be combined with anonymous comments, voting, and so on, to develop ideas more rapidly than may occur with systems in which the group members are at different locations.

One of the trends related to this topic is the use of the term group support systems (GSS), which encompasses all types of systems to support workgroups, rather than the more restrictive GDSS terminology. Another trend involves group videoconferencing, using cameras and sound boards to provide audio and video images of other people involved in the conference.

Executive Information System Software

Executive information system (EIS) software is also considered a specialized form of DSS. An EIS (also sometimes called executive support system, or ESS) uses some of the DSS features but was originally directed toward meeting the needs of top-level management. With an EIS, a company's highest-level decision makers can obtain critical data in only a few keystrokes.

The primary goal of an EIS is to allow immediate access to information about the topics that are most important to a particular executive. For example, an executive of a retail department store would be interested in reports indicating which products are selling well compared with similar products by competing firms, and which items should be priced lower to encourage more sales. Top executives need information in a more concise, summarized form than do some employees at other levels.

An EIS is specifically designed to be easy to use with little training, primarily through the use of graphics and summaries. EISs do not require keyboarding skills. Executives can use a computer mouse or a touch-sensitive screen for making selections, if they prefer.

EISs are available for use in all types and sizes of computers. Although early EISs used mainframe computers and were very expensive, current systems rely heavily on microcomputers, which are now capable of storing important data or accessing other computers. Because executives need information from outside sources, an EIS needs to be able to access databases containing both internal and external data. External sources may include news services, the federal government, and even competitors. Uncertainty exists in many executives' decisions, and an EIS can help them assess and perhaps control the risks involved with these difficult decisions.

One example of a typical EIS function involves calculating and displaying performance indicators, such as the average time required to complete a particular task. Some EISs use directional arrows to indicate whether the numbers are improving ($\uparrow$), staying the same ($\rightarrow$), or getting worse ($\downarrow$).

A good EIS allows the executive to examine further details in any areas that may need attention, branching (called drilling down) to additional details on which the initial data is based. An EIS lets the executive go from summary to detailed information, to get cross-tabulations, and to get graphical representations of summary data. The data being used can be subdivided or combined in different ways depending on the current situation.

Although EISs were intended initially for executives who need to navigate through data quickly and easily to obtain answers to strategic questions, the same concept is being used in developing similar systems for all levels of an organization. Some of these tools are referred to as OLAP (online analytical processing) tools, in which users can navigate through corporate data by drilling down, moving up or across levels in different subjects or dimensions of the data.

Artificial Intelligence Software

Artificial intelligence (AI) software, as the term suggests, attempts to mimic human intelligence, such as thinking and reasoning. Computers cannot actually think, but they can be programmed to follow some of the thinking processes used by humans. Robots, one form of artificial intelligence, are used widely for repetitive and hazardous activities, such as automobile manufacturing processes. Robots are not widely used for many of the other, nonmanufacturing types of business activities, although new uses for robots continue to be designed. Two types of artificial intelligence that have numerous business applications are expert systems and neural networks.

Expert Systems Software

Expert systems software includes a reasoning capability that traditional computer applications do not possess. An expert system acts as an automated consultant to provide suggested answers to questions or solutions to problems. The expert system searches through alternatives and considers various factors before reaching a conclusion or suggested solution.

Expert systems—usually designed for specific, rather narrow purposes—are intended to perform the way an expert would perform. Programs are based on data acquired from experts. The expert system is asked for advice and follows the same procedures that a human expert would use if asked for the same advice. When a person is discussing a situation with a human expert, clarifications or additional information are often needed by the expert. An expert system also asks for further information as needed during the process of arriving at a conclusion.

Some people make a distinction between an expert system and one referred to simply as a knowledge-based system. An expert system has a knowledge base, which is the knowledge collected from one or more experts and stored in the computer to be used in the problem-solving process. But an expert system includes more than just a knowledge base; it has additional, specialized information provided by experts who help the system to resemble human thought processes. Experts describe their reasoning processes for specific circumstances, indicating such things as a series of steps to follow, items to consider, or comparisons to make. Developers then include these processes in their expert systems. Expert systems help the computer user to consider many important aspects of a situation before making a decision.

Expert systems have been designed for use in a variety of fields where a large quantity of data may need to be analyzed and where the conclusion is extremely important, such as in making medical diagnoses, designing new products, and determining manufacturing processes. Expert systems can be used at all levels of an organization.

Here are some benefits of using an expert system:

▼ Recommendations are based on knowledge of one or more experts, so the system may provide a better solution than that of a nonexpert.

▼ Decisions may be made faster because the system can search through data faster than a human can.

▼ Decisions are likely to be more consistent, following the same procedures each time and not being affected by personal biases, personality differences, or stress.

▼ The knowledge of one or more experts can be stored and used by nonexperts for an unlimited time.

▼ The system can be made available to more than one person at the same time, while one human expert can be at only one place at a time and can handle only one decision at a time.

Here are some problems in using an expert system:

▼   Development and maintenance of the system are difficult and expensive.

▼   These systems cannot yet learn from their own experiences, so they are limited in their ability to substitute for a human expert.

▼   Expert systems are not good at creativity.

▼   Expert systems have difficulty copying the human senses often used in reaching a conclusion, such as the senses of smell, touch, taste, and sight.

▼   Expert systems are usually limited to problems that can be defined very clearly.

The usual components of an expert system are the knowledge base, the inference engine, the user interface, a knowledge acquisition facility, and an explanation facility.

The knowledge base contains knowledge or facts about some area of interest. These facts are obtained from human experts in the area and can also include information from other sources, such as books and reference manuals. The knowledge base includes as much information as possible that can be used to follow the same procedure(s) used by a human expert to reach a conclusion on some topic.

The knowledge base also contains reasoning procedures based on information obtained by the expert(s). Several methods exist for representing this reasoning procedure. One widely used method uses a set of rules. A rule is a statement that links a particular condition to an action. These rules are usually in the form of "If . . ., then . . ." statements, such as "If ___ condition exists, then take ___ action." The knowledge base rules indicate the procedures or processes the system follows to reach a conclusion based on information provided to the system.

Another method uses "case-based reasoning," which stores historical examples (cases), e.g., previous situations or performance data. This data can be analyzed to assist in making decisions in a new situation. When this new situation occurs, its description is entered so that the system can search the database for the most similar case. The stored set of procedures for handling the selected case can then be tried on the new case, although modifications may be needed. One difference in this system compared with the rule-based system is that the database can continue to be updated and expanded as each new case and its solution is added to the database.

The inference engine is the part of the system that handles the procedures for solving the problems that it is given. The inference engine takes care of processing the rules and facts in the knowledge base to reach a conclusion. It determines which rules are to be used in a given situation, locates the rules, executes the rules, interacts with the system user as needed when additional information is required, and eventually makes recommendations by applying the rules to the facts.

The user interface is the part of the system that allows the computer user to interact or communicate with the system. It translates the person's input into information that the computer can understand, and it also translates computer information into a form that the person can understand. The expert system needs to be able to interpret responses to its questions appropriately, and the computer user needs to understand the system prompts and any other information provided. In addition to screen prompts, the user interface typically includes other facilities for ease of use, such as a natural language processor, one or more data entry screens, and a report generator.

A knowledge acquisition facility is used in developing (acquiring) the knowledge base. This facility allows the developer to enter appropriate information and relationships into the knowledge base, with the facility often designed so that menu choices are used to assist in the development. This facility provides the means of entering the facts and rules into the knowledge base.

The person who collects the facts from human experts or from existing data and determines how they need to be represented in the system is often referred to as a knowledge engineer. The knowledge engineer knows how to develop and maintain an expert system, but is not the person who will actually use the system. The knowledge engineer determines from the experts and from other sources the specific problems to be solved, possible solutions to the problems, and the rules to be followed by the system in using the facts to reach a conclusion. For example, the knowledge engineer determines which thought process the expert uses to reach a conclusion from the data and uses that process in developing the system.

Most good expert systems also provide an explanation facility. The expert system should be able to provide information about how it reached its decision, in the same manner that a human expert might need to provide an explanation. The typical explanation facility can list or display all the facts and rules used in reaching a decision, often with a diagram indicating the path or series of steps involved in reaching the conclusion. Some systems can also indicate a level of confidence in the conclusion.

Differences of opinion exist as to the minimum requirements before a system should be called an "expert" system. Some believe it must contain a neural network (described in the next section), while others simply require that it have more extensive capabilities than a simple knowledge base. An expert system can be acquired by purchasing a complete system from a consultant or vendor or by developing a system in-house.

> ## Management Perspective
>
> Here are some points to consider before purchasing or developing an expert system:
>
> The problem must be one that can be defined clearly.
>
> The problem must be one that has a logical pattern from definition to solution.
>
> The problem should be complex enough to require the use of an expert.
>
> At least one expert must be available, willing, and able to provide the knowledge.
>
> The overall benefits should outweigh the costs, perhaps by being available for use by several people in a manner that will save considerable time or make major improvements in the final conclusions being made.

Neural Networks

Additional information about artificial intelligence is available at the Web site.

A neural network attempts to imitate some of the functions of the human brain, especially the capacity to learn. The human brain has billions of cells, which run in parallel and create trillions of connections per second. Computers typically have individual logic circuits that are each linked to one other circuit so that information travels along one path. The human brain distributes its information more widely, and neural networks simulate this process by being wired with connections between circuits. Human brain cells (called neurons) receive data and transform it into outgoing data that is transmitted. Brain cells can use their experiences to change the way they react to different items of data that are received. Neural networks try to copy this process by using an input layer for receiving data, a middle layer for analyzing data and studying the rate at which it comes in and its connection strength, and a final layer that transmits the processed data. Neural networks in use today are considered rather primitive in comparison to the human brain, but improvements continue to be made to increase a neural network's ability to learn and the speed of processing the data it receives.

Neural networks are designed to mimic the brain's ability to recognize and understand patterns, such as those in faces, voices, and written characters. Neural networks learn by example. For example, a neural network may be trained to speak by giving it sample words and sentences and preferred pronunciations. It gets better as it encounters more examples. A neural network can also be trained for visual activities. One report described the use of a neural network to sort apples. The neural network was regularly shown which was a good apple and which was a bad apple so that it could learn well enough to correctly direct a mechanical device to throw out the bad apples. Neural networks have also been combined with optical character recognition (OCR) systems to improve the visual accuracy of data input. Neural networks can be trained to read very sloppy handwriting.

Neural networks are considered more precise than expert systems. For example, an expert system was used in one organization to detect potential credit card fraud. The system looked for obvious changes in spending patterns. The problem with the system was that too many card users were flagged when their spending habits changed slightly. Changing to a neural network reduced significantly the number of credit card users who were flagged to be checked for possible fraud.

Neural networks are used in the design of data mining systems that are becoming widely used in data warehouse systems today. These systems are discussed in more detail in Chapter 9.

Artificial intelligence systems continue to be developed and expanded. Business managers find it necessary to read articles and reports regularly to be prepared to make decisions concerning the possible adoption of new software systems of this type.

EVALUATION OF APPLICATIONS SOFTWARE

When evaluating applications software to determine which best meet your needs, develop your desired criteria ahead of time. One method is to create a checklist of criteria and to rank each software package based on how well it meets the criteria. Since some factors listed as criteria are probably more important to your situation than other factors, you can give the individual factors a weighted value according to importance for your needs, using a scoring system to help you make a final decision.

Here are some questions that could be used as a starting point for developing a checklist of desired criteria:

1. What general types of applications are most needed?
2. For which applications do you need more extensive features, and which specific features are most important?
3. Do you already have hardware on hand? If so, will the software work with the current hardware? (Hardware requirements are stated on software packages.) Ideally, software would be purchased before hardware, but once you have the hardware, you will probably purchase additional software that should be tested on a similar configuration to your hardware.
4. Is the new software compatible with other software already in use (assuming that it will continue to be used), especially if data will be shared between applications packages?
5. Does the software fit your needs without too much modification?
6. What level of support is available from the manufacturer or vendor?

7. Is training available from the vendor, and does the software contain a built-in tutorial?

8. How much and what types of documentation are available? Is it well organized, and are instructions easy to follow? Are additional materials available from other sources?

When you are purchasing software for office use and have multiple people using it, you must also consider the various arrangements available.

Here are some commonly used methods of acquiring the number of copies you need:

▼ Purchasing a licensed copy for each computer.

▼ Purchasing a licensed copy for each user.

▼ Purchasing licensed copies for the maximum number of users at any one time.

▼ Purchasing a site license, which may include a discount on multiple copies of the software or may include permission to make unlimited copies of the software.

▼ Purchasing a licensed copy for a file server, which can then be accessed by some number of multiple users.

If you already have a particular type of software, such as a word processing package, you can "upgrade" (buy a newer version) with features you need at a lower price than the price of a full package. Sometimes you can also get a competitive upgrade, in which your upgrade is to a different brand of package from the one you have now. Software manufacturers and other vendors are trying to develop new options in licensing. One

Ethical Perspective

Most software packages are considered copyrighted works, unless they are designated as "public domain" software (belonging to the public) or as "shareware," where you are encouraged to try the software and share it with others, but are expected to purchase the right to use the software after reviewing it. (Shareware typically costs much less than commercial software, and is often as sophisticated and feature-laden as some commercial software. Some commercially available programs started as shareware.) When you purchase copyrighted commercial software, you are buying the right to use the software. The programs that make the software work are still the property of the copyrighted owner. Typically, you are allowed to make one backup copy of copyrighted software. Businesses have been held

(continued)

(continued from previous page)

Ethical Perspective

liable when their employees make illegal copies of software. For example, it is not legal to purchase one copy of a package and make additional copies for thirty other employees.

Businesses are expected to purchase software, either through individual copies or through site licenses, to fit the usage to be made of the software. One problem is that many businesses, especially smaller ones, are not likely to be checked to see if they are using software properly. As with any guidelines or laws, businesspeople should take responsibility for doing what is right even if they are not likely to be penalized for inappropriate usage of software.

option developed by some vendors is a plan that lets businesses negotiate a contract based on the number of desktop computers they have rather than on specific software packages in use; however, this is sometimes a more expensive plan than other options. Another plan is one in which a company purchases a license for a specified amount of usage. The vendor supplies a program that monitors the company's usage of the software and allows them to purchase more usage if needed.

You must also decide where to purchase your software. Several options are available, such as Internet sites, mail-order catalogs, and various retail stores. Businesses often use multiple sources for different software.

Summary

Office automation refers to the use of information technology to automate activities typically performed in offices. In addition to automating tasks that might otherwise be done manually, office automation sometimes provides capabilities that would not be possible with manual methods.

Office applications software is used to automate many office activities. Typical examples include word processing, spreadsheet, database, and graphics programs.

Word processing software is used primarily for projects that involve the use of text in paragraph form, such as memos, letters, and reports. Common word processing capabilities include editing, formatting, mail merge, spelling and grammar checking, and find and replace operations.

Spreadsheets are used frequently for activities involving numeric calculations. Spreadsheets are designed to contain a series of columns representing the items of interest and rows for entering data about each item. Typical spreadsheet activities involving numbers include financial, logical, and date calculations. Other capabilities, in addition to numeric calculations based on the spreadsheet data, include graphics, sorting, and querying.

Database software offers some capabilities that are different from word processing and spreadsheet packages, such as a more extensive ability to link data from different files and produce reports based on contents of multiple files. This capability decreases the need for including the same data in more than one file, thus reducing duplication of data (redundancy). The linking ability provides additional capabilities that are not possible manually, such as automatic searches and comparisons of data in multiple files.

Graphics packages are used to create pictorial representations as an aid in understanding a message. Presentation graphics is the term used to refer to the types of professional-looking graphics that are generally prepared for oral presentations. Graphics software usually includes a clip art library and symbols, along with capabilities of creating freehand drawings, multiple charts on a page, and three-dimensional illustrations.

Many additional types of office applications software are available, such as programs for forms processing, work flow, and calendaring/scheduling.

Decision-support tools are a more specialized form of applications software, used to assist people who make decisions in businesses. Some of the available programs are used for project management, decision support, group decision support, and executive information systems. Some forms of artificial intelligence are used for more complex applications.

Project management software is used to assist in managing a wide variety of needs in planning, scheduling, and controlling all the work involved in major projects of an organization. Features include time reporting, project accounting, and resource leveling. Gantt and PERT charts are traditionally used project management tools, and many additional forms of output have been developed.

A decision support system (DSS) is used for unstructured or semi-structured decisions, those decisions for which at least part of the information needed may not be clearly defined in advance. A DSS can meet the needs of several people who provide different input; it responds differently based on the data provided. A DSS is often used for "what-if" analysis, in which the user can make changes to see what effect the changes would have on other items of interest.

A group decision support system (GDSS) is used when multiple people need to work together by computer and need access to the same documents and to each other electronically. The Delphi technique is often used to reach a consensus.

An executive information system (EIS) provides relevant data that is easy to use, quick to obtain, and easy to interpret. The focus was initially on types of data needed by higher-level executives, often including more external data than would be needed for lower-level employees. A recent trend has involved incorporating EIS capabilities into applications needed by persons other than high-level executives.

Artificial intelligence uses computers to imitate human intelligence. Expert systems and neural networks are two types of artificial intelligence with business applications.

An expert system is designed to duplicate human functions such as reasoning. Components of an expert system usually include a knowledge base, an inference engine, a user interface, a knowledge acquisition facility, and an explanation facility. A neural network provides an important feature—the ability to learn. The network attempts to simulate the methods used by the human brain in distributing information through the system.

When you are evaluating applications software for purchase, it is helpful to develop the criteria identifying your needs and priorities before beginning the search. Once you identify the software that best fits your needs, you must decide where to purchase the software, based partly on factors other than cost, such as provisions for documentation, training, and other assistance. You will also have to consider what license arrangement to use if there are multiple users of the software.

Questions for Review and Discussion

1.   Describe an example of a business situation in which you should typically use spreadsheet software and a situation in which you should typically use database software.

2.   Compare what-if analysis with goal-seeking analysis; provide an example of each.

3.   Why is a "drill-down" capability an important component of software designed for assisting in executive decisions?

4.   Compare expert systems with neural networks.

5.   What licensing options are available if you are considering the purchase of software to be used by 50 employees in your office?

Selected References

Alwang, Greg. "Instant Groupware." *PC Magazine*, February 10, 1998.

Brandel, William. "Licensing Stymies Users." *Computerworld*, April 18, 1994.

Cole-Gomolski, Barb. "Users Look, But Don't Leap at Groupware on the Web." *Computerworld*, March 24, 1997.

Devoney, Chris. "Go for the Bandwidth." *Computerworld*, April 13, 1998.

Eckerson, Wayne W. "Decision-Support Tools." *Computerworld*, December 2, 1996.

"Is Your Software Properly Licensed? *LAN Times*, February 22, 1993.

Levin, Carol. "Holographic Thinking." *PC Magazine*, November 18, 1997.

Melymuka, Kathleen. "Virtual Realities," *Computerworld*, April 28, 1997.

Samuelson, Pamela. "Copyright's Fair Use Doctrine and Digital Data." *Communications of the ACM*, January 1994.

Spanbauer, Scott. "Electronic Forms Fill the Bill." *PC World*, August 1993.

Chapter 5 Key Terms

Office automation
using information technology to automate office activities.

Office applications software
programs designed to assist in performing many activities found in business offices.

Word processing software
software designed for use primarily in creating documents containing paragraph data, such as letters and reports.

Editing
software capability of changing data in a document, such as inserting, deleting, copying, or moving characters.

Formatting
software capability of changing the appearance of data, such as underlining or centering a group of words.

Macro
software capability of storing a series of steps that can be activated and used easily; macros save time when the same steps are used repeatedly for a particular activity.

Help screen
on-screen assistance in completing specific software tasks.

Menu-driven help screen
help facility that gives users on-screen options for choosing a topic with which they need assistance.

Context-sensitive help screen
help facility that, when activated, displays the help topic related to the current activity being performed.

Smart icon
on-screen picture representing a specific function; selecting the picture activates the function (e.g., the user selects a printer icon to activate a printing activity).

Spreadsheet software
software designed primarily for numeric activities and containing vertical columns and horizontal rows into which data is entered, somewhat like an accountant's worksheet.

Cell
the intersection of a vertical column and horizontal row on a spreadsheet, representing one location for entry of data.

What-if analysis
capability of changing data in one location to see its effect on related data.

Add-on package
software with special features that can be used along with a basic software program such as a spreadsheet or word processing package.

Database software
software designed primarily for use with many types of data that need to be linked in a variety of ways at different times.

Graphics software
software with a capability of creating many types of charts or pictorial displays.

Presentation graphics
software with a capability of creating graphic materials of high enough quality for use in making oral presentations.

Forms processing software
software with special capabilities related to use of forms, such as designing, completing, and transmitting forms electronically.

Work flow software
software with special capabilities related to automating the flow of many types of work processes.

Calendaring and scheduling software
software that electronically checks calendars and then schedules meetings to fit those calendars.

Project management software
software that assists in planning, scheduling, and controlling all aspects of important project activities.

Decision support system (DSS) software
software that assists users with decisions in which some or all of the information needed is not known in advance (semistructured or unstructured decisions).

Goal-seeking analysis
analysis that begins with a desired end result (a goal) and works back to determine the data or path needed to reach that goal.

Model
a representation of some business activity or system that allows changes to be tested on the model instead of on the actual system.

Group decision support system (GDSS) software
specialized DSS designed to be used when multiple persons are involved in making one decision; also referred to as group support system (GSS) software.

Executive information system (EIS) software
easy-to-use system designed to provide summary data to top-level executives, with a drill-down capability to view additional details as needed.

Artificial intelligence (AI) software
methods of using computer capabilities to imitate human thinking and reasoning processes.

Expert system software
a form of artificial intelligence software that includes a reasoning capability; designed to assist in decision making by basing recommendations on information provided by experts.

Knowledge base
the part of an expert system that includes facts based on information gathered from experts, as well as rules that indicate procedures to follow in using the facts.

Inference engine
the feature of an expert system that handles the processing of rules and facts to reach a conclusion, using either forward or backward chaining (path direction).

User interface
computer system capability that allows the computer user to communicate with the system, such as to respond to prompts or questions that appear on the display screen.

Knowledge acquisition facility
facility of an expert system that allows the knowledge engineer (developer) to enter appropriate information and relationships into a knowledge base.

Explanation facility
feature included in an expert system to provide additional information to the computer user, such as rules used or path followed to reach a conclusion.

Neural network
a form of artificial intelligence software that imitates some functions of the human brain, such as a learning capacity.

Online Activities

Refer to the companion Web site at www.wiley.com/college/simon for a variety of online activities: additional chapter content, *Wall Street Journal Interactive Edition* access, review materials, student assignments, and relevant links.

GO TO http://www.wiley.com/college/simon

 THE WALL STREET JOURNAL.

Your four-month access to the Interactive Journal allows you to research articles published within the last 30 days in the Interactive Journal, Barron's Online, and Dow Jones Interactive. A Help feature is available if you need assistance in specifying your search topic.

One of the best ways to become familiar with the Interactive Journal is to use the "Journal Atlas." This site map allows you to jump into any of the sections or subsections in one click.

Research each topic in the Interactive Journal and analyze the results of your search.

1.   Neural networks or expert systems for business activities. What types of technology are being used? What business decisions might be necessary in deciding to use a neural network or expert system?

2.   Project management software. What types of capabilities are currently available? Do you expect that this type of software will continue to be used by managers?

3.   Group decision support systems in businesses. What are the trends related to the use of this type of software?

CHAPTER 6

System Software Considerations

LEARNING OBJECTIVES

After studying the contents of this chapter, you should be able to

1. Explain the general purposes of system software.
2. Describe and contrast the different types of control programs and processing programs that may be included in system software.
3. Explain the purposes of language translators and utility programs.
4. Describe the general types of operating systems available for large, medium, and small computer systems.
5. Identify and contrast the specific types of operating system software options available for small computer systems.

PURPOSES OF SYSTEM SOFTWARE

Computer equipment cannot operate without software programs to give it instructions. Two general types of software programs are referred to as system software and applications software. The general purpose of system software is to manage the resources of the computer by supplying programs that cause it to work properly and efficiently, thereby reducing the need for programmers and other computer users to handle these tasks. Reducing the need for human intervention by creating software instructions for the computer has the effect of providing more efficient, more productive systems. Applications software could not be used without system software to manage all the input, processing, output, and storage activities.

The word *system* in system software helps to emphasize that the computer itself is simply a machine and is dependent on the other parts of an information system—specifically, software or instructional programs, data, people, and related procedures. The system software is designed to communicate with the hardware as well as with the applications software and sometimes with computer users, so it plays an essential role in an information system.

As depicted in Figure 6.1, the people using the computer system actually communicate by using applications software (software designed for a specific purpose or application, such as to produce written documents). System software then serves as an interface between applications software and the hardware; and it transforms applications program instructions designed to be understood by people into formats that the hardware can understand.

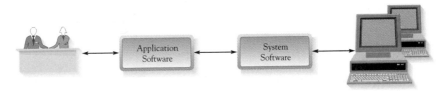

Figure 6.1 General Purpose of System Software

As hardware and software continue to become more compatible and to contain more advanced technological capabilities, businesspeople must be knowledgeable about system software and have an understanding of the available options. In the early days of desktop computers, software decisions primarily involved applications software. Now that computer users are more knowledgeable about their systems and these systems have much greater capabilities, the system software has become an important factor in decisions related to new hardware and new applications. Today there are even more choices when selecting operating systems, since they are available for use on multiple types of hardware (platforms), and since applications software programs are often developed for multiple operating systems. This chapter discusses the system software that makes it possible for the computer to do tasks such as processing, I/O, and other computer activities. Separate chapters deal with the hardware involved, such as processors, memory, communications, and storage. Adding new hardware capabilities will not have much impact on a computer's capabilities if there is no system software to direct the work of the hardware and to handle those capabilities.

CONTROL PROGRAMS

Control programs are used to handle scheduling of activities, to take care of input/output tasks, to communicate with computer users by displaying prompts or messages and to determine appropriate procedures when interruptions in programs or other unusual events occur.

When the computer is turned on or activated, the parts of programs most likely to be needed first are brought into its primary memory. This memory is a temporary work space inside the computer where programs and data are kept during processing. Those parts that are not as likely to be needed can be called into memory when needed, but are not resident within the main memory. Those parts of the program that are resident can call in other nonresident or transient parts of the program when they are needed. This procedure keeps more of the memory available for other purposes by not bringing in the parts of programs that have no immediate function. The memory and related processing activities are described in Chapter 7.

Computers of all types and sizes also contain methods of allowing programmers to write control programs, which are instructions as to how specific tasks are to be completed. These instructions are converted by the system into machine-language instructions that the computer can understand.

PROCESSING PROGRAMS

Processing programs make it easier for computer users to create and run programs or to use applications packages. Programs in the early computer systems used serial processing, which means that each program was executed one instruction at a time, one program after another. Because input/output devices (such as keyboards and printers) are much slower than the processing speed of the computer's central processing unit (CPU), the CPU was not being used efficiently; it could have been doing additional processing during the input/output phase if it were given some work to do. This inefficiency in the use of the CPU led to the development of programs for concurrent and simultaneous processing.

Concurrent Processing

Concurrent processing generally refers to a capability that allows the CPU to be working on more than one job at a time. One processor can actually perform only one processing task at a time, but a processor can perform a task so quickly that it has time to move back and forth from one activity to another, processing individual tasks so quickly that it gives the appearance of working on multiple activities at the same time.

System software is responsible for managing these activities. Although these software capabilities require certain hardware capabilities, the primary complexities involved in any form of multiple processing are often in the system software rather than in the hardware. The concepts are described in this chapter as they relate to system software, while Chapter 7 describes these features in further detail and includes some emphasis on the hardware involved.

Multitasking capabilities, in their most basic sense, allow the computer to work on more than one application at a time. Thus, the computer user can open a second application and perform tasks while the first application remains open. In larger and more sophisticated systems, the processor can handle multiple tasks by one person or by multiple users of the system. It processes only a portion of a task at a time, but can switch from task to task. Typically, the switch to a different task occurs when the processor reaches a logical stopping point, such as an input/output activity. Preemptive multitasking capabilities are becoming increasingly available; in this case the system software decides when to allow access to the processor and can change to higher-priority programs as needed. (A priority system is included within the programs for determining which programs have higher priorities.) Otherwise, one task could not be processed until another task was completed or for some other reason relinquished its access to the processor.

The form of multitasking in which the computer works on multiple tasks from a single computer user is also referred to as multiprogramming. The term time sharing is sometimes used to refer to multitasking that involves tasks from multiple users being worked on at the same time.

Figure 6.2 illustrates the concept of multitasking. At any given moment, the system software can be managing the processing of multiple tasks, even though only one processor is in use.

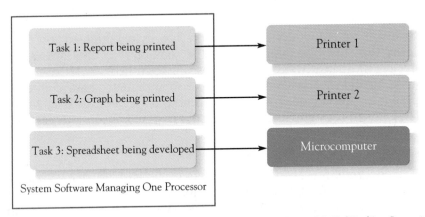

Figure 6.2 Multitasking Concept

One limitation of multitasking is that it requires programs being executed to be kept in partitions (subdivisions) in the computer's internal memory. Although memory capabilities of computers continue to increase, physical limits do exist, and these limitations are eased through the use of virtual memory. Virtual memory is somewhat like "virtual reality," in which something you are viewing seems real but really is not. Virtual memory is so named because the system software gives the appearance of unlimited memory by bringing into memory only that part of a program that is needed at a particular time, with the remainder stored on disk. This method allows more memory space to be available for parts of other programs; therefore, parts of more programs can be brought in to be processed during the same time period. When a new program part is needed, it can be brought in and its position added or exchanged with another part of the program that is not needed currently. The system software manages these exchanges.

Simultaneous Processing

Simultaneous processing is similar to concurrent processing, in that multiple tasks or multiple programs can be involved in processing at the same time, with the activities also controlled by the system software. The difference with simultaneous processing is that more than one task or program is actually being processed at the same moment in time.

Multiprocessing is a form of simultaneous processing that involves the use of more than one processor, in contrast to multitasking, in which several programs are being processed by one processor alternatively during some time frame. These multiple processors can be linked and coordinated, and several programs can be processed simultaneously since more than one processor is being used (Figure 6.3). Multiprocessing also can be used to divide up the processing of one large program task (Figure 6.4).

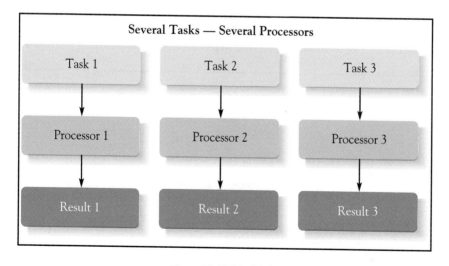

Figure 6.3 Multitasking: Several Tasks on Several Processors

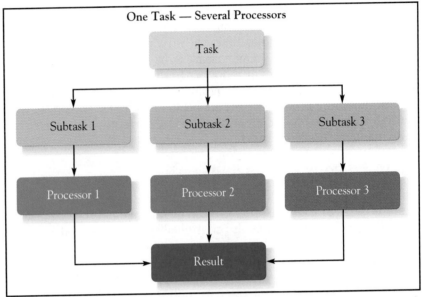

Figure 6.4 Multiprocessing: One Large Task

Multiprocessing can involve computers of the same size or of different sizes. One common method is to have one larger CPU linked to at least one smaller CPU. (The CPU is described further in Chapter 7.) The larger CPU is typically reserved for processing that requires greater capabilities, such as complex mathematical calculations. When a smaller or different CPU is used for coordinating input/output activities involving peripheral devices or other computer terminals and determining which activities are to be sent to the larger CPU, it is usually referred to as a front-end processor (Figure 6.5).

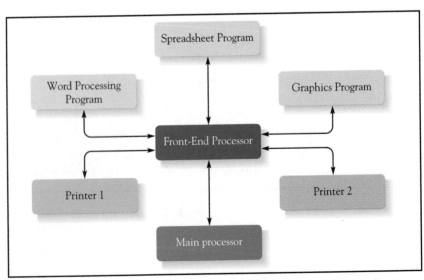

Figure 6.5 Use of Front-End Processor

When a separate CPU is used for maintaining or housing a database, it is usually referred to as a back-end processor. Although a smaller unit may be used as a front-end or back-end processor, systems exist in which the front-end processors are the same size as the main unit. In addition the back-end processor may need to be larger, due to the enhancements that have occurred to database systems recently. But front-end and back-end processors still serve the primary purpose of reducing the extent of demands on the main processor.

Ethical Perspective

One typical function of system software is to provide security. One current concern related to computers has to do with the number of files that are accessed by using social security numbers. With the increasing capabilities of file linking, as well as accessing other computers, knowledge of a person's social security number could provide a great deal of information. No clear-cut plan appears to exist within organizations that uniformly protects the privacy of individuals. One option organizations could consider is to select system software that can provide special types of security to fit their individual needs.

LANGUAGE TRANSLATORS

The general purpose of language translators is to convert programming language statements into machine language. Chapter 8 describes programming languages in more detail.

Machine language is limited to combinations of 0s and 1s, which is very difficult for humans to work with. Assembly language was developed to ease the programming burden of humans, but it was still very time consuming. Eventually, languages were developed that were easier for programmers to use. Anything that is not written in machine language must be converted (translated) to the 0s and 1s the computer can understand.

Assembly language uses an assembler as a translator. Other languages use interpreters and compilers for translating program code into machine-language format. An interpreter translates each program statement into machine-language statement(s) and executes each statement individually. The machine-language statements are not retained, so the program statements must be interpreted again each time the program is to be run. A compiler converts an entire program into machine-language format and retains the new code after execution, so that the compiling process is performed only once for each program. The original program code is often referred to as source code, and the machine language code is referred to as object code.

For a program that is not expected to be used more than once, one that uses an interpreter may be a feasible choice because of the overall time required. With a compiler, the program must first be converted to machine language, and then the compiled program is run. Compiled programs run faster, but that time savings exists only with the second and any succeeding uses of the program, for which it is not necessary to first convert the program statements into object code.

Every programming language must have a language translator. Most languages that are used for large or long-term business applications are designed to use compilers.

UTILITIES AND OTHER SYSTEM PROGRAMS

Utility programs are sometimes referred to as "housekeeping" programs, because their main functions involve changing the appearance or location of data. Utility programs provide functions such as rearranging files or transferring data from one file to another. They are used to change a file from one storage medium to another, such as from disk to tape storage. Utility programs also allow you to format disks, change the names of files, or delete files.

Some variations exist in the utility capabilities available, with larger systems typically having a greater need for more sophisticated functions. As with many system software capabilities, functions developed for use on larger systems have eventually become available for small and midrange systems.

Defragmentation refers to rearranging data in a file into sequential clusters (subgroups), which increases access speed when you are locating a file. When a file is stored on a disk, the first available cluster is used, then the next available cluster, etc., wherever they are found on the disk. This is a quick method, but it causes a file's contents to be scattered across the disk in nonsequential clusters, or "fragments." Defragmentation (sometimes referred to as defrag) puts the parts of a file back into adjoining locations, resulting in faster access.

A *data recovery* program is used to locate the clusters of a file when the file has been deleted accidentally from a disk. As long as no new files have been saved since the deletion activity occurred, the files are still on the disk. But the name of the file has been deleted from the directory, and the indication of the order of the file's clusters has been deleted from the file allocation table (FAT), which maintains a record of the locations of all parts of a file. The data recovery program locates the file's clusters and rejoins them in the appropriate order, reassigning the space so that any new files will not be saved in the locations assigned to this file.

System software features that were previously available only with larger systems have become available for smaller computer systems, such as desktop and laptop computers. These features offer additional security, including options of user identification, passwords, data encryption, and antivirus protection. Some features also make keyboard commands more accessible to people with disabilities (described in Chapter 7) and are mentioned here because they must involve some type of system software for the input to be processed.

Capabilities of utility programs continue to expand and increase. For example, these programs continue to improve their ability to fix problems that occur with data that somehow becomes "lost" or files that are damaged by a virus. Many of these utility programs are being included in new versions of operating systems, so you may not need to buy a separate utility program to take care of the more common problems that occur.

SPECIFIC OPERATING SYSTEMS

The group of programs that control or assist in the activities of the computer is generally referred to as the operating system. The operating system accepts instructions from the computer user or program and converts them to instructions that are understandable to the computer hardware. The operating system tells the computer what to do when the computer is started or activated, checks the computer to be sure the system is working correctly, and manages the overall procedure of receiving and interpreting instructions and performing desired activities. Operating systems have been developed and refined over many years to reduce the need for human intervention, thus increasing the speed and accuracy of the activities involved.

Operating systems serve many purposes, including

▼ Managing the operations of the CPU, such as scheduling jobs for execution.

▼ Allocating storage space as needed.

▼ Controlling input and output activities, such as displaying data on the computer screen, sending data to a storage device, or retrieving data.

▼ Determining priorities of the various computer activities.

▼ Communicating with the computer user about the status of jobs being processed.

This list illustrates that an operating system is a complex set of programs. Operating systems are getting even more complex as hardware capabilities increase and cause an increase in the managerial responsibilities of the operating system. The difficulties of developing operating systems account for the fact that new models of hardware are introduced much more often than new operating systems. Hardware is often obsolete in a few years, while some operating systems last for decades, although extensions or additional capabilities may be added to the software after the initial design, as hardware changes occur.

Global Perspective

Approximately three-fourths of software packages in use worldwide have been produced in the United States. One problem in using this software worldwide is that early computer standards for codes did not provide for all the written languages of the world. The most common coded character set for microcomputers is called ASCII, with 256 characters available. Code sets vary with different operating systems and language scripts. A standard called Unicode has been developed in an attempt to consolidate code sets and to provide a capability of encoding in all known written languages. Unicode has the capability of providing more than 65,000 characters; however, converting existing system software to Unicode is very expensive. Getting people to change is not an easy task, and a standard is not very standard if it is not followed.

Sorting order preference is another problem with operating systems being used worldwide, because of the many differences. For example, the U.S. sorting preference is from A to Z, but there are letters after Z in Denmark. The ch that would be treated as a double character in the United States is treated as a single character in Latin America and placed after c, preceding d. Other variations in preferences involve uppercase versus lowercase letters, accented vowels, and numerals.

Increasingly, programs are being developed that enhance the operating systems' ability to handle some of the global variations required.

The different operating systems available are compared here in groups according to general size of computer—large, midrange, and small. The operating systems for large systems generally are not compatible with those developed for midrange and small systems.

Operating Systems for Large Computer Systems

Mainframe computer operating systems (frequently called proprietary systems) have been around for many years and usually have been developed for a specific brand and capacity of computer, with little concern for compatibility. One reason for this lack of concern for compatibility was simply that businesses did not have a need for compatibility with other computers until recent years. In the earlier days of computers, businesses often had one mainframe computer that did not communicate with any other computers of any size.

Operating systems for mainframe computers must be able to control a computer system that typically has a great many computer users and many jobs. With these multiple users, the operating system must keep up with more input/output activities and more decisions about priorities than with one or a few system users. Security of the data is also a frequent concern, and mainframe operating systems typically have good built-in security systems. MVS®, one of the most widely used mainframe operating systems, is used on IBM® mainframe equipment.

Supercomputers have been developed more recently and are used primarily for very advanced calculations such as those found in large research projects. The operating systems for supercomputers vary in complexity, depending on the expected uses. Some supercomputers, for example, are designed primarily for scientific and engineering needs; others are designed to meet a wider variety of needs. UNICOS® is an operating system developed for use with some Cray supercomputers.

Operating Systems for Midrange Computers

Advanced features of operating systems that had been available only for mainframe computers have become more widely available for use with small and midrange systems. These features include additional capabilities involving multiple users and multiple tasks. These improvements are directly related to the increased capacities of these smaller systems.

Digital Equipment Corporation (DEC) minicomputers have traditionally used the VMS® operating system. VMS is considered by some to be a very sophisticated operating system that provides considerable help for inexperienced programmers, as well as flexibility and power for professional programmers. Now that the DEC Alpha processor is being used increasingly instead of the earlier VAX processor, the VMS operating system has been revised to work with DEC Alpha computers. Some of these computers are being used as "servers," providing programs and data to other computers ("clients") as needed. VMS has also added many of Windows NT's data structures and design elements; VMS servers are being used for some of the high-end computing for NT servers and workstations. (Windows NT is described below.)

The UNIX operating system was developed in the 1970s by AT&T for minicomputers. UNIX can be used on small and large computer systems, too, and has numerous memory management, file management, and utility capabilities. Multiple versions of UNIX are available. This operating system is described further in the next section, where comparisons are made of several operating systems now available for smaller computers.

Operating Systems for Small Computers

The most widely used operating system for microcomputers was developed, at least in its final form, by Microsoft. Its early versions were commonly referred to simply as DOS (disk operating system). Other operating systems that have been receiving increased use in businesses in recent years include Microsoft® Windows® (multiple versions), various versions of UNIX®, LINUX®, and Mac OS®. Expansions and enhancements of these systems have also been developed, and competition is fierce among developers. Decisions related to operating systems are becoming more important because operating systems are becoming more open—more able to operate with multiple types of hardware. In addition, businesses are relying more on small computers for their important applications now that these computers have more advanced processing and storage capabilities. In the following paragraphs, you will find descriptions of some of the operating systems that have been predominant, with the stipulation that enhancements and new operating systems continue to be under development and should be considered.

PC-DOS and MS-DOS

The original version of DOS for the IBM PC was named PC-DOS (Personal Computer Disk Operating System). A very similar system, MS-DOS® (Microsoft Disk Operating System), was designed for similar ("IBM-compatible") computers. The reason these non-IBM computers were compatible with IBM PCs is that they were all using basically the same operating system, as well as very similar hardware. These "DOS" systems were referred to as command-driven, because commands were generally executed by entering the name of the command desired, such as COPY or FORMAT.

The earliest versions of DOS were developed around 1980 for microcomputers with two floppy disk drives and typically no hard disk drive—the typical design of microcomputers at that time. Later versions of DOS began to support hard disk drives, networks, menus with mouse access, and access to a greater amount of memory. Although microcomputers have much greater memory capacity today than was true in the early 1980s, that memory is not automatically available—the operating system still must be capable of accessing it and managing it.

Microsoft® Windows®

One method of enhancing the capabilities of DOS was to install a separate "add-on" package. Microsoft (MS) Windows version 3.0, (followed by 3.1) was developed as an add-on package that became widely used with IBM PC and compatible equipment. (This software, as well as more recent versions, is often referred to as "Windows," but to avoid any possible confusion with other uses of the windows terminology, we will refer to the software discussed here as Microsoft Windows or MS Windows, unless a specific version clearly identifies it as a Microsoft product.) MS Windows 3.1 gave DOS users some limited multitasking capabilities, with "windows" or views into multiple applications. MS Windows included memory management capabilities so access to more memory was possible than with DOS alone.

Windows 95 (introduced in 1995) was designed to replace the original Microsoft Windows and compete better with other operating systems containing more advanced features. In contrast to Windows 3.1, Windows

95 was not an add-on for DOS but rather a "stand-alone" operating system. Some of the improvements included the capability to use longer file names, and a feature that lets microcomputers work automatically with added accessories (a "plug-and-play" feature—which means that you should be able to plug the accessory in and have it automatically set up and ready to be used).

Windows 98 was developed as an upgraded version of Windows 95 with improvements to some of these features. It supports the universal serial bus (USB), which allows many separate peripherals to be able to be used from a single port on the computer. USB peripherals are much better at "plug-and-play" performance, in which the peripheral starts working with your system as soon as you connect it. Another feature of Windows 98 is a capability of converting the hard drive to FAT 32 (File Allocation Table 32), rather than the traditional FAT 16. With FAT 32, the disk space is used more efficiently. In addition, FAT 32 recognizes any size of hard drive. In contrast, Windows 95 and earlier systems require you to partition a hard disk larger than 2 GB (gigabytes), usually designating one as Drive C and another as Drive D, then Drive E, and so on, depending on the total storage size on the disk.

Windows NT® is another Microsoft operating system that is widely used for computers operating on a network. Multiple versions of Windows NT have also been developed, with each designed to provide improvements to the previous version or to handle new technology as it becomes available. A recent version of Windows NT (called Windows 2000) allows Windows 95/98 computers to be upgraded to have NT's networking capabilities.

All versions of MS Windows contain a graphical user interface (GUI; pronounced "gooey") so that icons (pictorial representations of items to be selected) and a computer mouse can be used to issue commands. The term graphical user interface comes from the fact that computer users can interface or communicate with the computer by using graphical representations of their desired commands. The use of GUIs has been widely accepted because of the ease of learning and ease of use, and many commercial software developers are focusing their attention on development of GUI-based applications. A few problems have occurred with GUI developments, though. For example, it is becoming more difficult for developers to continue to come up with new icons that are easily recognizable. And not everyone prefers to use icons. In some situations, a person who is knowledgeable about DOS commands could accomplish a task faster by entering those commands through a keyboard than by going through a series of icon selections.

Many utilities that add extra features to MS Windows are now on the market. Since no operating environment can be exactly right for every user, Microsoft Windows can support a great many utilities that can be added to fit individual needs. (Newer versions require fewer add-on utilities because more have been included within the operating system.)

Microsoft Windows has many other advantages over DOS. DOS is limited in the number of TSR (terminate-and-stay-resident) programs and device drivers that can be loaded before running out of memory or encountering other problems. (A driver is a software program that tells the computer how to operate plug-in devices such as a mouse or a printer.) In Microsoft Windows, multitasking allows you to have many TSR programs, and DDE (dynamic data exchange) sets up a communications channel between applications that allows programs to talk to each other.

OLE (object linking and embedding) is a method of sharing data and functions among applications; objects that are stored contain data as well as information about what to do with the data, and multiple objects can be accessed and put together into one document. Object-oriented operating systems are the direction being taken by other systems, as well. Objects are interchangeable in different programs or applications. The use of objects makes systems more flexible, with programs and data that can be used wherever needed without requiring the development of a new program for each use.

UNIX and LINUX

The UNIX system initially developed for minicomputers can now be used on microcomputers because these machines have greater capabilities than earlier models. Versions of UNIX are available that can run MS Windows applications. Some operating systems, such as Solaris® and NeXTStep, do not use UNIX as part of the name but are UNIX-based systems. UNIX is not limited to specific types or brands of computers. UNIX is designed to "insulate" applications from the hardware specifications, which means that the application programs are handled the same way regardless of the hardware used for output (e.g., magnetic disk, magnetic tape, optical disk). A program runs the same way each time, even if the destination hardware changes.

With the original UNIX operating system that was designed around 1970 by AT&T, users had to enter lengthy commands, but more recent UNIX systems provide easy-to-use graphical interfaces. UNIX systems can be found today on all types of computers, from microcomputers to supercomputers. In addition to being able to handle the sharing of the CPU among several programs, UNIX can handle multiple users. UNIX does not have limitations of access to memory, and it can share files with different kinds of equipment on a network.

A relatively new operating system named LINUX has been increasing its market share significantly. One reason is that it can be downloaded free from the Internet. Another reason is that it has been getting good reviews from some businesses that have tried it and reported that it was more reliable than other systems they had used. A more reliable, more stable operating system reduces the costs of keeping the system running properly.

Mac OS

Apple® computers are known for their excellent graphics capabilities and their overall ease of use. The Macintosh® had extensive graphics-based capabilities (a GUI system) long before the MS Windows add-on became available for DOS systems. The reputation for ease of use is a major reason that Apple computers have been widely used in educational settings, starting in kindergarten (or younger).

The Macintosh operating system, or Mac OS, can handle the same types of activities as MS Windows and other microcomputer operating systems, such as accessing operating system commands. It uses a GUI system so the computer user is not required to know and enter command names. A computer mouse can be used for selections, so learning time and operating time are minimized. Other features include being able to see and exchange information from separate applications in different windows or divisions of the screen at one time, and being able to work on more than one task at a time (multitasking).

Table 6.1 is a list of several widely-used operating systems and the hardware on which these operating systems are primarily used. This type of information is becoming increasingly important as businesses try to link more systems to work together. New operating systems will be expected to communicate with multiple types of hardware and with other operating systems.

Additional information about operating systems is available at the Web site.

Operating Systems	Computer(s) Where Used
MS-DOS	IBM-compatible microcomputers
Mac OS	Macintosh and Macintosh-compatible computers, Power PCs
Windows 3.1	Added to PC-DOS and MS-DOS operating systems
Windows 95 and 98	IBM-compatible microcomputers
Windows NT and 2000	IBM-compatible microcomputers, usually on a network
UNIX	Supercomputers, minicomputers, and microcomputers; various versions available, such as Xenix and NeXTStep
VMS	Digital Equipment (DEC) minicomputers
MVS	IBM mainframes
UNICOS	Cray supercomputers

Table 6.1 Selected Operating Systems and Associated Hardware

SYSTEM SOFTWARE COMPATIBILITY

System software serves as an interface between the computer and the various application programs being used. Computer manufacturers develop programs for operating their computers and often for licensing to other manufacturers. These system programs usually include a variety of functions but can also be expanded or enhanced by knowledgeable users or programmers. Vendors also offer additional programs such as security and additional utilities that can be added to the system to provide extra features.

Although a great deal more compatibility exists now than in the early years of computer development, the system programs provided for one type of computer are not always usable on another type of computer. There is, however, a trend toward interoperability, whereby operating systems are connected so they can communicate with each other and transmit messages and data from one system to another. One refinement of this trend is referred to as open systems, in which it is not necessary to be concerned about which operating system is in use. Data and operating system commands can travel from one system to another without interruption. Because of these trends, it has become more important to pay special attention to the types of operating systems that are to be used on any new systems you are acquiring.

Management Perspective

Several considerations are important when choosing a new graphical user interface (GUI) environment. It should be one that is supported by a great many software developers and hardware suppliers (numerous applications should be available, as well as multiple brands of hardware). It must be one that can work with your current applications. Any new software you select must be written specifically for the GUI environment you choose. In addition, you should expect to encounter some needs for additional training, as well as a loss of productivity while computer users are adjusting to the new environment. You will also need to provide additional technical support to these people during the adjustment period.

Summary

System software provides an interface between the computer and the applications being used.

Control programs are used to schedule various computer activities, communicate with the user or with hardware, and generally oversee all the operations. This control process includes bringing into memory only those parts of programs that are needed so that remaining memory can be used for other purposes.

Processing programs are related to the actual execution of instructions within the CPU. Early computers used serial processing, in which one instruction was executed completely before the next instruction. Later developments in these programs allowed for the use of concurrent processing, which allows the CPU to work on processing more than one task at a time and thereby use its capabilities more efficiently.

Multitasking is a form of concurrent processing in which the CPU processes one program's instructions at a time, but can go quickly to a different program and work on its processing while an earlier program is involved in some other activity that does not require processing (such as input or output).

Multiprocessing is a form of simultaneous processing; it involves the use of multiple processors that are linked so their work can be coordinated. With more than one processor, several programs can be involved in an actual processing phase at the same time.

Language translators convert programs into machine language. Any programs not written in machine language must be converted. One type of translator is an interpreter, which translates each program statement and executes it individually, without retaining the translation. Another type of translator is a compiler, which retains the translated code after the execution of instructions has been completed.

Utility programs are used primarily to change the appearance or the location of data, such as transferring data from one file to another file or from disk to tape storage.

Purposes of operating systems include managing CPU operations, allocating storage space, controlling input/output activities, and determining the order of various activities according to priority.

Large computer systems include mainframes and supercomputers. Many of these operating systems are not compatible with operating systems for other computers. UNIX was developed as an operating system for minicomputers but can also be used on small and large computer systems. UNIX-based operating systems are not limited to specific types or brands of computers. LINUX is a fairly new operating system that has been increasing its market share.

PC-DOS and MS-DOS operating systems were designed as command-driven systems developed initially for microcomputers with more limited memory capabilities than today's computers.

Microsoft Windows was developed initially to be used with DOS systems, partly for its memory management capabilities and for its graphical user interface. Windows 95 and Windows 98 are stand-alone operating systems developed by Microsoft. Windows NT and Windows 2000 were developed for networked computers.

Mac OS is an operating system used by Apple Macintosh and Macintosh-compatible computers, which are widely known for their ease of use and graphics capabilities.

System software is generally acquired from the manufacturer at the same time the hardware is acquired. Additional system programs can be purchased from various vendors to add to the basic system features provided. Operating systems are becoming more compatible so that they can communicate with each other.

Questions for Review and Discussion

1. Explain the relationship between system software and applications software.

2. Contrast concurrent processing with simultaneous processing.

3. What is the primary reason for the use of a front-end or back-end processor?

4. Explain the purpose of (a) language translators and (b) utility programs.

5. Discuss some of the operating systems available for large, medium, and small computer systems; describe similarities and differences.

Selected References

Byers, T. J., and Rex Farrance. "Caches Pay Off," *PC World*, June 1993.

Davis, Dwight R. "Multiprocessor Software Plays Catch-Up." *Datamation*, June 1, 1993.

Heideger, Clark, and Mark Casey. "Get Ready for Windows." *Microsoft Magazine*, Fall 1997.

"How IS Can Explain UNIX to Meet Corporate Needs." Supplement to *Datamation*, September 15, 1993.

Kim, James. "Apple to Allow Mac Clones." *USA Today*, September 19, 1994.

Linthicum, David. "Operating Systems for Database Servers." *DBMS*, February 1994.

Mohan, Suruchi. "DLL, OLE, DDE: Making Sense of Alphabet Soup." *LAN Times*, January 25, 1993.

Poulsen, Tim. "What's New in Windows NT." *PC Magazine*, April 7, 1998.

Schmit, Julie. "Apple Takes Mac Operating System Forward." *USA Today*, May 12, 1998.

Schwartz, Bruce. "Windows 98 Is an Upgrade that Bears Scrutiny." *USA Today*, June 25, 1998.

Smith, Ben. "VMS: Alive and Well." *Byte*, November 1996.

Chapter 6 Key Terms

System software
software that serves as an intermediary between the hardware and the application software and people using the application software (e.g., by translating application commands into machine language and by providing on-screen information in a format that can be understood by humans).

Control program
instructions for the computer system that are designed to manage the various activities, such as input and output of data.

Processing program
instructions for the computer system that cause data to be changed or manipulated, which is a primary purpose of the system.

Serial processing
execution of instructions one at a time; inefficient and no longer used, after being replaced by concurrent processing.

Concurrent processing
a capability that allows more than one task at a time to be in some stage of execution, although one processor can actually be processing only one task at a given moment.

Partition
subdivision in a computer's internal memory (partitions are also used to subdivide disk storage).

Virtual memory
the appearance of having somewhat unlimited memory through a capability that allows only those programs that are needed to be held in memory at a given time and then exchanged with other programs when appropriate.

Simultaneous processing
using multiple processors to provide the capability of processing more than one task at a given moment; multiprocessing and parallel processing are forms of simultaneous processing.

Front-end processor
using a separate processor to coordinate input/output activities and thus reduce the activities performed by the main processor.

Back-end processor
using a separate processor to house and maintain a database and reduce the activities performed by the main processor.

Language translator
a facility that converts programs developed with higher-level languages (source code) into machine language (object code).

Assembler
a language translator that converts assembly-language programs into machine language.

Interpreter
a language translator that converts higher-level programs into machine language by translating and executing one statement at a time; the translated code is not retained.

Compiler
a language translator that converts an entire program into machine language and retains the translated code for future use.

Utility program
various "housekeeping" capabilities available for computer systems, such as rearranging data on a disk into a more efficient arrangement.

Operating system
the overall system that manages the computer activities; different operating systems have been developed for various types and brands of computers.

Proprietary system
operating system developed for a specific computer, typically a mainframe.

Command-driven system
an operating system format in which words (commands) are entered to indicate desired activities.

Graphical user interface (GUI)
an operating system format that includes pictures or icons from which users can select desired activities, rather than entering commands through a series of keystrokes.

Open system
an operating system environment in which computers can communicate with each other regardless of the type or brand of equipment involved.

Online Activities

Refer to the companion Web site at www.wiley.com/college/simon for a variety of online activities: additional chapter content, *Wall Street Journal Interactive Edition* access, review materials, student assignments, and relevant links.

| GO TO | http://www.wiley.com/college/simon |

 THE WALL STREET JOURNAL.

Your four-month access to the Interactive Journal allows you to research articles published within the last 30 days in the Interactive Journal, Barron's Online, and Dow Jones Interactive. A Help feature is available if you need assistance in specifying your search topic.

For career and company information, take advantage of careers.wsj.com. Use the Keyword search in Job Seek and search "information technology." Look over the types of positions available in this field. "Who's Hiring" offers links to company websites.

Research each topic in the Interactive Journal and analyze the results of your search.

1. Computer operating system, excluding Microsoft's. Identify who the manufacturer is, what systems it works on, any special features, etc. What are the chances that this operating system will become the predominant operating system for desktop computers?

2. Microsoft Corporation and Apple Computer, Inc. Why has Microsoft had a larger portion of the business market than Apple? Is there any chance that this will change in the next few years?

3. Digital Equipment Corporation (DEC) systems. How are they similar to or different from Microsoft operating systems? For what reasons would a business choose a DEC operating system rather than one from Microsoft?

CHAPTER 7

Computer Components and Options

LEARNING OBJECTIVES

After studying the contents of this chapter, you should be able to

1. Identify specific types of input and output, as well as their purposes and features.
2. Discuss important considerations for selecting appropriate input and output devices.
3. Describe the methods of magnetic storage, along with advantages and disadvantages.
4. Discuss optical disk storage options, including advantages and disadvantages.
5. Explain the general procedure involved in the processing of computer data.
6. Describe the components of the central processing unit.
7. Discuss significant developments related to chip technology.

OVERVIEW

One of the essential components of any information system is the computer hardware. With the increasing capabilities and expanded use of desktop computers for important business activities, decisions about hardware selections have increased significantly in importance. In addition to the communications devices described in Chapter 4, computers have input and output devices, a central processing unit, memory, and storage.

INPUT AND OUTPUT

In information technology, input refers to data and programs entered into the computer for some form of manipulation or processing. As part of this procedure, symbols understood by humans are converted to symbols understood by computers. Output refers to the information produced by the computer as a result of the processing. During this procedure, symbols understood by computers are converted to symbols understood by humans. These two procedures, often referred to as input/output (or I/O), are often discussed together because some input hardware can also serve as output hardware, and the hardware required for transferring data in for processing is primarily the same as that needed for sending the results out after processing. The hardware options available for input and output continue to improve and expand, making it increasingly more important for businesspeople to be knowledgeable about the considerations involved in selecting and using input and output devices.

The general concept of I/O is depicted in Figure 7.1. The processing activities, which are usually the reason for using the technology, are dependent on data and programs being brought in (input), with the results of the processing later provided in a desired form (output).

Figure 7.1 Input/Processing/Output Concept

Input

Input involves collecting raw data and converting it into a machine-readable form (a form the computer system can understand). The term source document is used to refer to the original source of the data input, such as an invoice, a handwritten set of notes, or any other document used as a beginning point or basis for input.

Computers can accept data and programs from a variety of input devices. Some of the most common forms of input are described in this section.

Keyboard

The most widely used input device is the keyboard, a device similar to a typewriter keyboard (but with additional keys), which a human uses to enter appropriate data by pressing keys on the keyboard. A screen or monitor is used with the keyboard so the person can view the keystrokes, but the monitor itself is an output device in this case. The primary disadvantages of the keyboard are the slowness of data entry when the person has limited keyboarding skills and the increased chance of error when entering commands. For people with physical disabilities that cause them difficulty in using keyboards, various adaptations are possible. For example, "sticky-key" software is available in programs that electronically lock and hold the Shift, Ctrl, and Alt keys when these keys otherwise need to be pressed at the same time as at least one other key. A picture of the keyboard can be displayed on the monitor, and a head-mounted pointer can be used to select the desired keys. Other adaptations include switches that can be activated by eye movements, breath control, or other muscle movements.

With an increasing number of workers now using computers in their jobs, some health concerns have arisen due to extensive use of computer keyboards and the potential for development of repetitive-motion injuries. One of the major repetitive-motion injuries resulting from long use of computer keyboards affects the wrists and is called carpal tunnel syndrome. The Occupational Safety and Health Administration (OSHA) has been working to develop regulations to control these injuries, such as giving employers the responsibility for taking actions to prevent injuries. Actions might include changing the schedules of data entry workers to reduce the length of time they perform keyboard entry activities without a rest break.

Several companies have developed keyboards that are designed to reduce wrist stress from extended data entry. Most of the new designs involve a keyboard that can be divided or is slanted to straighten the user's wrist position at the keyboard. When using the traditional keyboard, each wrist must be turned inward to use the straight sets of keys.

Pointing Devices

Pointing devices are widely used for a variety of input activities, such as making selections from options displayed on a screen or indicating a block of material to be moved or deleted. Pointing to items on the screen is often much faster than using the keyboard to indicate a desired function and does not require the user to remember which keys to use.

The computer mouse is the most commonly used pointing device for input. The mouse is attached to the computer system and is moved around to change the position of a blinking position marker called a cursor, an arrow, or some other pointing symbol displayed on the screen. One reason for the development of the mouse as an input device was to create a method of input that would be easier for people with little or no keyboarding skills. Unfortunately for those without good keyboard skills, much of the input continues to involve entry of paragraph or numeric data, rather than menu selections.

Ethical and Social Perspective

Title I of the Americans with Disabilities Act (ADA) prohibits employment discrimination against a qualified person with a disability. A qualified person with a disability is someone who can perform the essential functions of a position but may need some reasonable accommodation. Being able to use a standard computer keyboard for data input is sometimes difficult for people with certain disabilities. The ADA requires businesses to provide reasonable accommodation to a disabled person in testing and in other hiring procedures, as well as in performing the job. Therefore, a disabled person who is qualified for a job should not be disqualified as an applicant simply because of the disability if a reasonable accommodation could be provided so that the person could perform the job. One example of what might be considered a reasonable accommodation would be to read the questions on a paper-and-pencil test to a blind applicant. Another example would be to design a method, perhaps with Velcro™ straps, of positioning a computer mouse in the hand of a person who did not have the ability to grip the mouse but needed to be able to use the mouse to perform the job.

A trackball is similar to a mouse in concept (an upside-down mouse), with a ball device used to move the cursor or pointer displayed on the screen. Trackballs have become especially popular for use with small computers, such as the notebook-sized models, where they are often built into the computer near the keyboard. In other systems, they can be attached to the side of the keyboard.

Touch pads have also become popular for use with notebook-sized computers. The computer user simply touches the pad and moves the tip of a finger across the pad, with the cursor on the screen moving in the same pattern.

A touch-sensitive screen has a grid of invisible infrared beams, sound waves, or electric current that is broken when the screen is touched, allowing the computer system to determine the position and take an appropriate action. To use a touch-sensitive screen, you simply touch the screen at a particular point to select a command or desired action, and the computer knows what to do based on the location of the touch.

Pen computers are small, handheld computers that use the touch screen concept but use a pen as the pointing device. You select from items on a screen by pointing to the desired item and touching the screen in that position with the pen. The computer identifies the selection by determining the coordinates of the points on the screen being touched by the pen. Although some pen computing systems accept only numbers, others also accept alphabetic data and other symbols, in handwritten form.

Scanners

A scanner is an input device that can be used to convert data to a machine-readable form without data entry from a human. This method is much faster and more accurate than having a person use a keyboard to enter material from a printed page. Scanning can convert text or graphical data into digital input. Scanners and the other input devices described in this chapter have become essential to many businesses with large transaction processing systems requiring fast, accurate input of massive quantities of data.

The scanner sends the digital data to storage in the computer system so it can be used in whatever form is desired, such as a graphics program or an optical character recognition (OCR) program. OCR techniques have been used for a number of years to read characters that are in typewritten or printed form. Some OCR systems can read handwriting. Most OCR systems are designed to read the bitmap created by the scanner and determine the pattern or map of the page, locating various parts such as paragraphs, columns, headings, and graphs. A bitmap is a matrix of pixels (picture elements or screen dots).

Once the data has been converted through use of the OCR, it can be saved in any of several formats, such as those appropriate for use with word processing or spreadsheet packages. Some OCR software uses the Microsoft Windows object linking and embedding (OLE) technology, which allows the computer user to scan in documents and automatically import them into a word processing document or into a spreadsheet.

One problem with the increasing availability and capabilities of scanners is that they can be used in unintended ways. The American Bankers Association indicated that counterfeiting of fraudulent checks is a major crime problem facing banks. Criminals feed images of checks drawn on good accounts into their computer systems. They can then change the date and name of payee and print copies of the fake checks on laser printers that have check paper (this type of paper is available at most stationery stores). Many businesses are printing their checks on their own laser printers, with their own logos; crooks can get laser printers, inexpensive scanners, and graphics software to copy the check designs rather easily. Because there is no standard design of checks, they are easier to counterfeit than cash.

Point-of-sale (POS) terminals use scanning technology and are widely used in retail stores. Many of these terminals include a "wand" reader that can be passed over the price tag to automatically enter the product code into the computer system, which is then matched with a price stored in the system for that product code. A keyboard is used for additional input, a cash drawer is included, and a form of printer provides a receipt. These terminals are often connected by a communication line to large computer systems located elsewhere that maintain sales information and inventory records.

Magnetic ink character recognition (MICR) is a scanning procedure that was developed over thirty years ago for use by banks, in which magnetic ink characters are placed on checks. The characters can be read by humans but can also be read very quickly by a magnetic ink character reader. The use of this equipment greatly increased the speed of processing checks. MICR readers read a check by magnetizing the magnetic characters and sensing the signal as each character passes by the read head.

Speech/Voice Recognition

Another type of input is available through the use of the human voice. Speech (or voice) recognition units analyze and classify speech patterns and convert them to digital codes for use by the computer system. One goal of speech recognition is to be able to dictate text to a computer, but one that some people see as an even bigger goal is to reduce the need for a mouse by being able to issue voice commands instead of clicking on an icon. In the type of voice recognition sometimes referred to as a speaker-dependent system, the computer has to be "trained" to recognize particular words and voices. Anyone using the system must spend considerable time training the computer to recognize that person's voice patterns. These systems work by storing a person's spoken words as electronic patterns, which are later compared with sounds or electronic patterns received through voice input. The computer can take the appropriate action once it "recognizes" specific words. A majority of the software available today uses this system predominantly.

Some voice recognition systems can recognize words from a variety of voices. Most of these systems have limited vocabularies but can recognize different voice patterns that use words in its vocabulary. This method is often referred to as a speaker-independent system. Improvements continue to be made in this type of system to increase the vocabulary and the ability to recognize different-sounding voices, including regional accents.

Voice and speech recognition has been available for decades but has been too costly to pursue until recent years, with a need for very expensive software as well as expensive computer hardware. These systems require considerable processing power and storage space. The software is fairly complex, since it must analyze each sound and determine the most likely words in a particular situation. Algorithms are used to match patterns, and these systems need to be able to recognize variations in tone, pitch, rate of speaking, and so on. Several systems have been developed for dictating text to a computer, but they still need work before they can replace either the keyboard or mouse. Two programs that are currently available are Dragon Systems' Dragon Naturally Speaking, and IBM's ViaVoice.

Additional uses are being made of voice or speech recognition systems. Some translate words from one language to another. Some are used for security because a person's voice pattern (voice print) can be used as an identifier, similar to the way a fingerprint is used. Automobile manufacturers are developing methods of using voice commands for several activities, such as adjusting the volume of the radio or lowering a power window. These recognition systems free the hands for other purposes and also can be used by people who are disabled. Input systems of this type continue to be developed and are expected to improve significantly in their recognition capabilities over the next few years. Some people are predicting that voice technology will eventually replace the mouse as a predominant input device

Other Forms of Input

Satellite signals are being used for input into some computers, especially for navigation purposes. The signal is picked up by receivers (located on aircraft, ships, land vehicles, or in handheld units, for example) containing a computer that determines time, location, and speed. Automobile manufacturers are installing these systems in some dashboards. If you have a receiver on your dashboard, the information about time, location, and speed is transmitted to a large computer at a base station. The information is displayed on a map that is relayed to your car so you can see your position on your computer screen, as well as appropriate routes to your destination. Rental car companies were among the first users of these capabilities when they became available for automobiles. Many ground transportation businesses are using systems of this type to aid in the rapid delivery of products and people.

Additional information regarding input devices is available at the Web site.

A smart card is another form of input (as well as a form of storage of data). It looks very much like a credit card and contains a computer chip that stores data that can be used for security purposes, such as personal identification data. Smart cards are being used as identification cards and for charge purposes. They are considered fairly secure because they are difficult to duplicate. For monetary transactions, these cards are used to retain a record of the current balance in an account, and the card is used as input into vending and other machines to allow spending without carrying cash or writing checks for small amounts.

Output

Output involves converting computer system data into a form that is usable by humans, usually either displayed on a screen (called soft copy) or printed on a page (called hard copy). Output can also be in an audio form, or it can be directed to a storage device. As mentioned previously, some forms of input also serve as forms of output. Even the punched cards described as an early input device also served as an early output device, with the cards stored for future reference. Many more methods of output are available to us today, and the most widely used forms of output are described in this section.

Screen Displays

The computer's visual display or monitor appears on a screen that is similar to a television screen and is sometimes referred to as a VDT (video display terminal), CRT (cathode-ray tube), or simply screen. Images on the screen are created through the use of points of light called pixels. A pixel can be turned on or off and can be in different shades or colors. The number of pixels per inch (density) determines how clear the images are, and is referred to as screen resolution.

Early monitors on desktop computers were primarily monochrome, meaning that only one color was available for displaying data against the background (such as white or green on black). Most businesses and individuals now use microcomputers with color monitors.

Most desktop computers use CRTs for the display devices. The CRT is the oldest but still most common type of monitor. The CRT is basically a vacuum tube. Monitors for desktop computers can display graphics as well as text, along with color.

The VGA (video graphics array) monitor has 720 by 400 pixels for text and 640 by 480 pixels for sixteen colors. In addition, 256 colors are available with a resolution of 320 by 200 pixels. Super VGA (or SVGA) displays up to 256 colors with at least 800 by 600 pixels, with some models having 1,024 by 768 resolution. The numbers continue to increase.

The standard VGA monitor uses 4-bit technology, and the SVGA uses 8-bit technology. Since computers use the binary (base 2) system of 1s and 0s, 4-bit technology refers to a way of expressing 2^4, which indicates the total number of 1 and 0 combinations that are available (16 in this instance). High-color cards are available that use 15-bit (2^{15} or 32,768 colors) and 16-bit (2^{16} or 65,536 colors) boards and are good for using photographs as part of the display. A 24-bit card (referred to as true color) that can display over 16 million colors is available for those situations in which the most lifelike color images are needed.

If the work you are doing does not require high-quality color capability, you can get faster performance by using a card with a smaller number of colors. The cost, of course, increases as you increase the quality of color output.

Smaller, more portable computers often use liquid crystal display (LCD) devices, similar to the type of display on small calculators. CRTs are too large to fit in small computers with flat-panel displays. Work continues on improving the screen display of portable computers. Some of the technology, referred to as an active-matrix screen, makes the screen easier to see by providing greater contrast, a wider viewing angle, and a faster refresh rate than the passive-matrix screen design. But the active-matrix screen typically uses more power and is more expensive to purchase.

Although most desktop computers still use CRT monitors, some manufacturers are developing monitors that use flat-panel display technology. Monitors could be much lighter in weight and physically smaller with this technology. However, the cost is still considerably higher than the CRT technology. If other computer technology costs can be used as a predictor, this flat-panel technology can be expected to decrease in price in a few years.

You should be knowledgeable about options related to color displays before selecting a monitor. Here are some things to consider:

▼ Screen size: larger sizes of desktop monitors (such as a a 17" or 19" screen) usually take up more desk space (referred to as a larger "footprint") but are increasingly popular. If the monitor size is not mentioned in an advertisement, it is probably a smaller size.

▼ Dot pitch (dp): spacing between dots on the screen that produce an image. Most people recommend that the dot pitch should be 0.28 mm or less, although lower numbers equate to higher prices.

▼ Screen resolution: number of pixels on the screen. A higher resolution generally provides a sharper image; for example a 1024 x 768 screen is recommended for people spending a great deal of time looking at the monitor.

▼ Refresh rate: how many times per second the full image is redrawn. Generally, 70 hertz (Hz) rate or more will provide images without a noticeable flicker.

▼ Video card support: the video memory available to support higher resolution needed if more colors are used. At least 1 MB (megabyte) of video memory is usually needed.

Printers

Printers are the most widely used form of output other than display screens. Printers produce copy by receiving electronic signals from the computer system. Numerous improvements have been made over the years in printer speed and quality of the printed document. In addition to standard paper output, many printers can print on other materials, such as labels, envelopes, and transparencies.

The laser printer is one of the most widely used printers for small as well as large computer systems. Laser printers create images on a document through the use of a laser beam.

Laser printers can produce both text and graphics of very high quality and much more quickly than some other types of printers. Results look very professional. Color laser printers are available and offer high quality of output, but they are still rather expensive for situations in which only occasional use of color is required. One prediction is that color laser printers will be widely used in businesses once the price gets low enough to justify the cost, because they offer high quality and a capability of printing on varieties of paper.

Another type of widely used printer is the ink-jet printer. This printer directs ink toward the paper. Ink-jet technology is not new; IBM produced an ink-jet printer over thirty years ago, but printing was rather slow and the ink often smeared. In addition, the holes that the liquid ink must pass through often clogged. Many improvements have been made in recent years, including a reduction in the problems of the ink smearing on the page.

Color ink-jet printers have increased in quality in recent years, while the price has been decreasing. These printers usually have four colors (one is black) that can be mixed to provide a wide variety of color options.

Here are some topics to consider when selecting printers:

▼ quality and speed of output, primarily dots per inch and pages per minute

▼ ease of use, such as an easy-to-see and easy-to-use control panel

▼ your need for color, as well as the quality and extent of color needed

▼ compatibility of the printer with your software

▼ capability of printing on different sizes of paper, on envelopes, or on transparencies, depending on your needs

▼ capability of handling specialized fonts or other format options you require

▼ cost comparisons for all of the above versus importance of each factor (cost comparisons should include paper and replacement materials that will be needed, such as new ribbons, ink cartridges, or toners)

Audio Output

Audio (voice) output from a computer is often obtained through the use of a voice synthesizer. Sounds previously provided by humans are stored in the computer and generated electronically when appropriate. Examples include the recorded message that gives you a telephone number when you call directory assistance, and the car voice that tells you that your car door is open. The quality of audio output is often excellent, so good that some people actually want poorer quality because they want to know when the voice is computerized.

Audio output has become more widespread in recent years as multimedia usage has increased, especially with the extensive use of Internet Web sites that have these capabilities. As with voice input described above, increased noise could become a concern in offices with multiple employees, especially if it causes distractions to occur that decrease productivity of other workers.

SECONDARY STORAGE

Secondary storage is required because the primary memory within the computer (described later in this chapter) does not provide permanent storage for the data and programs that are needed by most businesses or individuals. Data is stored separately in a variety of forms that allow permanent storage of data and programs, with the storage capacity limited only by the amount of space available for housing the storage media. This permanent storage is described as nonvolatile because it is not erased when the computer's power is turned off. Most primary memory is volatile—its contents are erased when the power is turned off.

The types and capabilities of secondary storage available are becoming increasingly important as hardware and software capabilities increase. As we progress to more extensive systems such as imaging systems and computers with very large processing capabilities, we will need storage systems big enough and fast enough to access and transfer data efficiently and effectively. Many businesspeople are now expected to be knowledgeable enough about current storage options to make appropriate decisions about their usage.

Encoding Systems

Data and programs must be stored in a form or code that the computer can understand. Digital computers use a binary system, which is the basis for the most widely used encoding systems for computers. This chapter's topic of storage is a logical place to describe encoding systems, since they are used for data storage. Keep in mind, though, that the concept is not limited to secondary storage. References to these systems occur in discussions of all aspects of information technology and are especially important in making comparisons of computer system capabilities.

The binary system of two options (0s and 1s) is used to represent data because it fits the two-option situations found in computers. For example, electricity can be either on or off. Semiconductor circuits are either conducting or nonconducting. A magnetized spot can be either a positive charge or a negative charge, depending on its direction or polarity.

The binary system of 0s and 1s can be used to convert every type of character, including values and special symbols, into a form that the computer can understand. Each 0 or 1 is a binary digit, referred to as a bit (combined from binary digit). Bits are combined into groups, called bytes, to represent individual characters. In contrast to the decimal system that uses powers of 10, the binary system involves powers of 2.

Some values concerning the capabilities contained in computer advertisements are directly related to powers of 2. The number of different options represents all the combinations of 0s and 1s that can be created for the number of positions available. An 8-bit card has 256 (2^8) different combinations of 0s and 1s, and a 16-bit card has 65,536 combinations. You may have noticed that these are some of the same numbers

Additional information about encoding systems is available at the Web site.

that were used to describe monitor capabilities in the previous section. Capabilities are determined by the number of combinations of 0s and 1s that can be stored.

Here are some related terms:

A kilobyte (abbreviated as K or KB) represents 1,024 storage positions because it is based on the binary (base 2) system and represents 2 with a power of 10 (2^{10}).

A megabyte (abbreviated as M or MB) represents 2^{20} bytes, which is 1,048,516 bytes.

A gigabyte (abbreviated as G or GB) represents 2^{30} bytes, which is 1,073,741,824 bytes.

Two encoding systems for computers that have been widely used are Extended Binary Coded Decimal Interchange Code (EBCDIC, pronounced IB-sae-dik), used on many IBM and similar minicomputers and mainframes, and American Standard Code for Information Interchange (ASCII, pronounced AS-key), widely used on microcomputers. EBCDIC is an 8-bit code, therefore containing 256 possible combinations of characters. ASCII was originally a 7-bit code, with 128 characters (2^7), developed cooperatively by several manufacturers in an attempt to create a standard code. An 8-bit version (called ASCII-8 and able to represent 256 characters) was later developed that can be used with computers designed to use an 8-bit code. The extra bits beyond alphabetic letters and numbers in the ASCII and EBCDIC codes are used to create special symbols or sounds. ASCII has become the standard encoding system for microcomputers in the United States. A standard encoding system allows files developed with one software package to be usable with another package. It also allows you to use the data if you change from one computer to another—as long as they all use this standard.

Tape Storage Media

The two general media used for secondary storage are tapes and disks. Both methods continue to be used, with selection decisions typically based on the type(s) of access to the data that will be needed compared with the costs involved. Tape storage is the method that was developed first for storing computer data.

Magnetic tape allows a large amount of data to be stored in a small space. Tape storage devices are sequential access devices, which means that everything is recorded in serial order, one after another. Retrieval also must take place in a sequential order, moving from the current or starting position to the desired position. The same concept applies if you are viewing video tapes; you can "fast forward" to get to a desired position, or you can rewind to go back and see something again, but you cannot jump from Scene 2 to Scene 16 without passing by Scenes 3 through 15. Tape storage media are available primarily in two forms: reel-to-reel magnetic tapes or magnetic tape cartridges.

Reel-to-Reel Magnetic Tapes

Reel-to-reel magnetic tape has been used in large computer systems ever since we started storing computer data for business applications. Magnetic tape is similar to other types of recording tapes, using a continuous strip that is wound onto a reel. Reel-to-reel magnetic tape storage uses two reels, a supply reel and a take-up reel. Reel-to-reel magnetic tape systems are used today primarily for long-term storage or for large-system backup data.

Most magnetic tape storage is organized into nine parallel rows, called tracks. Each track contains the value of one bit (0 or 1) at a particular location on the tape; across the width of a 9-track tape at any one position would be a total of 9 bits. A combination of 8 bits is used to represent a single character. The ninth bit is used as a parity bit—a way of checking for errors when bits are transmitted from one place to another.

Tape density is measured in bytes per inch (bpi), which is the number of bytes that can be stored in one linear inch of tape. Reels vary in price, depending on storage density and length of tape. Capacities and storage needs versus cost of storage are important factors when businesses are selecting tape storage systems.

The tape drive onto which the magnetic tape is mounted when it is to be used contains a read/write head that can read or detect the magnetized bits as the tape passes by and can then convert them into electrical pulses to be sent to the central processing unit (CPU). These blocks of data are often preceded by a header block containing data about the block of data to follow, such as an identification number, number of characters included, and format of the block of data. When being used to write, the read/write head magnetizes spots on the tape and erases any data previously stored there.

Magnetic Cartridges

Magnetic cartridges are based on the same storage concept as magnetic tape. A trend has developed in recent years toward increased use of cartridges instead of reel-to-reel systems, probably because of the convenience of use. Magnetic cartridges typically use 1/4-inch-wide tape, and tape drives that meet the standard format that has been established are referred to as QIC (quarter-inch cartridge) data cartridges. Storage capabilities are quite high on some cartridges, with some having several gigabytes of capacity. Prices vary depending on quantities purchased and size of tape storage, but the cost per byte is quite low (not quite as low as reel-to-reel tape, but lower than other storage options).

Cartridge backup systems are used for microcomputers as well as for midrange systems. In addition to the low cost of storage, other reasons for their popularity are that

▼   they provide more secure backup than magnetic disks.

▼   some tape cartridges can store considerably more than one reel of magnetic tape and require less space for storage of the tape.

▼ increased capacity of microcomputers has made their data and applications more important to the operations of various organizations, thereby increasing the need for backup systems.

Magnetic Disk Storage Media

Magnetic disk devices are direct access storage devices (DASD). With direct access (also called random access), each storage position has a unique address and can be accessed without having to search through all data recorded previously. Therefore, disks have greater access speeds than tape storage media, which explains why tape storage is typically used only when frequent access to specific items is not expected to be needed, such as for backup systems.

Microcomputers have always used some form of magnetic disk for data storage. These disks have several features that make them preferable to magnetic tape for desktop computers, primarily because data on disks can be accessed either directly or sequentially. In addition, data on the disks can be replaced by new data and used over and over. These disks are inexpensive, although they are more expensive than magnetic tape in total storage cost per byte of data. Numerous improvements have been made since the first microcomputers and their disks, and today we have more types of disks to choose from as well as greater storage capacities.

As shown in Figure 7.2, tracks on magnetic disks are divided into invisible sections or pie-shaped wedges. Each subsection in a wedge on a track is a sector. In this illustration (the traditional arrangement that began with the first IBM PCs and compatible equipment using 5 1/4-inch disks), each track contains eight sectors. The Macintosh design also used sectors, but the design is different; outer tracks contain more sectors than inner tracks. Tracks and sectors are numbered and used as part of the address where data is stored so that access can occur directly.

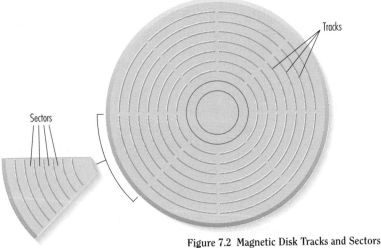

Figure 7.2 Magnetic Disk Tracks and Sectors

You may see references to tracks and sectors at various times when you are using a computer, perhaps when you are checking a disk for a possible problem. Track and sector numbers simply identify specific locations on a disk.

The two most common forms of magnetic disk are generally referred to as floppy disks and hard disks. The computer must contain a disk drive that is appropriate for the type of disk being used. The disk is the location where data is stored, and the disk drive contains the technology that allows the storage and later retrieval of data to occur.

Floppy Disks

Although various floppy-disk sizes have been in use, the predominant ones at first were the 5 1/4-inch size, followed later by the 3 1/2-inch size. Most new microcomputers no longer contain a 5 1/4-inch disk drive (unless special-ordered) because of the preference for the 3 1/2-inch disks. Instead of the early designs of 5 1/4-inch and/or 3 1/2-inch disk drives, many these desktop computers now contain a CD-ROM drive and often a Zip drive (discussed below), in addition to a 3 1/2-inch disk drive.

As is true with magnetic tape systems, a disk drive contains electronic heads that can "read" or "write" data (called read/write heads). The read/write head on a disk drive is located on an access arm, which moves back and forth over the disk. When you want to read or write to a particular file, a seek operation occurs first, in which the access arm moves the read/write head to the appropriate track. The search operation then occurs, in which the diskette is rotated to the appropriate position. The time span from the beginning of the process, when the request for data in secondary storage is made, to the time when the search operation has been completed is called access time. Access time is generally very fast, frequently less than 25 milliseconds, and is affected by the time required for the seek and search procedures. Another factor affecting the total time involved before the data is actually available for use is the time it takes to transfer the data from the disk to primary memory (transfer time). Access and transfer times have become important considerations for businesses that depend on speed of their systems as a major factor in their competitive success.

The read/write head copies data from the disk to the computer's internal or primary memory by converting the magnetized spots to electronic signals. Reading from a disk does not change the data stored on the disk. Data is changed only when new data is written onto the disk into the same location as previous data. When you save a file using the same name as a previous file, the computer erases the earlier file as it stores the new file.

Technology related to capabilities of floppy disks and their disk drives continues to improve. For example, some high-density disks used today have storage capacities of about 2MB. In contrast, the Zip disks introduced more recently provide 100-250MB of storage, which has caused them to be used sometimes for backing up data on desktop computers.

Iomega, which provides Zip disks and drives, also has Jaz drives. Jaz disks have 1-2GB storage capacity. The Zip disks are widely available for standard desktop computers, with the Jaz drives typically used when significantly larger disk storage capacity is needed. Both Zip and Jaz drives are available for internal installation or as external drives.

Hard Disks

A hard disk drive contains at least one metal disk (often more than one) that holds programs and data through the use of magnetic spots and can also read and write data in the same manner as a floppy disk. A hard disk has considerably more storage capacity than a flexible disk. Most hard disks are built into the computer cabinet and are not visible to the computer user. These disks are not removed from the computer cabinet after each use; they are permanently installed, although they can be removed if necessary—perhaps for repairs or to be replaced by a higher-capacity disk system.

One advantage of hard disks is that they are tightly sealed with no need to be constantly exchanging the disks in and out of the computer, thereby reducing the chance of damage to the disk. The operation of the disk is very similar to that for the floppy-disk drives described earlier, with a motor to rotate the disk, an access arm with read/write heads, and a seek operation and search operation. Access to data on a hard disk is faster because the disk can rotate faster than a flexible disk, which could actually get too warm if it were to spin too fast.

Management Perspective

Many of the improvements in storage technology are related to speeds of accessing and transferring data. You have several hard-disk options to consider when making computer purchases. Unfortunately, advertisements and brochures for hard drives often use acronyms with no explanations, such as SCSI (pronounced "scuzzy"), IDE, and others. When you are evaluating potential computer purchases, be sure to notice the type of hard-disk drive technology included. Small computer system interface (SCSI) drives and integrated drive electronics (IDE) drives include controller electronics in the drive itself to further increase transfer speed. SCSI drives use technology that is considered more versatile than IDE, but many computer users do not need those capabilities. You should not pay extra for something that your employees do not need. Capacity of the disk drive is partly determined by the size and number of disks but also by the technology used. Make comparisons of costs for your needs versus different types of technologies before making your selections.

Disk packs are widely used with larger systems, such as minicomputers, mainframes, or a microcomputer that is connected to other microcomputers in a network to provide data or programs for other microcomputers. These disk packs are hard disks containing several platters that are positioned above each other.

Space is allowed between the disks for access arms. With two read/write heads on each access arm, extra capacity is provided because one head can read the surface above while another reads the surface below. In some designs, the top surface and the bottom surface are not used. Those outer surfaces have a higher risk for damage, and the access arm design with two read/write heads per arm can be used for all disk surfaces involved if the outer surfaces are not used. With this design, a disk pack with ten disks, for example, would have eighteen surfaces (not twenty) on which to read and write data because the surfaces on the top and bottom of the entire pack are not used.

All the disks in a disk pack rotate together. The read/write heads are positioned over the desired track by the movements of an access mechanism. All the heads move to the same position on all the disks. The same track location on multiple disks forms a vertical line called a cylinder. Therefore, the number of cylinders equals the number of tracks per disk. The number of tracks in a cylinder equals the number of usable disk surfaces. A disk pack with ten disks and eighteen usable surfaces would have nine access arms, eighteen read/write heads, and eighteen tracks per cylinder. The cylinder number is used as part of the disk address for an item of data.

A technology option related to multiple disks is called RAID (redundant array of inexpensive disks or redundant array of independent disks). This type of storage system involves the use of multiple disk drives. High data transfer rates are possible because several write operations are performed simultaneously. Disks used can be standard 3 1/2-inch disks, which are inexpensive forms of storage. The "I" in RAID was originally for "inexpensive," since the disks themselves were inexpensive. However, some people believed that was a misleading term because the overall systems are fairly expensive. Therefore, some people now use "independent" as the word being represented by the "I."

Removable hard-disk media is an additional storage option. The applications available today have so many features that they can fill up the space on your internal hard drive rather quickly. Using removable media gives you the option of increasing your storage capacity without replacing your internal hardware. Some removable hard-disk drives use a cartridge design; these removable cartridge hard drives have an external case that includes the read/write head mechanism and the drive electronics, along with a magnetic cartridge that contains the disk.

If you use all the storage space on a removable hard disk, you can buy another one and interchange them as needed. If you are using the cartridge media, you simply buy additional cartridges. Another advantage of

Additional information about storage options is available at the Web site.

removable media is that you can physically remove confidential or restricted data or programs to a secure location if other persons have access to the computer system.

Optical Disk Storage Media

Optical disk technology has continued to improve, and businesses (and individuals) have begun to take advantage of the available features. An optical disk can store large quantities of data, including pictures or images that can be accessed and displayed directly on a computer screen. Optical disks are often being used for permanent (unchangeable) storage of data, through the use of laser technology. A laser beam is used to burn small pits or tiny holes in the surface of the disk to represent data. (The two-option binary concept is still in use here: either a pit is located in a certain location or it is not.) A lower-powered laser beam is used to read the disk to determine the existence of pits in specific locations and send the data to the computer chip for conversion. Optical disks used for changeable data typically use a combination of laser and magnetic technology (see "Rewritable Disks," later in this section).

Optical media have a longer shelf life than magnetic media and are less susceptible to poor environmental conditions, such as high temperatures. Estimates of the shelf life of optical media range up to 100 years, although the technology has not been around long enough for us to check this out yet. One disadvantage of optical disks versus magnetic tape is the cost of storage. Magnetic tape costs are estimated to be significantly lower per megabyte, although cost estimates continue to change as technological advances occur.

Banking institutions have become major users of optical-disk storage systems. Optical technology gives banks a way to store large amounts of data and access it easily. Many types of bank documents can be scanned into the system and stored on optical disks. Documents such as canceled checks can be disposed of once an image has been stored. The documents can be viewed on screen, with a copy printed if needed. Banks have reported savings of millions of dollars in paper costs after changing to optical-disk storage. Additional savings occur in labor costs involved in accessing data. Customer service has also improved because of the quickness of the system in locating data compared with previous paper systems.

In general, optical disks are available in two forms:

▼ disks that can be written on only once.

▼ disks can be erased and reused.

Of course, your computer must have a disk drive (internal or external) designed for the type of optical disk technology you want to use.

Write-Once Disks

Early optical technology was referred to as WORM (write once, read many) technology because it could not be changed once data was written on the medium. WORM disks are used for archival storage and for long-term backup, since the data cannot be erased (you cannot refill the pit that was created by the laser beam). WORM disks can be used as evidence in many courtrooms because the recorded data cannot be altered.

WORM-type disks are also used in some imaging systems, such as the bank document system described earlier in which images of documents are stored and retrieved on screen as needed. Large systems may use a jukebox, which uses the same concept as an old-time music jukebox, in which an order for a record caused the desired platter to move out from a storage slot onto a horizontal surface for access. Disks in many imaging systems are stored in slots or racks. When data from a disk is to be read, a mechanical arm moves the desired disk to a disk drive for reading and then returns the disk to its slot. The user can then view the image or do various types of processing without changing the data stored on the disk. Jukeboxes vary in the number of disks they hold. Some have capacities of fewer than ten disks; others can hold over a thousand disks. (Jukeboxes are also used with systems of multiple rewritable disks such as those described in the next section.)

CD-ROM (compact disk read-only memory) began its life as a form of WORM technology. This type of disk can be used on a microcomputer with a CD-ROM disk drive (the traditional spelling in the music industry is compact disc). One primary difference is related to who stores the data on the disk—WORM data is recorded by the business or individual, while CD-ROM data was initially recorded by publishers and others who mass produce the data for distribution to anyone who wants to purchase the disk.

Another difference is that you can continue to write to a WORM-type disk until it runs out of storage space; you just cannot erase anything previously written to the disk. With most CD-ROM disks, the entire writing process takes place at one time. The CD-ROM disk drives can be installed internally in a disk drive slot of a microcomputer, or they can be external disk drives.

Disk drives for microcomputers are now available that allow the computer user to write once to a compact disk. These disk drives are being used extensively for multimedia presentations (e.g., sound and animation added) and various forms of desktop publishing in businesses. The disks are typically called CD-Recordable (CD-R). Additional uses are being made of these disks, such as for backup systems and for data distribution. Although they are more expensive for backup copies than magnetic tape systems, CD-R systems allow for fast, random access to data, which is not possible with magnetic tape. Now that so many desktop computers contain CD-ROM disk drives that can read CD-R disks, a disk onto which numerous business images or other large files have been stored could be duplicated and sent to various persons within the organization as needed.

The primary benefits of CD-ROM and CD-R are the same as for other forms of optical disk storage—storage capacity and permanence of data. The main disadvantage is that access times are typically slower than with hard-disk drives, although the technology continues to improve.

Digital Versatile Disks (DVDs) are now being mentioned as technology that may replace CD-ROMs, as well as magnetic disks. DVDs are similar to CD-ROMs in their appearance, but DVDs can store considerably more data. DVD disks have more tracks per disk; the tracks on DVD disks are thinner, with pits that are not as deep as those on CD-ROMs. Initial DVDs were designed to be read-only, referred to sometimes as DVD-ROM. WORM versions being developed are often referred to as DVD-R, in which data can be recorded once per disk. DVD-RAM and DVD+RW are rewritable formats of this technology (competing manufacturers use different terminology). It is expected to be several years before this rewritable format (described below) overtakes CD-Recordable technology in usage level.

Rewritable Disks

Additional information about storage is available at the Web site.

In recent years, optical disks have been developed to allow data that is recorded on them to be erased, with new data then recorded on the disk (often referred to as CD-Rewritable or CD-RW disks). Most of these disks use magneto-optical (MO) technology, which combines some features of magnetic technology with optical (laser) technology. Data is recorded magnetically, and a laser is used to make changes. The surface of the disk cannot be changed magnetically at room temperature. Instead, a laser beam heats very small points on the disk surface to the temperature at which its magnetic properties change, and the magnetic writing head then changes the polarity of the area. For reading, the laser operates at low power and the disk rotates beneath the light. Reflected laser light rotates either clockwise or counterclockwise, depending on the polarity in each spot. The rotation is determined by the drive and converted into digital data.

These disks are durable because the surface is touched only by light. MO disk drives typically have faster access times than floppy-disk drives but are slower than hard-disk drives. The main disadvantage of MO disk drives is their cost, which may be several hundred dollars more than a Zip drive. However, it has several advantages, such as transfer rates that are similar to those of hard-disk drives.

MO technology is a method favored by some well-known standards organizations. A standard called Continuous Composite has been accepted by the European Computer Manufacturers Association, the International Standards Organization (ISO), and the American National Standards Institute (ANSI). Having these standards helps make it possible for the disks to be interchangeable among disk drives from different vendors in different countries. It is always a good idea to select products that follow accepted standards.

Additional Storage Options

Several additional options exist for improving secondary storage capabilities. Some that appear to be increasing in usage are described here.

Smart Cards

Smart cards are credit-card size but contain a built-in computer chip for storing data (also used for input, as described above). Data may be of many types, such as financial data or medical data. These cards are widely used in Europe and are expected to increase in usage in the United States in the next few years. This technology continues to improve and includes the capability of encrypting crucial data while also consuming very little power.

Smart-card technology is being used to protect computerized data. For example, one system provides a smart card and a smart-card reader that is attached to the desktop computer and used to protect the stored data. The computer user must insert the card into the reader and enter a related personal ID number before gaining access to the data. Cards of this type are being used for more security of Internet shopping as well as electronic mail. These cards will become more widely used in the United States if retail stores decide to replace their magnetic-strip readers with smart-card readers.

One report indicates that about one-third of all Visa cards are expected to have these built-in chips by 2002.

Holographic Storage

Holographic storage is being considered as a possible solution to the problem in the storage industry of eventually reaching an ultimate limit in disk drive capacity for the current technology. (The bit density of hard disk drives has been doubling every year and a half since 1991.) With holographic storage, data is stored within optical layers, rather than only on the disk surface. It uses the cubic volume of a crystal or polymer to store data. Several large manufacturers, as well as universities, are working on developing holographic storage systems.

PROCESSING

Processing requirements are an extremely important consideration when making decisions about computer hardware acquisitions, both for business and personal uses of a computer. In a business situation, the computer equipment must have the processing capabilities to perform work that is critical to the organization's continuing success. At a minimum, the business must be able to give its clients or customers a level of service or quality of product that is equivalent to what they could acquire somewhere else. As processing capabilities improve, businesses must take advantage of these changes to make the appropriate strategic decisions to continue to be competitive.

Computer processing involves activities needed to convert data into desired output, such as doing calculations or reformatting data. To make good decisions related to computer systems, it is helpful to have a basic understanding of processing terminology. The computer system unit in which data processing takes place has two main parts:

The central processing unit (CPU), where the actual processing occurs.

The primary memory, also referred to simply as memory, where data, programs or instructions, and processed information are held temporarily. Other terms used to refer to this temporary internal storage location include main memory and primary storage. In this chapter, we use primary memory or memory to distinguish clearly between this internal temporary storage location and the external permanent storage location, which we refer to as secondary storage (or simply storage).

Some descriptions of computer systems include primary memory as a component of the CPU, because memory is essential to the overall procedure. The important concept here is that processing capabilities require the use of memory. The CPU and the primary memory work together to handle processing. Primary memory is located on separate circuit boards that are connected to the CPU. During processing (see Figure 7.3), the data and programs needed for a particular task are brought in from their external storage locations (secondary storage) and placed temporarily in primary memory. Results can be displayed on the computer screen, printed, or both; they can also be placed in secondary storage.

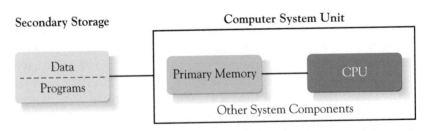

Figure 7.3 Conceptual View of Processing

Primary Memory

Anyone considering the purchase of either hardware or software needs to know the difference between primary memory and secondary storage. Many people get the two items confused, probably because both are related to a computer's capability of retaining data. Primary memory and secondary storage capacities are both normally expressed in quantities of bytes. In most systems, a byte is made up of eight bits that are used in various combinations to represent different characters (alphabetic, numeric, or other symbols). Therefore, a byte is the equivalent of one character.

Primary memory usually has a relatively small size compared with secondary storage. For example, many desktop computers currently available have memory in some number of megabytes (e.g., 128MB) and storage now available in several gigabytes. The memory is located on chips inside the machine, with data erased when you turn off the computer. Secondary storage is usually on disks and can contain the same data as in memory, but turning off the power does not erase data stored on a disk.

Primary memory temporarily stores instructions, data, and results of processing. All data and programs must be placed in the primary memory before being used in processing. Results generally remain in memory until they are replaced or transferred to an output device. One reason that the concept of primary memory as a temporary storage location is important is that any stored contents in memory are erased if the power to the computer is turned off (primary memory is said to be volatile because of its temporary nature). Therefore, results need to be stored regularly on a secondary storage device to avoid the risk of losing data.

Each location in memory is assigned an identifying number that represents its address, and data and programs are stored at individual address locations in memory. Accessing data or instructions in memory is called reading. Storing new data or instructions in memory is called writing. When instructions or data at specified addresses are "read," they are merely accessed or "fetched" for use and are not erased from an address; therefore, reading is referred to as a nondestructive process. But when new data or instructions are written to specified addresses in primary memory, they replace whatever was previously in those locations, so writing is referred to as a destructive process. (These terms also apply to disk storage; i.e., writing or saving a file on a disk is also a destructive process, but simply reading data from a file is not destructive.)

There are actually two main forms of memory within a computer, called ROM and RAM. Both are essential, but most advertisements and discussions related to memory capabilities are referring to RAM.

ROM

Read-only memory (ROM) contains permanent instructions that cannot be changed by other instructions. These instructions are "hard-wired" by the manufacturer and can be changed only by actually changing the wiring of the circuits. Instructions in ROM are not erased when the computer power is turned off (ROM is nonvolatile). Since ROM is built into the hardware, it operates faster than RAM because its contents do not have to be brought in from a secondary storage location.

Most of us do not plan to change from the standard ROM provided by the manufacturer, but it is useful to know that variations in ROM have been developed so that users with special needs can create their own ROM programs (special equipment is required). One option is programmable read-only memory (PROM), which can be programmed after it has left the manufacturer. Once the programs are stored, they cannot be changed. Other options that have been developed are erasable programmable read-only memory (EPROM), and electrically erasable programmable read-only memory (EEPROM), which allow ROM programs to be erased and changed if that flexibility is needed.

RAM

Random access memory (RAM) is the part of memory that is used to store instructions and data temporarily during processing. The access to data and instructions is considered random or direct because the data can be located based on its address rather than by searching memory locations sequentially.

In recent years, RAM has been referred to as DRAM or SRAM, depending on whether it was dynamic RAM or static RAM. In the past few years, RAM technology has made significant improvements, with several new architectures that provide higher speeds.

Cache (pronounced the same as "cash") is a part of the memory that increases the speed of processing by providing a temporary storage area for instructions and data. Generally, it stores data that was read from disk most recently. This procedure speeds the processing by putting into this memory area the items that are likely to be needed again, rather than repeatedly accessing these items from the disk.

Central Processing Unit

By now you should be aware of the importance of the computer's memory in providing a temporary place for data and programs or instructions. But nothing would happen to the data if it merely sat in memory. Without processing capabilities, your computer would not be able to perform any of the typical activities—such as creating a message or performing calculations. When you pressed keys or moved a mouse, nothing would happen.

The term CPU (central processing unit) came into existence years ago when businesses were using only mainframe computers; it is sometimes referred to as the "main brain" of the computer. When microcomputers were developed, they included the same types of components on a small chip, referred to as a microprocessor chip (described in more detail later in this chapter), with the term CPU used widely to refer to microcomputer systems, too. The development of microprocessor chip capability had a significant impact on the computer industry, because it became possible for small computers to have large processing capabilities. Figure 7.4 illustrates how the components of the CPU work together as well as with primary memory to complete the processing functions. A register is included in this figure for conceptual purposes; registers play an important role and are described later in this chapter. Th CPU contains two main rocessing components: (1) the arithmetic-logic unit (ALU), which performs the computations, and (2) the control unit, which interprets program instructions and handles the execution of instructions, including the sending of data to and from input and output devices.

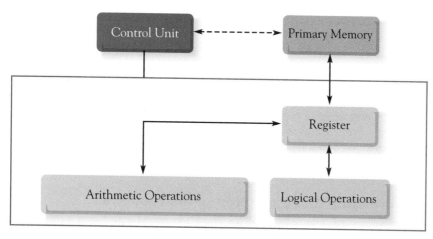

Figure 7.4 Processing Components

Arithmetic-Logic Unit

Manipulation of data occurs in the ALU, which performs all arithmetic and logical operations. Arithmetic operations include all types of mathematical calculations, such as addition, subtraction, multiplication, division, and exponentiation. Logical operations are comparison tests, such as comparing two items to see if one is greater than, less than, or equal to the other. Other logical comparisons are greater than or equal to, less than or equal to, and not equal.

You could probably think of many examples of ALU activities. Here are a few basic ones:

▼ Making calculations arithmetically, such as multiplying an employee's pay rate by the number of hours worked.

▼ Making calculations logically, such as comparing an employee's total hours worked with 40 to see if overtime pay was earned.

▼ Sorting data into whatever arrangement is desired, such as sorting alphabetically by employees' names.

Because all alphabetic characters are converted to combinations of 0s and 1s, logical operations can be performed on alphabetic data just as easily as on numeric data. Sorting of names alphabetically is an example of a logical operation, in which comparisons are made of codes representing each character to determine the appropriate arrangement.

Data may be transferred back and forth between primary memory and the ALU many times during processing.

Control Unit

The control unit regulates the activity of the CPU by directing the sequence of operations. It interprets a program's instructions and produces the electronic signals that cause the instructions to be executed.

The control unit takes care of directing the input device to transfer instructions and data into memory. The control unit then directs the retrieval of one instruction at a time from memory, interprets it, and sends the appropriate electronic signals to the ALU and memory so that the instructions are performed. Signals sent may cause data to be transferred back and forth from primary memory to the ALU and eventually to an output device.

Interpretation and Execution of Instructions

The sequence of events needed for the CPU to interpret and execute an instruction is measured in units called a machine cycle. (The control unit oversees or coordinates the procedure.) During each machine cycle, pulses generated by the internal clock cause special circuitry elements to sense and interpret instructions and move them from one component to another of the CPU (the items being moved are in the form of electrical pulses at this time). The number of electrical pulses emitted by the CPU's internal clock determines the timing of basic operations such as obtaining and interpreting instructions. The process of interpreting and executing an instruction involves getting everything ready and then performing the operation, referred to as an instruction cycle and an execution cycle (see Figure 7.5).

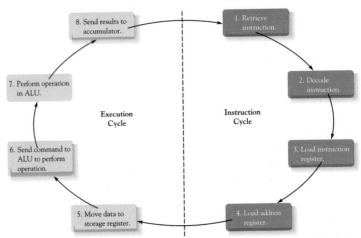

Figure 7.5 Machine Cycle

The instruction cycle is the process of obtaining an instruction from primary memory and interpreting it. An instruction must first be retrieved from primary memory and then translated into a code that is understandable to the machine. Instructions and addresses of data are transferred into registers (refer back to Figure 7.4). Registers are used as a quick-access "working memory" in the ALU and control unit. More expensive systems often have a higher number of registers. Separate registers are used for instructions, for addresses of data to be used, and for storage of data retrieved from primary memory. Registers keep each item only briefly and transfer it as soon as the control unit sends the instruction to do so. In general, the instruction cycle is the phase that prepares the computer to perform (or execute) the desired operation.

The execution cycle involves performing whatever operations are indicated from the instruction cycle. The instruction and needed data move through the CPU during the execution of an instruction. Data is retrieved from primary memory and moved to a storage register for use during the operation. Then the desired operations are performed in the ALU and the results are sent to an area sometimes referred to as an "accumulator," in which the machine forms (or accumulates) the result of an operation. The instruction and execution cycles are repeated as often as needed until all instructions have been executed.

Although this description of a machine cycle is rather brief and omits some technical aspects, it should serve its intended purpose—to instill an appreciation for the variety of tasks being performed in small fractions of seconds. The time required to complete a cycle and the amount that can be accomplished are very important in many business applications. Computer speed is often expressed in MIPS, an acronym for millions of instructions per second, for large systems and in megahertz (MHz) for desktop computers (discussed further in another section of this chapter).

Large System Processors

The processor in a large computer may use many circuit boards contained in a "frame" somewhat like a box, which is said to be the origin of the term mainframe. The various components of the CPU are connected by special electrical connections.

Some large computer systems use a multiprocessor design, in which multiple processors are connected in some way so that the processing needs can be shared. (There are also desktop-sized, multiprocessor-design computers available, but these are usually relatively expensive and are purchased for specialized tasks such as computer-aided design.) The use of multiple processors provides greater capabilities but also increases the cost of the equipment, largely due to the complexity of the connections and the required internal coordination of the activities. There are several types of multiprocessor designs. For example, one processor may be considered the main processor, communicating directly with the operating system, while the other processors assist or support the main processor.

Or the design may be one in which all processors can be used for any activities, with the operating system managing the work and monitoring the processors' work loads.

In the design involving parallel processors, multiple processors are organized so that many instructions can be executed at one time. A multiprocessor system can complete entirely separate programs at the same time. A parallel processor system typically processes one program by subdividing it into different parts for each processor. Once the program is subdivided, each processor operates independently. With this design, processors typically do not have to share memory.

IBM has introduced mainframes using parallel-processing technology. Instead of the traditional mainframes with processing boards the size of a telephone book, these new machines use less expensive microprocessor technology. Two primary advantages of this new design are that the cost based on MIPS is much lower, and the physical size is reduced considerably.

An expansion of the concept of parallel processors is called massively parallel processing (MPP). Instead of "several" processors operating in a parallel configuration, MPP systems may have thousands of simple processors operating in parallel. One definition used for MPP indicates that a minimum of 1,000 processors is required for a system to be considered "massive." The memory sharing of the traditional multiprocessor design provides limitations to expansion that are not a problem with the parallel processor design.

Microprocessors

Processors for microcomputers are on a single chip called a microprocessor. The part of the microcomputer that contains the CPU is sometimes referred to as the system unit. This system unit contains the following components:

The motherboard or system board, which is a flat board that normally contains the CPU and often some primary memory chips.

The microprocessor and other chips (The chips—integrated circuits—and circuitry for input/output devices are attached to metal or plastic containers with pin connectors that can then be plugged into sockets on the board.).

▼ Microprocessor speed is affected by several factors similar to those for large systems, including the following:

▼ Clock speed, which is the number of electronic pulses the chip produces each second.

▼ Number of bits that can be processed by the microcomputer at one time (referred to as word size).

▼ The number of bits that can travel at one time (bus width); a "bus" is the path on which data and instructions travel and is explained below.

▼ The amount of data and instructions that are available in primary memory.

▼ cache size and type

Clock speed is measured in megahertz (MHz). (Mega means million, and hertz refers to the number of pulses or cycles per second.) One MHz equals 1 million beats or cycles per second. The electronic pulses affect the execution speed of instructions. As mentioned earlier, larger systems use other methods of stating processing speed, such as MIPS. Additional methods include megaflops (millions of floating-point operations per second) and gigaflops (billions of floating-point operations per second). A floating-point operation is an instruction that represents numbers of various sizes by using exponents as in scientific notation, such as a number multiplied by a power of 10.

A bus is physical wiring that links parts of the CPU together and links the CPU with other hardware. Bits of data travel on bus lines. A 32-bit bus means that the line or path is 32 bits wide and can transfer 32 bits of data at a time, while a 16-bit bus would allow fewer data bits to travel at a time.

Global Perspective

United States computer manufacturers must be aware of export laws related to technology. Some newer computers are considered too powerful in their processing capabilities to be shipped to certain foreign countries. The U.S. Bureau of Export Administration is responsible for determining locations where such technology cannot be exported. Manufacturers are then responsible for knowing what is prohibited in various locations and following appropriate procedures.

Chip Technology

Because computer chips have become so prevalent in our lives, both personal and professional, this section is devoted to describing some of the chip designs that have affected our computer decisions. Chips are generally produced for one of two purposes—for memory or for processing. An awareness of current technology should help prepare you for changes that are likely to occur in the future, especially as the competition increases among manufacturers. In the future, the types of chips included in hardware are predicted to be more important considerations than the brand names for people making business decisions about hardware and software purchases.

Silicon chips are manufactured by machines that can etch very thin wires onto slivers of silicon. These wires form transistors, which are tiny switches packed tightly together. As technology has made it possible to use smaller wires, more transistors can be packed onto a chip, thus increasing capability on that chip. The decrease in needed size of a chip also means that more chips can be made from one wafer of silicon, thereby reducing chip cost.

Have you heard of Moore's Law? It was a prediction in the 1960s by Gordon Moore, who was a cofounder of Intel, that the number of transistors that could be squeezed onto a single silicon chip would double every 18 months. (Actually, he noticed at first that it was doubling every year, but he later revised it.) That prediction is still pretty accurate, although it is expected to slow down. Early chips contained only a few thousand transistors, compared with some recent Pentiums that have over 7 million transistors. As the density of transistors increases, the distance between transistors decreases, which shortens the travel distance and thus increases the speed.

Memory Chips

One use of memory chips is for a computer's random-access memory (RAM). Improvements in recent years allow more data and instructions to be stored in the memory, so that there is less need for data to be swapped back and forth from secondary storage. Trends toward increasing memory capacity so that entire sets of data can reside in memory are causing significant improvements in getting data into memory for processing.

One relatively recent development is flash memory, a memory chip developed by Toshiba in the mid-1980s. Flash memory is lightweight and durable and can store data at a high rate of speed while using little power. It is therefore excellent for use in portable computers and other hand-held equipment requiring memory and battery power, such as pocket calculators. Flash memory can store data indefinitely; it does not lose its stored data when the power to the computer is turned off. It can also be erased and reprogrammed. It is similar in concept to EEPROMs, but flash memory is usually bigger and can erase and write larger blocks at a time, making it faster than EEPROMs—it does its work in a "flash"! Flash memory is slower than RAM, especially for writing and erasing operations.

The potential for using flash memory rather than magnetic disks as secondary storage in small computers has been considered. But changes like these will not occur until the capabilities and cost of flash memory are competitive with the use of magnetic disks.

Microprocessor Chips

Some of the most widely known microprocessor chips are referred to by product numbers—not by chip capacity. For example, many IBM-compatible computers used Intel chips numbered in the 80000s—such as 80286, 80386, and 80486—although they were often referred to by the last three digits of the product numbers. The higher product numbers generally represent an improvement in this "family" of chips; the "386" was an improvement over the "286," and the "486" was an improvement over the "386."

Motorola chips are used in several types of computers; for example, until recent years, the Apple Macintosh series used numbers in the 68000s, with the 68040 being the most powerful. Intel deviated from its numbering plan when it introduced a design called the Pentium. A competing chip called the PowerPC (now used in Apple Macintosh computers) was developed by Motorola, IBM, and Apple. And DEC developed its own chip design, named Alpha. Chip type is becoming more important to businesspeople, because software is developed to fit specific chip designs. Businesspeople must be sure the software they are considering is available for use with their current (or expected purchase) computer chip design.

The current Intel chips include the Pentium with MMX™ technology and the Pentium II. MMX technology is available on most chips by major vendors today. It uses fewer instructions for some jobs and makes significant improvements in speed when working with multimedia software that uses these MMX instructions, such as Adobe Photoshop and Macromedia Director.

Intel and Hewlett-Packard have jointly developed a 64-bit microprocessor architecture that uses several advanced techniques to provide capabilities for increased parallelism in processing programs. Probably the most important concept is to be aware of the need to keep up-to-date with the continuing developments in chip technology so that you can make intelligent acquisition decisions.

Additional information on chip designs is available at the Web site.

Summary

Input refers to data and programs that are entered into the computer to be manipulated or processed. Output refers to the results of the processing.

The keyboard is a widely used form of input but has more chance for error than some other forms of input.

Pointing devices used for input include the mouse, trackball, touch pad, touch screen, and pen.

A scanner is an input device that can convert data to a machine-readable form without the need for human data entry through a keyboard. OCR programs are often used in conjunction with scanners to identify the characters that have been received into the system.

Speech or voice recognition systems are also used as forms of input. Some systems can expand their vocabularies as more voice patterns are added.

Screen displays represent one very common form of output. Laser printers are used extensively for high-quality output. Ink-jet printers are also widely used as an alternative to the more expensive laser printers; the quality of ink-jet output is usually poorer than most laser printers. Color output is available with both ink-jet and laser printers.

Audio output is another option. Human sounds are stored in the computer and generated as output as needed.

Secondary storage is a permanent (nonvolatile) location for data and files, as opposed to a computer's internal or primary memory, which is temporary or volatile.

An encoding system must be used for data and programs to be understood by a computer. The binary system of 0s and 1s is used to represent data and programs. Adaptations of the binary system that are used within computers include ASCII and EBCDIC codes. ASCII is the predominant encoding system used in microcomputers.

Reel-to-reel magnetic tape has been used as a method of secondary storage for many years. Magnetic cartridges have been developed in more recent years as an alternative to the reel-to-reel system of tape storage. Tape systems are sequential access devices and continue to be used as excellent methods of providing backup systems.

Magnetic disks provide direct access to data and are widely used with microcomputers. The commonly used forms are referred to as hard disks and floppy disks. Some large systems use multiple disks, called disk packs.

Optical disks are increasing in use in businesses, partly because of their durability. Some forms of optical disks can be written on only once, which provides security for the original data. CD-ROM is a form of optical disk that is increasing in use with small- and medium-sized computer systems. Other forms of optical disks are rewritable or erasable, primarily using magneto-optical technology.

The central processing unit (CPU) and the primary memory work together to handle processing. The data and programs needed for a task are brought into primary memory from secondary storage during processing. The results remain in primary memory until they are replaced or transferred to an output device, or until the computer's power is turned off.

Primary memory and storage capacity are usually stated in quantities of bytes.

Reading data is a nondestructive process; writing data is a destructive process, because whatever was stored previously in that location is replaced.

Data stored in primary memory temporarily is in the area referred to as RAM. The area of primary memory containing permanent instructions is referred to as ROM.

The CPU's two main processing components are the arithmetic-logic unit (ALU) and the control unit. The ALU performs arithmetic and logical operations, and the control unit directs or controls the sequence of operations of the CPU.

The machine cycle is the sequence of events involved in interpreting and executing an instruction. The instruction cycle is the process of obtaining an instruction and interpreting it, and the execution cycle is the process of actually performing whatever instruction was specified.

Large computer systems may have designs that include a multiprocessor design, in which the computer has several processors with individual control units, or it may include a parallel processor design, in which multiple processors can work simultaneously and independently on parts of the same program.

A microprocessor is the chip used in microcomputers for processing. Microcomputers contain other chips in addition to the microprocessor chip.

Microprocessor speed is affected by several factors, including clock speed, word size, bus width, cache capabilities, and the amount of data and instructions available in the primary memory at one time.

Questions for Review and Discussion

1. Describe the major advantages and disadvantages related to the use of various forms of computer input.

2. What are the major advantages and disadvantages related to the use of audio capabilities for input and output?

3. For what main reason did one or more forms of optical disk become admissible as evidence in court proceedings?

4. Identify and provide a brief explanation the two main parts of a computer system unit.

5. Discuss recent developments related to RAM technology.

Selected References

"Adaptive Chips." *PC Magazine*, February 24, 1998.

Bannon, Peter J. "Alpha Arrives at the Desktop." *Byte*, May 1997.

Blevins, Andy. "MPP, A Strategic Weapon." *DM Review*, February 1998.

"Companies to Watch: MicroTouch Systems." *Fortune*, October 19, 1992.

Dillon, Nancy. "Benched 'Til After the Millenium: Benefits of Rewritable DVD Put on Hold." *Computerworld*, June 1, 1998.

"Does it Mean 'Toothpaste'? Or 'Rat Poison'?" *Fortune*, February 17, 1997.

Flohr, Udo. "The Smartcard Invasion." *Byte*, January 1998.

Girard, Kim. "Universal Bus Awaits Windows 98 Drivers." *Computerworld*, December 8, 1997.

Helle, Steve. "Massively Parallel: Reaching Critical Mass." *Database Programming and Design*, June 1993.

Hill, Jonathan. "To Write or Rewrite?" *PC Magazine*, March 10, 1998.

Himowitz, Michael J. "The Best Way to Store Data." *Fortune*, March 16, 1998.

Hogan, Mike. "A Gig in Your Pocket." *PC World*, March 1998.

Hummel, Robert L. "DVD Remains a Moving Target." *Byte*, December 1997.

Levy, Doug. "Pentium II Chips Zing up Notebooks." *USA Today*, April 9, 1998.

Locke, Keith. "Storage Squeeze." *Software Magazine*, January 1998.

Maney, Kevin. "Setting up a PC-Mouse Trap." *USA Today*, April 30, 1998.

Novakovic, Nebojsa. "Memories of Things to Come." *Byte*, January 1998.

Pendery, David. "When Data Explodes." *InfoWorld*, May 18, 1998.

Pickering, Wendy. "Computer: Take a Memo." *Datamation*, January 7, 1994.

Poor, Alfred. "Watch What You Say." *PC Magazine*, March 10, 1998.

Port, Otis. "Gordon Moore's Crystal Ball." *Business Week*, June 23, 1997.

Pountain, Dick. "Amending Moore's Law." *Byte*, March 1998.

Randall, Neil. "Image Problems." *PC Magazine*, April 7, 1998.

Schmit, Julie. "Smart Cards Coming to Home Computers." *USA Today*, June 10, 1998.

"Secondary Storage: A Look at Existing Technologies and New Ones on the Horizon." *PC Quest*, March 1, 1997.

Stone, M. David. "Removable Storage." *PC Magazine*, April 21, 1998.

Swoboda, Frank. "OSHA Drafts Broad Rules on Repetitive Motion Injuries." *The Commercial Appeal*, November 6, 1994.

Szlendak, John J. "File Saving Not an Alternative to Full System Backup." *Storage Management Solutions*, May 1998.

"The Essential Guide to Choosing a Monitor." *PC Magazine*, October 7, 1997.

Wildstrom, Stephen H. "Eeeek! A Better Mouse." *Business Week*, December 1, 1997.

Chapter 7 Key Terms

Input
data and programs entered into a computer system for manipulation or processing.

Output
information that results from computer manipulation or processing of data.

Input device
hardware used for entering data into a computer system (e.g., keyboard, mouse, trackball, touch pad, touch screen, light pen, or scanner).

Bitmap
an identification of the location of each pixel involved in creating a character or shape.

Pixel (picture element)
individual dot; various combinations of dots are used to create characters and graphics.

Optical character recognition
software used to read or recognize text and nontext input from a scanner.

Point-of-sale (POS) terminal
technology used in many retail stores that includes a scanning system and cash drawer to obtain sales data automatically as each sale occurs.

Magnetic ink character recognition (MICR)
system designed primarily for processing checks in which special ink is used so that some preprinted data can be entered automatically.

Speech or voice recognition unit
technology that allows input to a computer system through use of the human voice.

Satellite signal
technology allowing input of data from satellites.

Smart card
a card onto which data can be stored, allowing the card to be used for many purposes, such as for identification or for monetary transactions.

Output device
hardware that provides information for human use; examples are monitors and printers.

Monitor
the computer display screen, which is also referred to as a video display terminal (VDT) or cathode-ray tube (CRT).

Screen size
size of monitor, indicated in inches (measured diagonally).

Dot pitch (dp)
measurement of distance between screen dots; a lower dot pitch provides a sharper image.

Screen resolution
clarity of images; resolution is a reference to the number of pixels, and a higher number of pixels (higher density) creates a clearer image.

Refresh rate
how often the screen image is redrawn.

Video card support
amount of memory available for higher resolution as needed.

Voice synthesizer
output device that contains stored voice sounds that can be generated electronically.

Secondary storage
permanent or long-term storage of data outside the computer's CPU; referred to as nonvolatile because the contents are not erased when the computer power is turned off.

Nonvolatile/volatile
reference to the temporary (volatile) nature of primary memory versus the permanent (nonvolatile) nature of secondary storage.

Binary system
uses two options, 0 and 1.

Bit
one binary digit, either 0 or 1.

Byte
a combination of bits (typically 8 bits) used to represent a single character.

Kilobyte
equivalent of 1,024 bytes.

Megabyte
equivalent of 1,048,576 bytes.

Gigabyte
equivalent of 1,073,741,824 bytes.

EBCDIC
acronym for Extended Binary Coded Decimal Interchange Code; an 8-bit code used on IBM mainframes and other large computers.

ASCII
acronym for American Standard Code for Information Interchange; a 7-bit or 8-bit code (ASCII-8) used in microcomputers and some larger computers.

Sequential access
data is retrieved in serial order, or the order in which it was stored; data stored on magnetic tape must be retrieved or accessed sequentially.

Reel-to-reel magnetic tape
sequential access storage system that uses two reels, with magnetic tape wound from one reel to the other during use.

Track
location onto which data can be stored; tracks on magnetic tape are parallel rows, and tracks on magnetic disks are concentric circles.

Read/write head
a device that can either access (read) data stored magnetically or save (write) data onto magnetic media.

Magnetic cartridge
magnetic tape system in the form of a small case (cartridge) rather than on large reels.

Magnetic disk
a platter used for storing data magnetically that can be in the form of a hard disk or a floppy disk; widely used with microcomputers.

Direct access storage device (DASD)
storage method available with disks in which data can be located by its address rather than sequentially.

Sector
a subsection of a magnetic disk, used as part of the address to identify the location of stored data; a disk is divided into pie-shaped wedges, and an individual track within a wedge forms one sector.

Disk drive
hardware that contains the technology for storing and accessing data on a disk.

Access arm
hardware on disk drive that moves over disk to desired location; contains read/write heads.

Access time
the time required for locating desired data on a disk.

Transfer time
the time required to transfer data from storage to primary memory.

Disk pack
multiple platters (disks) used for secondary storage in one system.

Cylinder
track location on multiple disks that is in the same vertical position.

RAID
acronym for redundant array of inexpensive (or independent) disks; secondary storage system that uses multiple disk drives, which allows multiple write (data storage) operations to occur at the same time.

Optical disk
Secondary storage platter that uses laser technology for data storage and is capable of storing large quantities of data, including images.

WORM
acronym for write once, read many; a form of optical disk onto which data can be stored (written) only once but can be accessed as often as desired.

Jukebox
storage system for optical disks, which holds multiple disks and delivers a requested disk to the disk drive for use.

CD-ROM
acronym for compact disk read-only memory; a form of optical disk onto which data has been stored and can be viewed but not be changed.

Magneto-optical technology (MO)
use of magnetic technology for storing data on an optical disk, combined with laser technology for making changes to stored data.

Holographic storage
storage technology using optical layers rather than a single-surface image.

Central processing unit (CPU)
hardware component where processing of data occurs, along with control activities for other components.

Primary memory (or "memory")
internal location where data and programs are held temporarily for use in processing activities.

Address
location in primary memory where data or instructions are held temporarily.

Reading
accessing data or instructions; a nondestructive process.

Writing
storing new data or instructions; a destructive process.

ROM
acronym for read-only memory, a special memory area containing permanent instructions that the computer uses when it is turned on.

RAM
acronym for random-access memory, the part of memory that can be accessed directly and used for temporary storage of data and programs.

Cache
extra temporary storage that increases processing speed.

Arithmetic-logic unit (ALU)
CPU component that performs logical comparisons and arithmetic calculations.

Control unit
CPU component that coordinates the activities of other components.

Machine cycle
a sequence of activities that occurs in the computer when interpreting and executing an instruction.

Register
a temporary area used during execution of an instruction to hold needed items, such as data, instructions, and addresses.

MIPS
acronym for millions of instructions per second, a method of measuring computer speed; widely used measurement in larger systems.

Multiprocessor
a system using multiple processors, which allows several programs to be processed independently while sharing memory.

Parallel processor
a system using multiple processors, each with its own memory, which allows one program to be subdivided and completed by separate processors operating independently.

Microprocessor
a microcomputer processor chip.

Clock speed
the number of electronic pulses per second, measured in megahertz.

Word size
the number of binary digits that can be processed at one time.

Bus width
the number of bits that can travel at one time.

Megahertz (MHz)
a measure of clock speed; 1 megahertz equals 1 million cycles per second.

Bus
wiring that links parts of the hardware to each other; bus lines are used for transferring data.

Online Activities

Refer to the companion Web site at www.wiley.com/college/simon for a variety of online activities: additional chapter content, *Wall Street Journal Interactive Edition* access, review materials, student assignments, and relevant links.

GO TO http://www.wiley.com/college/simon

 THE WALL STREET JOURNAL.

Your four-month access to the Interactive Journal allows you to research articles published within the last 30 days in the Interactive Journal, Barron's Online, and Dow Jones Interactive. A Help feature is available if you need assistance in specifying your search topic.

Don't overlook the work of the Interactive Journal columnists. Their insights can magnify a topic and interpret its affects through clever analysis and sometimes humor.

Research each topic in the Interactive Journal and analyze the results of your search.

1. Flash memory. Is it expected to increase in usage in the next few years?

2. Speech/voice recognition technology in business. Is the use of this technology expected to increase? Where would you find the hardware and software needed?

3. Computer chip manufacturers. Can we expect continued increases in capabilities and decreases in size of chips?

Part IV

DEVELOPMENT AND MANAGEMENT
OF INFORMATION SYSTEMS

Part IV describes the process of developing information systems, including designing desired systems, writing programs, developing databases, and other aspects of system development. The development aspects are followed by a discussion of the many considerations involved in managing all the information resources effectively. Management of information resources has become a very important concern because of the value now placed on the information maintained in these systems.

Chapter 8   Programming Languages

Chapter 9   Database Development and Management

Chapter 10   System Development Procedures

Chapter 11   Information Resource Management Strategies

CHAPTER 8

Programming Languages

LEARNING OBJECTIVES

After studying the contents of this chapter, you should be able to

1. Identify the general purposes of programming languages.
2. Compare and contrast the major developments in each of the generations of programming languages.
3. Explain the commonly used terminology related to programming languages.
4. Describe current trends related to programming languages.

GENERAL PROGRAMMING CONCEPTS

Programs are sets of instructions (sometimes called statements) that are usually executed in sequence, one statement after another. But there are exceptions to this sequential process. The statements may include comparison activities that could cause a change in sequence (see Figure 8.1). A statement might have a path to take if the answer to a question is "Yes" and a separate path to take if the answer is "No." Some computer systems can process more than one program at a time, but the general order or sequence within a program still proceeds from beginning to end. Programming, then, involves developing these sets of instructions for the computer to follow and to do the task the same way as many times as needed.

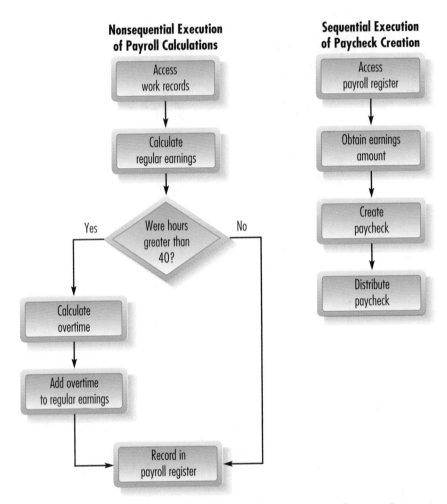

Figure 8.1 Sequential versus Nonsequential Execution of Program Statements

A programming language is used for developing desired programs to accomplish some task or activity. Programming languages are used widely to create custom applications that meet unique needs of a particular business. Programming languages have symbols and rules, very similar to sentence construction rules used in the English language. For example, English-language sentences use alphabetic characters as symbols for words and have rules such as using a plural verb with a plural subject and beginning each new sentence with a capital letter. Programming languages have their own sets of symbols and rules (a code). Standardization of symbols and rules within a language makes the program code easier to convert to instructions the computer can understand; it also makes the language more portable, meaning that the programs can be moved from one type of computer to another with only minor changes.

The evolution of programming languages is generally considered to have included at least four generations (some writers describe five generations while others include the same languages within four generations). The developments in programming languages have been consistent with the overall emphasis on "user-friendly" computer applications—the more recently developed programming languages typically require fewer statements or instructions and are easier for humans to use. But all generations of programming languages continue to be used in businesses today. One reason is that many businesses have very large and very important (mission-critical) programs, developed over many years, that would be difficult or impossible to replace without a great deal of expense.

Businesses must make changes to their programs regularly, partly to remain competitive by taking advantage of new capabilities, but also to adjust to new needs of their customers or their own internal staff. Making alterations and upgrades to current programs is often less time-consuming than writing entirely new programs, regardless of the programming language being used. For example, many of the online transaction processing (OLTP) systems used by airlines have been written in assembly language to take advantage of the execution speed. These systems are quite extensive in size and must be available 24 hours a day, so changes are typically made by altering the current programs rather than by trying to replace them. With OLTP systems, transactions can be entered directly into the computer system, which allows processing to occur immediately.

Global Perspective

Attempts have been made to build software industries in the Middle East and various less-developed countries, in part to improve their economies and in part to reduce programming costs by using an available pool of relatively inexpensive programming professionals. Some of these efforts have been quite successful, with large software industries in India and several other countries. The time differences can be used as an advantage, because program directions can be sent at the end of the working day in the United States to a country where programmers are arriving for work, and their work may be back by the next U.S. working day. One primary problem with global programming involves problems that occur with technology, due to the differences in quality of computers available for use and the quality of transmission of programs.

In the following sections, a historical perspective is used to give you a picture of programming language options available, as well as some of the changes that have occurred.

FIRST-GENERATION PROGRAMMING LANGUAGES

Machine language is considered the first generation of programming languages. Machine language, which uses the binary system represented by 0s and 1s, is the only language that the computer can understand and execute. Early programs created for computers in the 1940s were written in machine language because nothing else was available. The two parts of a machine language instruction indicate what to do and with whom to do it:

The operation code (sometimes called "op code") tells the computer system what operation to perform.

The operands identify for the computer system the location (address) of the data to use as a basis when the operation is performed.

Machine-language programs contain detailed instructions for each task, including the storage location for each instruction and each item of data used. Machine-language programs are referred to as low-level language programs, because they are written on the level the computer "understands"—the 0s and 1s. Although something called "low level" in other areas might be considered the simplest or easiest for someone to use, the opposite is true of computer programs. Low-level programs are written in a language more easily understood by the computer system but more difficult for programmers to write or use. High-level programming languages are easier for programmers to write but require translation to machine language. High-level languages are easier for humans to view and understand because of more English-like wording. But they are less efficient in speed and memory utilization of the computer, because they must be translated (converted to machine language). Generally, the easier the language becomes for humans, the more extensive the translation job becomes.

In the early days of computers, little thought was given to the use of multiple types of computers, so the fact that there is no standardization for machine-language programs was not considered an important issue. Machine-language programs are "machine specific"—programs written for one type of computer are not likely to be usable on another type of computer. The programmer must know the language for the specific brand and model of computer to be used before writing the program, because the 1s and 0s are used to indicate switch settings for whatever processor is in use.

Creating program statements in codes containing combinations of 0s and 1s is a slow, tedious process. Mistakes are difficult to notice visually. Programmers today do not write their programs in machine-language code. Considerable time can be saved by using one of the languages described later in this chapter, which can then be converted to machine-language instructions. All programs other than machine-language programs must be converted to machine language before the instructions can be executed.

SECOND-GENERATION PROGRAMMING LANGUAGES

Assembly-language programs, available since the early 1950s, are considered the second generation of programming languages. The major improvement from machine language was the capability of using alphabetic and numeric symbols rather than being limited to combinations of 0s and 1s, thereby making assembly language easier to learn. Assembly language uses mnemonic devices for instructions. Mnemonic devices are memory aids that may be abbreviations of words. If you have taken music lessons and learned to read music, you may have used mnemonic devices to help you remember the letters of sharps and flats on the scale. Mnemonic devices used in programming are much easier to view and analyze than machine-language statements. For example, RET might be used to represent RETURN, which in machine language would be a series of 0s and 1s, such as 0110 1100 0110 0000.

Like machine-language programs, assembly-language programs contain an operation code and one or more operands. In addition, assembly-language programs may contain a location name indicating where the instruction is to be stored. A program known as the assembler is used to convert assembly-language programs to machine language. Each assembly-language instruction is translated (assembled) into a single machine-language instruction. Assembly-language programs are considered low-level languages because they are written based on machine-language code, substituting more meaningful characters for the 0s and 1s. The capability of assigning names to memory locations was an important improvement over machine-language programming, making it easier to know the contents of various locations and to refer to a location by a logical-sounding name rather than by a series of 0s and 1s.

One problem with assembly-language programs is that the mnemonic codes used have not been standardized among different types of computers. The assembler must be able to translate the assembly-language programs to the appropriate machine language of the computer. Therefore, assembly-language programs written for one computer are unique to that type of computer and probably will not run on a different computer; the programs are not "portable" to other systems. Assembly language is considered less difficult to learn to use than machine language but more difficult than third-generation languages.

THIRD-GENERATION PROGRAMMING LANGUAGES

Third-generation programming languages (3GLs) marked the beginning of the development of high-level languages, which are intended to be easier to use for writing programs than assembly language. Although the programs created cannot be read directly by the computer, system software programs are available (compilers and interpreters) to convert the programming language statements to machine language. Thus, compilers and interpreters for high-level languages serve a purpose similar to assemblers used with assembly language programs.

A compiler translates programs into a code that can be used again whenever needed (the compiling process does not have to be repeated). An interpreter does not save the translated code, so the program would need to be interpreted again each time it is used. Each of these programming languages needs its own compiler or interpreter in order for its instructions to be converted to machine language, and the version must be one that is appropriate for the specific machine involved. Programming languages designed to be compiled generally cannot be interpreted well, and languages designed to be interpreted may not compile well.

Refinements in many of these languages have been made as standards have been developed by the American National Standards Institute (ANSI). Programs written for use on one type of computer are more likely to be usable on another computer than was true initially.

A few third-generation programming languages are briefly described here, for comparison.

FORTRAN

FORTRAN (FORmula TRANslator) was developed in the mid-1950s. Its primary uses have been in engineering and scientific applications and in statistical analyses. FORTRAN is very effective in handling tasks requiring extensive mathematical capabilities, such as forecasting, but it has limited capabilities in performing database manipulation tasks. As is true of most programming languages, FORTRAN has undergone some enhancements since its initial development. Efforts at standardization have been made, with ANSI standards developed in the 1960s. Getting the cooperation of manufacturers and programmers in adhering to the standards is a problem that developers of this language and many others have encountered.

COBOL

COBOL (COmmon Business-Oriented Language) was developed around 1960 for business applications. Its language was designed to be similar to English-language statements, and it is still used in many businesses. Some estimates suggest that billions of lines of program code have been written in COBOL and represent many "programmer-years" of work. These COBOL programs include some critical applications, such as payroll and general ledger activities.

COBOL is designed to perform all types of business applications, such as file processing needs or data searches. ANSI standards have been developed (and updated) for COBOL. Although it was originally used only with large systems, COBOL is now usable on all types of computers, including microcomputers.

COBOL programs include sentences that are fairly easy for a novice to read and understand. This ease of understanding makes it simple to locate specific sections when updates or alterations in the programs are necessary. One disadvantage of the very descriptive, English-like wording is that the programs are usually longer than programs in some other languages. Also, COBOL is not considered a good choice when intense mathematical applications are needed.

Rumors of the demise of COBOL have been around for quite a few years, and faculty at some educational institutions have debated the merits of continuing to teach COBOL programming courses. However, those billions of lines of COBOL program code mentioned above had an effect on the demand for COBOL programmers in the second half of the 1990s decade. Actually, the "Year 2000 (Y2K) problem" was a major reason for a heavy demand for COBOL programmers, as well as for those with other programming language skills.

The Y2K problem occurred because programmers, database developers, and others have saved storage space for years by using only the last two digits of a year when saving date data. Typically, they have used two digits for the month, two for the day of the month, and two for the year. The difficulty occurred because most of the systems were developed to interpret the year 00 as 1900 instead of 2000. Numerous problems began to occur with business data that eventually caused people to realize the extensive problems that could occur. For example, programs performing calculations of mortgage payments in future years were not working properly, sometimes calculating charges for late payments since 1900.

A wide variety of business data includes dates, which are often the basis for decisions. Many programming applications are based on dates, such as an employee's age, years of employment, vacation days earned, and on and on. Data related to customers, vendors, equipment records, and so on, all involve dates, and the associated programs may have thousands of lines of code that specify the year as two digits. The problems with years stored as two digits were discovered to be so extensive that entirely new businesses were formed to aid businesses in changing their programs. Most businesses and government offices did not have enough programmers on hand with the time needed to check all their programs and make needed changes.

BASIC

BASIC (Beginner's All-Purpose Symbolic Instruction Code) was developed in the early 1960s for use in any type of application, including both scientific and business applications. BASIC is a language supported by microcomputers, although it can be used on larger systems. But it is somewhat limited in dealing with large sets of data.

As indicated in its name, BASIC was intended to be easy to learn and use. It was developed primarily as a learning device for students and represented a simplified version of FORTRAN. One popular feature of BASIC is that it is interactive, which means that the programmer or user can interact or communicate with the computer in response to prompts during the testing and using of programs.

C

C was developed in the early 1970s and has received wide acceptance as a language that is highly portable. It can be used on all types of computers, so it is sometimes referred to as a language for an "open system." As other programming languages such as COBOL have become more compatible with various types of computers, they have also become known as open system languages.

C has some efficiency benefits similar to assembly-language programs, as well as some features of high-level languages (e.g., easier to learn than assembly language), so it is sometimes referred to as a middle-level language. C is often believed to be more difficult to learn to use than COBOL, partly because of its greater capabilities. C is sometimes used in developing system software, and its use is increasing as well for small-computer and large-computer applications of all types—business, mathematical, and scientific uses. C and COBOL are both considered languages for professional programmers, while BASIC is more widely used for small projects that are often used only once. Thus, BASIC was developed for use with an interpreter, while C and COBOL (and many others) were developed for use with a compiler.

FOURTH-GENERATION PROGRAMMING LANGUAGES

Fourth-generation programming languages (called 4GLs) are a little difficult to define because not everyone agrees on what they are. Some 4GLs used primarily by professional programmers are referred to as very high-level languages.

Fourth-generation programming languages use English-like instructions and require fewer instructions because many of the procedures are built into the system. With third-generation languages, the steps or procedures to achieve the desired result are specified; therefore, they are said to be "procedure oriented." In contrast, 4GLs are nonprocedural. The desired result is specified and the language provides the appropriate steps. As a minimum, 4GLs usually include a query language, a report generator, and an application generator.

A query language allows the computer user to ask questions or to issue commands using English-like words. The program then obtains the information from the database and displays the results of the query on the screen. Some 4GLs include a natural language interface. If natural language capabilities are available, the computer user can enter a query in a variety of normal sentence patterns and the computer can interpret the meaning and provide the correct response.

Results can also be displayed in the form of a report (report generator) by simply listing desired criteria of data to be used, along with a report title, column headings, and any totals desired. Other report-generating options are available in many of these packages.

Application generators are sometimes called code generators, because they are used to create or generate some of the program statements or code. Application generators can save time in creating basic program statements. These program statements can be altered and other program statements added as needed. The application generator prompts the programmer for certain information that is then used to determine the type of program, the data to be used, and the desired result. The program statements are generated based on responses to the prompts.

Some of the newer application generators are used to create on-screen windows. A type of painting or drawing tool is used to design the desired form of a graphical user interface (GUI) screen. Once the screen is designed and saved, the application generator is used to create the behind-the-scenes code that will allow the GUI screen to work properly.

Some software packages advertised as 4GL contain only one tool, while others contain a series of special tools. But most people agree that the intended purpose of 4GLs is to make the development of application programs easier, whatever tools are included. The first 4GLs were rather slow in processing speed, but they have improved in speed because of improvements in software and hardware technology. Many 4GLs are limited in their flexibility and functions; 4GL programs often require an additional operation involving conversion of the programs to C or other third-generation languages. The third-generation languages are then used in developing programs to perform additional functions, with these programs eventually compiled for use by the computer.

PROGRAMMING LANGUAGE TRENDS

Several trends are developing related to programming languages, primarily tools to help in program development and expansions of capabilities of the languages available. A few trends are described in this section.

3GL Tools

In recent years, changes have occurred in the way COBOL is used. Microcomputers rather than mainframes are being used more often, and tools and utilities are being developed for use in COBOL program development. Some of these "workbench" tools include a text editor, a compiler, a code generator, a debugger, and a graphical user interface. Similar tools have been developed for many 3GL languages in recent years, as these languages continue to represent a large segment of business programs.

More information on 4GL tools is available at the Web site.

Object-Oriented Programming Languages

The most predominant trend involving programming languages is the continuing development and expanding use of object-oriented programming (OOP) languages. Instead of writing a program to perform a particular task, the primary emphasis is on the objects or elements involved. Related data (attributes), instructions, and other procedures (methods) are grouped together as a module, with the group referred to as an object.

All parts of an object stay together so that one module (object) can be used in multiple locations whenever that particular set of data and instructions would be appropriate. For example, an "Employee" object might have attributes of social security number, name, address, telephone number, job type or classification, and date of birth. One procedure that would be appropriate to group with these attributes would be a calculation of the employee's current age. Figure 8.2 illustrates this concept. Or the calculation could be wages. Once a method is defined for this calculation, it could be used with all objects that need to do this calculation.

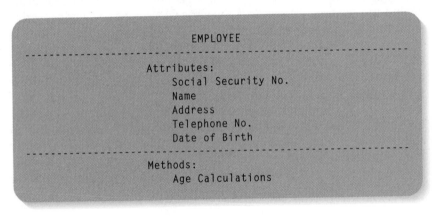

```
                        EMPLOYEE
-----------------------------------------------------
                Attributes:
                    Social Security No.
                    Name
                    Address
                    Telephone No.
                    Date of Birth
-----------------------------------------------------
                Methods:
                    Age Calculations
```

Figure 8.2 Sample Object

Table 8.1 compares some characteristics of machine and assembly languages with classes of languages that have been developed more recently, including third-generation (3GL), fourth-generation (4GL), artificial intelligence (AI), and object-oriented (OO). The numbers in each column represent typical rankings for a characteristic among the types of languages available. (Definitions of the characteristics are provided immediately below the table.) You could assign a weighting to each characteristic, depending on its importance to your situation, and then use these rankings to help you determine the best language choice for your needs. As you can see, machine language is ranked first for its performance but sixth for level of developer sophistication required. Third- and fourth-generation languages provide considerably greater developer productivity because of ease of use but at some sacrifice in the performance category. It is not surprising to notice that initial productivity has the same rankings as developer sophistication.

Language	Performance	Initial Productivity	Portability	Developer Sophistication
Machine	1	6	6	6
Assembly	2	5	5	5
3GL	3	2	1	2
4GL	5	1	4	1
AI	6	4	3	4
OO	4	3	2	3

Table 8.1 Comparison of Characteristics* of Programming Languages

*Definitions of Characteristics:

Performance–Time required for computer to execute business function (1 = fastest time).

Productivity–Time required for programmer to maintain or extend a business process (1 = shortest time).

Portability–Existence of industry standards across platforms (1 = most portable).

Developer sophistication–Years of experience required to become expert (1 = fewest years needed).

In selecting programming languages, additional factors would affect the results, such as the phenomenal price and performance gains in computer processing power during the past few years. But the hardware speed is now a less important factor than the difficulty of finding and training good programmers.

Management Perspective

When selecting a programming language, here are some of the most important considerations:

Compatibility with the computer to be used, if already purchased

Compatibility with any programs already in use, if coordination among programs is needed

Types of applications for which the programs are needed

Knowledge and capabilities of the programmers or users

Ease of use

Portability

Speed requirements

Additional information on object-oriented programming is available at the Web site.

Object-oriented programs are expected to continue to increase in use because of the reusable feature of the coded modules, which saves valuable time in program development. One disadvantage is that these programs have high memory requirements and slower execution times.

C++, Smalltalk, and Java® are examples of object-oriented programming languages. C++ is considered a hybrid language because it was derived from C. Smalltalk is considered the purest object-oriented language.

Java is comparatively new (introduced by Sun in mid-1995). It was also based on C. It represents the first language designed to take advantage of networks of computers and has received considerable publicity because of its use for some Internet-based applications. Programmers can write a single program that can work on most any kind of computer, through the use of the "Java Virtual Machine" (JVM).

The JVM is a small program that enters into a computer and translates Java programs into whatever form the particular computer needs. Therefore, the Java programs are "platform independent," i.e., they can be used on most systems without worrying about the specific hardware in use. One disadvantage of Java is related to its brief life. There has not been time for as many development tools and other enhancements to be added to the language as are available for use with other languages.

Many of the early Java programs were "applets," which are programs that can be used on a Web page. Partly because of the platform independence, an increasing number of businesses are finding Java useful for developing complete business applications; they are spending more of their Java programming resources on large application programs than on the creation of applets for Web pages.

Shown below is a very simple program written in Java. Although most Java programs are more extensive, this example is sufficient to emphasize the concept of an object-oriented language.

```
import java.applet.Applet;
import java.applet.Graphics;

public class Example extends Applet
{
    public void paint (Graphics g)
    {
g.drawString("This is an example",20,20);
g.drawString("of a Java applet program.",20,40);
}
}
```

This program creates a Java applet, which could then be used on a Web page. One of the main things to notice about this program is that it specifies what is to be done but does not specify how to do it (it does not specify the procedures).

The program indicates that two lines (strings) of text are to be displayed (drawn) on the screen, something like this:

This is an example
of a Java applet program.

The lines at the top of the program bring in (import) Java "classes" that can be used for performing the desired tasks. This program "inherits" built-in capabilities of those classes, which allows the program to create an applet that displays text on the screen.

Visual Programming Tools

Partly because of the difficulty some persons have had in learning to use programming languages, a related trend has emerged. Microsoft and others have begun to develop tools to simplify programming, such as by using more visual programming. Visual programming allows the program developer to use methods similar to those available for other easy-to-use applications, such as "drag-and-drop" and "point-and-click" methods of indicating preferences. Software elements can be linked together visually, and programmers can test different links to see the results. PowerBuilder®, Visual Basic®, Visual C++®, and Visual J++® are tools that can generate some code automatically, including a graphical user interface for the eventual user of the program. Additional program code usually will be needed, but these tools reduce the amount of development required. A knowledge of programming languages is still required to use the visual programming tools effectively.

Scripting Languages

Scripting languages are being used to customize Web pages on the Internet. These languages provide additional capabilities not available with standard HTML (hypertext markup language), which is the basis of Web pages. These scripting languages provide features that can enhance the appearance of the Web page, as well as automate some activities. For example, one commonly used script is used to test user input for types of data entered, with an on-screen prompt appearing if the user has entered something incorrectly.

Microsoft's VBScript and Netscape's JavaScript are two of the scripting languages in wide use today. Below is very simple example of JavaScript.

```
<SCRIPT LANGUAGE = "JavaScript">

Today = new Date();
WeekDay = Today.getDay();

If (WeekDay > 0) && (WeekDay < 6)
{
document.write("Today is" + WeekDay + "; Welcome!");
}
</SCRIPT>
```

JavaScript is based on Java but is easier to use, and the code does not need to be compiled. It can be inserted directly into an HTML file for use on a Web Page. Although this example does not show the extensive options available with JavaScript, it demonstrates how easy it is to understand the code.

In this example, today's date is stored in a variable named Today, and the day of the week for today's date is stored in WeekDay. (The language knows how to obtain today's date from the computer system.) A message is displayed on the screen if the day of the week is between 1 and 5 (between Monday and Friday). The message would look something like this, if it were Wednesday:

Today is Wednesday; Welcome!

JavaScript is an object-based system. The code in this example does not tell how to create the information on the screen but uses a built-in object (document) and one of its methods (write) to produce screen output.

5GLs

As mentioned earlier, not everyone agrees on the existence of fifth-generation programming languages (5GLs). Most who mention 5GLs suggest that they involve programming languages using artificial intelligence (some attempt to mimic the human thought process). Natural languages are also an important part of these languages, meaning that everyday wording can be used instead of special commands. PROLOG and LISP are two programming languages mentioned as having natural language development capabilities. But some problems have occurred in using these languages for business applications. 5GLs generally are not considered entirely new languages, but combine reasoning strategies with other programming language capabilities previously available.

Ethical Perspective

Ownership of programs that are written for a business has become a question of ethics in some organizations, in cases where a disgruntled programmer has sold the program code to a competitor or has taken the code to a new job when leaving a company. (Some of these situations are also legal issues.) Organizations argue that the work they paid for belongs to the organizations rather than to the individuals. Many organizations now require their programmers (as well as others) to sign agreements that restrict their use of their work if they leave the organization.

Summary

Programs consist of statements that are executed one by one. Programming languages are software used to create desired applications in an organization.

A portable programming language is one that can be moved from one type of computer to another.

At least four generations of programming languages have occurred, with the general trend being toward languages that are easier to use.

The first-generation programming languages involved machine-language programs, with programs that used only 0s and 1s. Low-level programs are based on the binary concept of 0s and 1s and are therefore rather difficult to write. Machine-language and assembly-language programs are both considered low-level programs.

Assembly-language programs represent the second generation of programming languages and use more meaningful symbols, called mnemonic devices, for instructions in place of the 0s and 1s.

High-level languages that are easier to write represent the third generation. Examples include FORTRAN, COBOL, BASIC, and C. These languages must be converted to machine language through the use of a compiler or interpreter, which takes extra computer time. But human time is usually saved because the languages are easier for programmers to use than low-level languages; fewer errors are made, and those errors that do occur are easier to correct.

Typical features of fourth-generation languages include (1) a query language, so that questions can be entered using normal sentences, such as a "natural language"; (2) a report generator, to create printed materials simply and quickly based on selected data; and (3) an application generator, which can create program statements.

A predominant trend in programming languages involves the use of object-oriented programming languages, including the development of modules of interest to the organization that contain related data, instructions, and other procedures. Individual modules or objects can be placed wherever appropriate and used repeatedly without the need to create new programs.

Another trend in programming development involves the use of visual programming tools, such as Visual Basic. Users can do some of the development activities by selecting screen icons and by moving objects from one location to another, with program code developed automatically based on these selections.

Scripting languages, such as JavaScript, are used for customizing Web pages and automating some activities.

Questions for Review and Discussion

1. Describe the general similarities and differences in these terms: assembler, compiler, interpreter.

2. Explain the difference between a procedural and a nonprocedural programming language.

3. Identify capabilities usually found in fourth-generation languages.

4. What is an "object-oriented" programming language? Name two examples.

5. Describe current trends related to programming languages.

Selected References

Coffee, Peter. "Java Applications." *PC Magazine*, April 7, 1998.

Coffee, Peter. "Scripting." *Windows Sources*, January 1997.

Halfhill, Tom R. "Today the Web, Tomorrow the World." *Byte*, January 1997.

Hicks, J. D., "The Complete Developer's Toolkit: 3GL Solutions." *DM Review*, April 1998.

Hicks, J. D. "The Complete Developer's Toolkit: 4GL Advances." *DM Review*, May 1998.

Kalish, David E. "0, 0 – Here Comes 2000 and a System Unraveler." *The Commercial Appeal*, January 25, 1998.

Maney, Kevin. "CEO McNealy Sets Sights on Microsoft." *USA Today*, July 14, 1997.

Perlepes, Serafim T., "An Overview of Object Oriented Programming." *Software Engineering*, Winter 1995.

Simpson, David. "Objects May Appear Closer Than They Are." *Client/Server Today*, August 1994.

The, Lee. "Visual C++: A More Approachable C." *Datamation*, August, 1993.

Chapter 8 Key Terms

Program
a set of instructions or statements for a computer.

Programming language
a group of specific symbols and rules used to develop a program.

Machine language
the only programming language that can be understood and executed directly by a computer, consisting of various combinations of 0s and 1s; considered a first-generation programming language.

Low-level language
designation for programming languages that are easy for a computer to use; examples are machine and assembly languages.

High-level language
programming language that is easier for programmer to use rather than easier for computer to use; considered third-generation programming languages (3GL).

Assembly language
a programming language based on machine language but using character symbols to substitute for combinations of 0s and 1s; considered a second-generation programming language.

Very high-level language
a programming language that is easier for programmers to use than high-level languages, for example, by accepting English-like wording (natural language) and by allowing the programmer to indicate the desired result without specifying the exact procedures; often referred to as a fourth-generation language (4GL).

Query language
a type of fourth-generation language capability that can be used to access data and obtain answers to specific questions without knowing specific programming language commands (uses natural, English-like wording).

Report generator
a fourth-generation language capability that allows reports to be created somewhat automatically, without writing a series of programs.

Application generator
a fourth-generation language capability that can be used to create (generate) some program statements (code) automatically.

Object-oriented programming (OOP)
a programming method that identifies specific items of interest (objects) and groups the data, instructions, and methods for one object.

Visual programming
a programming capability that allows the developer to use on-screen icons and other visual tools for creating programs.

Scripting language
used for customizing Internet Web pages.

Fifth-generation programming language (5GL)
uses artificial intelligence and natural language to include reasoning strategies.

Online Activities

Refer to the companion Web site at www.wiley.com/college/simon for a variety of online activities: additional chapter content, *Wall Street Journal Interactive Edition* access, review materials, student assignments, and relevant links.

GO TO http://www.wiley.com/college/simon

 THE WALL STREET JOURNAL.

Your four-month access to the Interactive Journal allows you to research articles published within the last 30 days in the Interactive Journal, Barron's Online, and Dow Jones Interactive. A Help feature is available if you need assistance in specifying your search topic.

Don't overlook the work of the Interactive Journal columnists. Their insights can magnify a topic and interpret its affects through clever analysis and sometimes humor.

Research each topic in the Interactive Journal and analyze the results of your search.

1. Fourth-generation-language (4GL) tools. What new capabilities are available? Are increases expected in the use of these tools?

2. Object-oriented programming languages. Why would a business decide to use such a language?

3. COBOL. Why is COBOL still in use? Is it expected to be used for new projects that businesses develop?

CHAPTER 9

Database Development and Management

LEARNING OBJECTIVES

After studying the contents of this chapter, you should be able to

1. Explain the general concept of databases and file linking capabilities.
2. Describe ways in which data may be organized and accessed.
3. Compare the conceptual data model with the logical data model.
4. Identify advantages and disadvantages of the various database structures used for logical data models.
5. Discuss the purposes of a database management system.
6. Describe advantages and disadvantages of the use of distributed databases.
7. Explain the relationship between data warehouses and data mining.

DATABASE DEVELOPMENT OVERVIEW

Data has become a highly valued resource for businesses. Data is not likely to be available for purchase externally, except for items such as reference materials and mailing lists. Much of an organization's data is unique, such as information about its own products, services, and customers. Individual sets of data are usually developed during the operation of the business and are used for many purposes.

Design and development of these sets of data are the focus of this chapter, especially as the process relates to the overall development of a new or revised system. Data to be used in a new system may be in place within the business but may need to be converted to the new system. At other times, a new set of data may be needed. Whether you are a system user, a developer, the manager of some area of an organization, or one of many others who might be involved in determining the needs of a new system, a basic knowledge of database design concepts and terminology can help you in clarifying your needs and desires. Important considerations include how data will be stored, accessed, used, and managed.

GENERAL CONCEPTS AND TERMS

Each item of interest to an organization is stored within a field. All of the specific data about one particular person, such as customer's name, address, and credit limit (a collection of fields), for example, becomes an individual record. Each customer approved for credit would have a separate record, and the entire collection of similar records is referred to as a file. Related files (sometimes referred to as tables or data sets) are kept in a grouping referred to as a database.

Related data items in a database have some reason to be associated with each other, and the database also contains metadata, which is data about the data—descriptions of the data and its relationships. A database may be shared by multiple computer users, although it may be perceived in different ways by different people. The appearance of data on the monitor or in printed reports can be entirely different depending on formats developed and types of data used.

As an example of related files in a database, you might have one file containing background information about customers, one file of historical data about purchases and product interests, and another file containing payment records. Of course, many other possibilities exist, but Figure 9.1 is an abbreviated illustration of basic files that could be used. Note that the column headings represent the names of the fields, and the individual data on each line below the headings represents records. In this example, the customer number can serve as an identifier in one file that can be used as a link to data in another file. Only one file needs to contain name and address data, because that data can be accessed by customer number when needed. In addition to wasting time and storage space if name and address data were kept in every file, another problem is the likelihood that the data would not be consistent from file to file; an address might get changed in one file but not in others.

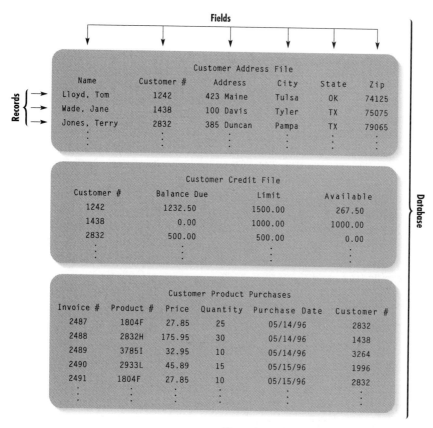

Figure 9.1 Related Files in Customer Database

Each person, place, or thing that is a basis for maintaining data is typically referred to as an entity. For example, a customer would be an entity. The individual characteristics about the entity are referred to as attributes. The names of the fields represent the attributes about a particular entity.

An important aspect of database design that has been used widely is to store data independently of the programs that are developed to use the data. In that way, changes can be made to data without needing to know anything about the programs that use the data. Also, programmers can make changes to the programs much more easily when the programs do not include the data.

FILE ORGANIZATION

File organization has to do with the way data is stored—the relationship between a record and its location within a file. The actual storage location for a record is referred to as its address.

Two types of addresses are:

▼ the physical address

▼ the relative address

The physical address on a magnetic disk, for example, would include the specific cylinder, track, and sector used. The relative address refers to the record's position in the file, such as the fifth record. In other words, it is a number (such as 4) indicating the record's position relative to the beginning of the file. Relative addresses are sometimes used for linking purposes; one record may contain the relative address of another record. What you then have in this system is a series of pointers, or a linked list. You could have a record containing the relative address of the next record that contained the same item of interest. That next record could contain another relative address pointing to the next record in the series that contained this item. If you wanted to access records in the customer address file in order alphabetically by city, a series of pointers could be included to provide this arrangement.

Three basic types of file organization are:

▼ sequential

▼ indexed sequential

▼ random (also called direct)

In a sequential file organization, records are stored in some specific order, such as alphabetically, by customer number, or by date.

With an indexed sequential file organization, records are divided into groups, which are then arranged in a sequential order within groups. Telephone book yellow pages are an example of this arrangement. You could go directly to the group of pages of interest, such as the section labeled "Automobile Dealers," and there you would find an alphabetical list of names of dealerships.

In the random organization, the physical location is not related to the logical location. Records may be stored in alphabetic or numerical order, for example, but they could be in any other order and could still be located. In other words, records could be located or accessed in any order without physically arranging them in that order first.

FILE ACCESS

Two options for actually locating or accessing files are:

▼ direct (also called random)

▼ sequential

File access has to do with retrieving files, perhaps for viewing, as well as updating or making other changes (processing). When sequential files are accessed, they are presented in order from the first or current record to the last record in the designated order.

For data to be arranged for direct access, there must be one field (or combination of fields) that uniquely identifies a record. This identifier is referred to as the key. More specifically, you have what is called a primary key and usually one or more secondary keys. The primary key uniquely identifies a record so that it can be separated from other records in a file. A social security number could be used as a unique identifier. Secondary keys can be any other fields, and they do not need to be unique identifiers. With secondary keys, you can base your access on additional specific fields within records. A city name or a ZIP code might be used as a secondary key, for example. Sometimes a combination of fields is used to create a key.

DATA MODELS

A model is basically a representation of something. A data model involves designing a database using a series of models that are related. The general process is to develop a high-level model of some activity, from which a more detailed model of what is desired is defined. Eventually the more detailed model is transformed into a model that specifically identifies all the implementation details. Starting with a data model helps to be sure that the problem is clearly understood before the system is developed.

When a database is being designed, considerable communication should occur between designers and people who will use the database. Initially, a "requirements determination" step occurs to identify and review all the needs from the system users' viewpoints. These user views can then be transformed into a conceptual data model, which describes user needs without regard to any specific database structure. This process provides information about the entities needed, the attributes of those entities, and the relationships or associations among the entities. The entity-relationship (E-R) model is an example of a conceptual data model and is described in more detail in Chapter 10.

Once the conceptual model is clearly presented to represent system users' needs, it is used as a basis for a logical data model, which includes a description of the items that need to work together and how they should appear. (Actual physical design of a database occurs only after the logical design has been developed and agreed to by all parties involved.)

Three database structures that have been used extensively for logical data models are hierarchical, network, and relational. In recent years, a model called object-oriented (OO) has been introduced, which often involves the use of the E-R model to identify the objects for the design. These data models often provide the basis for communications between developers and system users, so a basic knowledge of these structures can be very useful.

Hierarchical Structure

The hierarchical model uses a top-down structure, sometimes called a tree structure. If you turned a tree upside down, you would have the shape of a hierarchy. As shown in Figure 9.2, the main data element is the root at the top. This structure contains a single path to get from the root or base of the tree to a particular subdivision or segment.

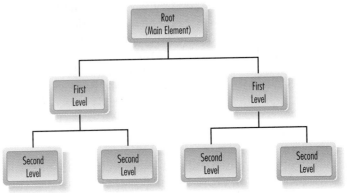

Figure 9.2 Hierarchical Structure

In a hierarchical structure, the sources from which data can be received are controlled and limited. Such a structure works well when the data actually flows in this way, in a top-down fashion that always follows the same path. Processing of data is typically easier and therefore more efficient with this structure, because of the clear-cut relationships that do not change. A disadvantage is the lack of flexibility, which is why other structures are available from which to choose the best "fit" for the specific situation.

Figure 9.3 is an example of a portion of a hierarchical structure that could be used in a retail department store. In this example, the Men's Clothing department is used as the main point of interest. Subdivisions could include a variety of topics of interest, such as employee records, customer records, and job descriptions.

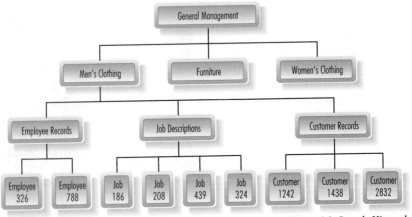

Figure 9.3 Sample Hierarchy

Employee records and job descriptions may be appropriate to design in the hierarchical structure shown in Figure 9.3. But most department store customers shop in more than one area. A hierarchical structure for customers would have the potential of creating a great deal of duplication for those customers who purchase items in multiple departments.

Network Structure

The network structure has multiple paths for data flow. This structure makes it possible for customer records to be accessed from any department needing them. This design is referred to as a many-to-many relationship, with the hierarchical design called a one-to-many relationship (data flowing from one source to multiple destinations versus from multiple sources to multiple destinations).

As you can see from Figure 9.4, more relationships are possible in the network structure than in the hierarchical structure. Access paths are still clearly defined when the database is designed. An advantage of the network structure over the hierarchical is the reduction in unnecessary duplication of data (redundancy) when many-to-many relationships exist. The main disadvantage of the network structure compared with the hierarchical is that many-to-many relationships are more complicated to design and manage.

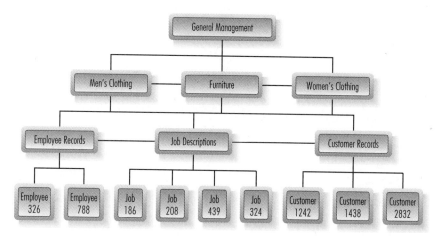

Figure 9.4 Network Structure

Relational Structure

In the relational structure, data is organized so that relations are shown in the form of two-dimensional tables. Attributes that are identified become the columns in a table. This method combines a simple method of organizing data with a structured query language. Data in one table can be linked to data in another table by having one column of data that is the same in both tables. This method is quite flexible and does not require that relationships be identified ahead of time.

The relational structure has become the most widely used database model. Figure 9.5 contains the same files or tables that were shown in Figure 9.1. These customer files can be linked because they contain one element (Customer #) in common that can be used to connect a record in one file with a record in another file. The field name does not need to be the same in the different tables. All you need is some item within each record that can be matched for linking purposes. Also, you do not have to use the same data element for every link. You might have a separate file of product information that could be linked to the Customer Purchases File through the use of the product number.

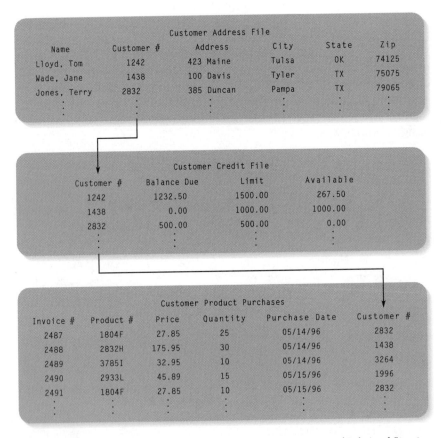

Customer Address File

Name	Customer #	Address	City	State	Zip
Lloyd, Tom	1242	423 Maine	Tulsa	OK	74125
Wade, Jane	1438	100 Davis	Tyler	TX	75075
Jones, Terry	2832	385 Duncan	Pampa	TX	79065

Customer Credit File

Customer #	Balance Due	Limit	Available
1242	1232.50	1500.00	267.50
1438	0.00	1000.00	1000.00
2832	500.00	500.00	0.00

Customer Product Purchases

Invoice #	Product #	Price	Quantity	Purchase Date	Customer #
2487	1804F	27.85	25	05/14/96	2832
2488	2832H	175.95	30	05/14/96	1438
2489	3785I	32.95	10	05/14/96	3264
2490	2933L	45.89	15	05/15/96	1996
2491	1804F	27.85	10	05/15/96	2832

Figure 9.5 Concept of Relational Structure

You could, of course, develop one giant table containing all your customer data. But a large table has the potential for a great deal of redundancy, and one large table generally takes longer to retrieve. Processing and storage operations usually take longer, too. Most activities do not require that you access every item of data you have about some entity, so it is more efficient to retrieve only those parts that are appropriate for a particular activity. In addition, access to sensitive data is easier to control when you have different types of data stored in different tables.

Social Perspective

Businesses should establish guidelines related to acceptable usage of data collected by the business. For example, one policy might be to maintain in a database only those items needed by that business. For example, data may be available about customers that does not need to be stored by this organization; this data would add to storage requirements unnecessarily and would have to be monitored as to appropriate uses, thus wasting time, energy, and space. Businesses also should take responsibility for ensuring the security of any private data stored, as well as for the accuracy of their records; this can be accomplished by including various checks and balances in the database monitoring system.

Object-Oriented Structure

Object-oriented design has received increasing interest in recent years, although relational design continues to be the most widely used database structure. Relational designs are good for simple data models but do not support as wide a variety of features as an object-oriented design.

In object-oriented design, a class is a person, place, or thing of interest to the organization. An object is an instance of a class and contains a collection of related data and methods or procedures for operating on that data. All objects within a particular class are of the same form but contain different data. For example, you might have a class called "Person," with attributes of "Name," "Address," and "Telephone Number" (or anything else of interest). An object could be created from this class to store data about a particular person.

Another characteristic of an object-oriented database is called inheritance, which means that new classes can be developed that make use of characteristics of existing classes. The Person class could have a subclass called "Customer." This subclass could have an attribute of "Credit Limit." The Customer class would have its own attributes but also inherit the attributes of the Person class, such as Name, Address, and Telephone Number. Encapsulation refers to a technique in which data is packaged together with corresponding procedures; the object is the mechanism used for encapsulation.

One of the basic concepts of the object-oriented design is reusability—developing systems or parts of systems that can be used over and over wherever and whenever they are appropriate. Object-oriented design concepts are also discussed in the chapter on programming languages.

Management Perspective

Businesses must ensure that their databases are developed in ways that enhance the operation of the business without causing unnecessary problems. Database development should include methods of checking that data is entered correctly and is kept up to date. Limitations should be placed on the development of individual databases in single departments that are not monitored by the overall organization. Without organizational controls, numerous problems can occur; e.g., these databases may be developed poorly, may be used inappropriately, may not be maintained correctly, may conflict with other organizational databases, and on and on. Regardless of the size of the database, organizational controls should be in place to control its development and use.

DATABASE MANAGEMENT SYSTEMS

A database management system (DBMS) does just what its name suggests—it is a complex set of programs designed to manage the database(s), usually found in relatively large systems. (A small business with few employees might not need a DBMS.) The DBMS handles numerous management tasks, including:

Controlling access so various data items are viewed only by authorized personnel

▼ Coordinating the shared use of data
▼ Maintaining the quality or integrity of data
▼ Managing input/output operations so they are as efficient as possible
▼ Monitoring performance of the overall system

A DBMS is especially useful in managing a database shared by many users who are depending on it for up-to-date information. Figure 9.6 is an example of a problem situation that can occur when many users access a database at the same time (concurrent use). In this example, the Shipping and Receiving departments both accessed the database to determine the quantity of part X1 in inventory. Shipping subtracted 100 units and obtained a new count to be stored in the file during the same time that Receiving was adding 200 units to the file. Whichever change occurs last becomes the current record. In this example, the shipment of 100 units was not included in the final count because Receiving was not aware of the transaction.

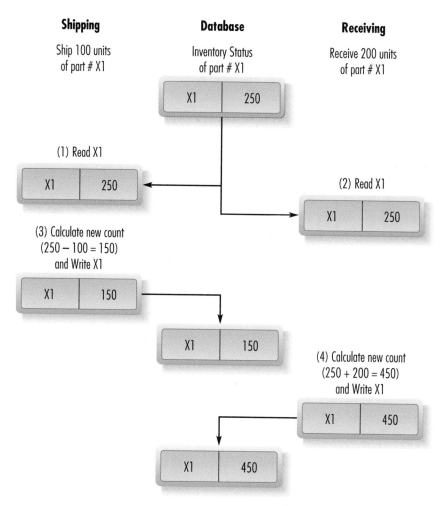

Figure 9.6 Need for Concurrency Control

A DBMS can coordinate access to data so that one person cannot change a record until another person using that same data has completed the transaction. Systems in which data is shared have significant advantages, such as storage savings and security capabilities, but also require careful management, which is one function of a DBMS.

Global Perspective

Transferring data across international borders is an important issue in a company's global strategy. Many legal, cultural, political, and technological concerns have become a part of database design decisions. U.S. companies expanding to Europe must review a variety of laws to determine what types of data can be transferred as well as where it can be transferred. Data security and data protection regulations vary, and laws in some countries are more strict than in others.

With the current capabilities for allowing people to access computers from other locations worldwide, data security concerns have increased. Persons from these other countries might access powerful computers in the United States and generate information that they can then export. The equipment is not physically exported, but its capabilities are accessed and the results exported. Various access controls are being added to prevent this type of unauthorized accessing and exporting of data. Continuing improvements in equipment and increasing technological competence of computer users are making it more difficult to monitor global access to and use of data and equipment. An awareness of the potential problems is the first step in making improvements.

Traditional DBMSs have been based on the relational model. With the increased interest in object-oriented database design, we now have new developments occurring related to DBMSs. An object-oriented database management system (OODBMS) has various features to support advanced object-oriented database applications. Since many businesses have a large amount of data in relational databases, another option is an object-relational database management system (ORDBMS), which allows current relational databases to continue to be used. These systems do not require the development of new databases; however, they are limited to data stored in relational databases, so some of the expected advantages of object-oriented systems, such as improved performance, have to be sacrificed.

Additional work continues to be done on the development of new types of DBMSs to fit new database designs.

DISTRIBUTED DATABASES

Distributed databases involve spreading an organization's database(s) over different geographic areas in a network. Distributed systems have become more widely used in recent years as desktop computers and other computers have become technologically capable of handling larger database activities and have become linked in networks. A distributed database system can be designed in one of two general ways:

1. various parts of a database are housed in the location where they are most needed

2. the entire database is replicated for separate locations

In either system, all the data would be available to users as needed regardless of their location, assuming they have adequate authorization. In addition, the demands on the network may be reduced by having databases housed locally where they are most used.

One of the advantages of the use of distributed databases is that a power failure or similar problem at one location will not shut down the entire system. Some designs, especially those with replicated databases, can automatically shift to alternate sites when problems occur at the originally intended site.

One of the biggest disadvantages of distributed databases is that the technology involved in setting up the system and in managing it is much more complex than a centralized database system.

DATA WAREHOUSES AND DATA MINING

In the days of mainframe-only systems, databases had no option except to be in a centralized environment. After we began to use distributed systems for many business activities, there was a related trend toward distributed databases. In the past few years, we have seen a trend back to centralized systems for some activities, often to take advantage of capabilities now available for analyzing large sets of data stored in one place—called a data warehouse. The process of analyzing the data in this warehouse to gain additional useful business information is called data mining.

Additional information on data mining and data warehouses is available at the Web site.

Data Warehouses

A data warehouse serves a purpose that is different from an operational or transaction-based database. Typical differences are listed in Table 9.1.

Operational/Transactional Database

    Used for split-second decisions, such as those by an airline reservations agent

    Usually requires up-to-the-minute data

    Often contains data for use with a specific type of application

    Houses detailed data for the operation

Data Warehouse

    Used for long-range decisions, primarily for management planning, competitive strategies, etc.

    Contains recent but also historical data

    Contains integrated data from multiple business activities

    Houses both detailed and summary data

Table 9.1 Operational Database versus Data Warehouse

Although much of the data in a data warehouse comes from the business operations, the data becomes a collection of nonvolatile data to assist in decision making. This data is stored separately from any volatile (constantly changing) data being used for immediate operations.

When data goes into the warehouse, it is integrated with other data so that the data is uniform and stored in a way that it can be used easily to provide additional but accurate information. For example, it needs to be stored so that it is clear what items are customer data, what items are from transactions, what items are vendor data, etc. Then it needs to be possible to combine data for analysis, such as combining customer data with geographic data.

Data in this warehouse is typically arranged by subjects. Keeping the data warehouse up and running is not an easy task, because it will continue to expand. The subject areas will continue to expand and the depth of data on a subject will increase. As the data warehouse expands, the demands on the system will also increase.

Data Mining

Data mining involves examining the data in the data warehouse to find useful information for the business, such as patterns and relationships that occur between various items that might not otherwise be noticed. Data mining takes the concepts of decision support systems a step further than their initial capabilities when they appeared a few decades ago.

Decision support systems tools have improved in recent years to include capabilities for online analytical processing (OLAP) and for analysis of contents of a data warehouse. Much larger sets of data can now be analyzed. One of the primary differences between OLAP and data mining has to do with their treatment of data. OLAP tools are designed to allow data to be broken down and summarized, such as to determine sales by geographic area. Data mining tools, in contrast, are designed to look at ratios and patterns, as well as other influences in a set of data. Both types of analyses are quite useful to a business in getting as much useful information as possible.

Data mining takes advantage of some of the advances in artificial intelligence, such as neural networks. Neural networks attempt to imitate the human brain, with one primary goal being an attempt to learn from what occurs. Data mining tools that use neural network techniques are designed to train themselves to adjust, according to examples that are encountered. Data mining activities frequently combine a wide range of decision support tools with neural networks for extensive analyses of data. For example, data mining tools can be developed to identify sales for the previous month by geographic location or by age group or income level, or a combination of all of those items. Or, with neural networks, it can be used for explaining behaviors or making predictions about customer behaviors following an anticipated advertising campaign.

Data mining is an expensive activity. Developing the tools can be very time consuming. Once the tools are developed, a series of tests of the data must be performed to be sure the results are logical and fit the data being used. One report told of a situation in which the data mining tool determined that customer ID numbers would be the best predictor of interest in the next marketing campaign—not a very logical recommendation. The problem was attributed to using tools that were not adequate for that particular task.

Data mining software and services are becoming more prevalent. And these tools are becoming easier to use. A majority of the tools available thus far are directed toward marketing activities, such as:

▼ finding opportunities for cross selling of products

▼ finding opportunities for new products

▼ developing effective retention plans for customers

▼ improving marketing campaigns

One reason for the emphasis on marketing is the basic fact that businesses need to retain and increase their customers. In addition, a great deal of data is already collected from customer transactions and is available for analysis once the tools are defined and refined. For example, these tools can help to determine the types of products that customers usually buy together or the items that should be bundled together to promote customer loyalty.

Data mining has been used successfully in other fields. For example, it has been used to detect insurance fraud, to diagnose failures in manufacturing processes, and to assess risk patterns regarding consumer credit loans.

The development of data warehouses and associated data mining tools is expected to continue to evolve and expand in an effort to help in the decision-making process. One addition is expected to involve the inclusion of some of the useful data that is not currently being placed in data warehouses, such as desktop computer data and data on Web servers.

KNOWLEDGE MANAGEMENT

Traditional data storage has involved data from transactions; it has not included knowledge that employees have gained from working in the organization, knowledge that can be an extremely valuable resource. Knowledge management is a term that is related to database systems and an organization's use of available information. Generally, knowledge management refers to systems in which the knowledge of various employees is stored and made accessible to others, usually to assist in business decisions and/or to improve customer service. For example, this employee knowledge may include policies and procedures they have developed for various activities or particular methods that have been successful. It might include information obtained from the Web or from electronic mail systems.

One of the biggest difficulties in taking advantage of the concept of knowledge management involves getting employees to share their knowledge. They must see some benefit for doing this, and any system used for storing their knowledge must be easy to use (and also easy for others to access). Suggestions for developing a knowledge management system include:

▼ Reward employees who share their knowledge

▼ Make this knowledge visible throughout the organization

▼ Get commitment from top management that encourages workers to share information

▼ Involve workers in the design of the system

Some companies are using text-search software for their knowledge management systems. Some of these systems can find information on the Web, as well as from standard databases and messaging systems. This is another information systems topic that continues to be refined and expanded.

Summary

Data is an extremely important resource, and it is typically stored in databases of related items.

Unique identifiers in files can be used as links to data in other files.

Storage locations of records are referred to as addresses; two types are a physical address and a relative address.

Files may be organized in one of these orders: (1) sequential (2) indexed sequential, or (3) random (or direct).

Files may be accessed in direct order or in sequential order. If direct access is desired, an identifier called a "key" is used.

A conceptual data model is developed to describe user needs and to serve as a basis for a logical data model, which identifies items that need to work together and how they should appear.

Database structures include the hierarchical, network, relational, and object-oriented structures. The relational structure has been used most widely for a number of years.

A database management system is used to coordinate and manage various aspects of databases.

Distributed databases are those in which databases are spread over different geographic locations within an organization.

A data warehouse is a large, centralized repository of data, both detailed and summary. It is typically arranged by subjects.

Data mining refers to sophisticated methods of examining and analyzing data in a data warehouse. Its purpose is generally to find information that might otherwise not be noticed but that could be used to improve a company's operations, customer services, decision making, and so on.

Knowledge management refers to storage of employee knowledge on an extensive range of topics.

Questions for Review and Discussion

1. Explain the difference between a physical address and a relative address of stored data.

2. Discuss similarities and differences between "file organization" and "file access" options.

3. Identify major advantages and disadvantages of the various database structures used for logical data models.

4. Why is a DBMS especially important when data is shared among many users?

5. Define and discuss "data warehouses" and "data mining."

Selected References

Blevins, Andy. "Data Warehousing: A Strategic Business Driver." *DM Review*, December 1997.

Cranford, Stephen. "Data Mining–The Intelligence Component." *DM Review*, May 1998.

Cranford, Stephen. "Why Manage Knowledge?" *DM Review*, March 1998.

Curry, Tom. "Knowledge IS." *Software Magazine*, January 1998.

Edelstein, Herb. "Data Mining: Let's Get Practical," *DB2 Magazine*, Summer 1998.

Grimes, Seth. "Modeling Object/Relational Databases." *DBMS*, April 1998.

Hackathorn, Richard. "Farming the Web." *Byte*, October 1997.

Inmon, Bill. "Wherefore Warehouse?" *Byte*, January 1998.

Mena, Jesus. "Data Mining FAQs." *DM Review*, January 1998.

Richman, Dan. "Data Mining: Still No Piece of Cake." Special Supplement to *Software Magazine*, December 1997.

Srinivasan, V., and D. T. Chang. "Object Persistence in Object-Oriented Applications." *IBM Systems Journal*, Vol. 36, No. 1, 1997.

Stedman, Craig. "Data Mining for Fool's Gold." *Computerworld*, December 1, 1997.

Stonebraker, Michael. "Betting on ORDBMS." *Byte*, April 1998.

White, Colin. "Warehouses Webicum: Evolution of a Species." *DB2 Magazine*, Spring 1998.

Wilkerson, Phil, and Richard Tanler. "The Intranet Data Warehouse Providing Content-Driven OLAP." *DM Review*, February 1998.

Chapter 9 Key Terms

Metadata
descriptions of data and identification of relationships among data.

File organization
the relationship between a record and its location within a file.

Address
identification of a storage location (same term used in referring to location of data in primary memory).

File access
a method of locating files, such as directly or sequentially.

Key
the unique identifier of a record, usually involving one primary key and one or more secondary keys.

Hierarchical structure
a database structure with one path from the highest level to a segment at the lowest level (one-to-many relationship).

Network structure
database structure similar to hierarchical structure but with the addition of horizontal relationships from one segment to another (many-to-many relationship).

Relational structure
database structure that organizes data into a two-dimensional table, with a capability of linking data in one table with data in another table.

Object-oriented (OO) structure
database structure that organizes data within objects, in which data, methods, and procedures are kept together and retrieved together.

Redundancy
unnecessary duplication of data.

Class
person, place, or thing of interest in an object-oriented system.

Object
an instance of a class in an object-oriented system, containing related data and procedures.

Inheritance
feature of object-oriented system in which new classes can use characteristics of an existing class.

Encapsulation
a reference to a technique in an object-oriented system in which data is packaged together with its corresponding procedures.

Database Management System (DBMS)
a system that manages the access to, use of, and storage of data.

Data warehouse
large collection of data from business operations, as well as from other sources, that is used for extensive analysis.

Data mining
the process of analyzing data in a data warehouse by using special tools to find information useful for business decisions that might otherwise not be discovered.

Knowledge management
systems that contain useful knowledge acquired by employees, such as successful methods of handling specific business activities.

Online Activities

Refer to the companion Web site at www.wiley.com/college/simon for a variety of online activities: additional chapter content, *Wall Street Journal Interactive Edition* access, review materials, student assignments, and relevant links.

| GO TO | http://www.wiley.com/college/simon |

Your four-month access to the Interactive Journal allows you to research articles published within the last 30 days in the Interactive Journal, Barron's Online, and Dow Jones Interactive. A Help feature is available if you need assistance in specifying your search topic.

One of the best ways to become familiar with the Interactive Journal is to use the "Journal Atlas." This site map allows you to jump into any of the sections or subsections in one click.

Research each topic in the Interactive Journal and analyze the results of your search.

1. Distributed databases. Why would a distributed database be used by a business instead of a centralized database?

2. Knowledge management. How are businesses developing systems to take better advantage of the knowledge existing within their organizations?

3. Data mining in businesses. What types of technology are needed? How would a business decide if it would be advantageous to them to develop such a system?

CHAPTER 10

Systems Development Procedures

LEARNING OBJECTIVES

After studying the contents of this chapter, you should be able to

1. Identify in general the phases involved in developing a system and relate them to business applications.
2. Explain the importance of a feasibility study and the types of considerations involved.
3. Describe the features and uses of tools such as data flow diagrams, entity-relationship diagrams, and prototyping.
4. Compare and contrast the logical and physical designs.
5. Discuss methods of acquiring hardware and software and factors considered in using these methods.
6. Explain the primary concerns during the system installation.
7. Identify and discuss the importance of activities involved in system maintenance.
8. Describe current trends related to systems development.

SYSTEMS DEVELOPMENT OVERVIEW

Regardless of your position in an organization, you can benefit from having a basic understanding of systems development. It enables you to participate productively in discussions of current or proposed systems or to make strategic decisions regarding these potential changes. If you were a new management trainee for a hotel, for example, you might begin your experience by handling reservations, where you would be trained in the proper procedures for entering data into the system. At first, you would be concerned mostly with learning how to perform your job. As you became more proficient and more knowledgeable, you might be included in discussions about ways to improve or change the system from the perspective of a person who uses it. Other people involved in the discussions would have other perspectives, such as people responsible for developing the proposed system, those responsible for managing it, and those considering the long-term strategic effects for the organization. A basic understanding of the procedures involved in developing systems would help you to contribute as much as possible to this process (and might also help you with career advancement opportunities—you might later be managing a system or deciding on the systems needed).

A person who is involved in discussions from the information systems perspective is often referred to as a system analyst. Some system analyst positions are actually referred to as "system analyst/programmer," because the job may involve both the analysis of the current system and the development of new systems. A wide variation exists in the activities that occur in these jobs, depending partly on the size of the organization and on the size of the project under consideration. A report published in *Forbes* indicated that the system analyst occupation is predicted to have one of the largest increases in jobs between now and the year 2006. Of the ten occupations on the list of those with the largest job growths expected, system analyst was the only occupation for which a bachelor's degree is usually required.

The development of a large system is a lengthy process, possibly involving several years of development time. The technology that must work together for such a project to be successful can become quite complex. Our discussion in this chapter focuses primarily on the development process for large systems because they are usually the most strategic systems for a business. If you understand the basic procedures involved in a large system-development project, you will also be prepared for the process of developing smaller projects.

Several steps or phases are typically involved in system development, from determining that a need exists to eventually installing and then maintaining a new or revised system. Once a request occurs to consider a new or changed system (someone identifies a need), the feasibility of the project is investigated. If the project appears feasible, the proposed project continues to the next phase and proceeds through a series of phases as long as it is still perceived as a viable project. Figure 10.1 identifies various phases of the traditional system development process. A project could be abandoned at any stage of the development process if it is determined that it cannot or should not be continued. In addition, some phases may be repeated several times or combined with others as needed, depending on other events that occur during the development process.

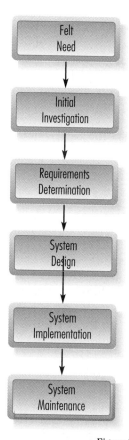

Figure 10.1 System Development Phases

These phases may be referred to by different labels or names in different organizations, but the overall procedures are generally the same. These phases represent a procedure or methodology for analyzing a situation and possibly identifying and developing a solution. Keep in mind that this process is not sequential in reality but the phases described here represent the types of activities that are involved. Some steps may need to be repeated several times, and some steps may occur at the same time as others.

FELT OR IDENTIFIED NEED

The process of developing a new or revised information system generally begins when someone suggests that a need exists (a felt need refers to the fact that someone felt there was (or identified) a need for this proposed change). If you were handling reservations at a hotel, for example, a need might be established for a new database that would be a part of the company's overall reservation system and would provide information that could result in better services for guests and a better marketing strategy.

These are desired "end results"; i.e., what is wanted as the final outcome. Desired end results represent the usual starting point for considering a new or revised system.

A variety of needs may be identified at different times and by different people within one organization. For example, someone may feel there is a need for any or all of these attributes:

▼ Increased processing speed
▼ Greater security of data
▼ Reduced operating costs
▼ Faster retrieval of information
▼ Better information
▼ Integration of work from different areas

The initiator of a project proposal can be anyone who feels there is a need (e.g., current users of a system, top executives, department managers, suppliers, or even customers). Background information is often included with the request, such as a description of the problem, the importance of the problem to the organization, potential solutions, and sources of additional information.

INITIAL INVESTIGATION

The purpose of the initial investigation phase is to gather enough information to decide whether it is feasible to undertake the proposed project. The two major aspects of this phase are

▼ determining the exact problem to be solved.
▼ conducting a feasibility study to see if it is practical and possible to try to solve the problem.

Although the term problem is used here, it does not necessarily indicate that something is wrong; it may be a suggested method of improving the system to provide an additional benefit. In the hotel example mentioned above, the "problem" might be to develop a method of storing and using data about guests that would provide better guest services and new marketing capabilities. Once the problem is defined clearly, employees may expend considerable time and effort in deciding if a database could be developed and added to their system without investing more dollars than the potential benefits would return.

Problem Definition

A clear statement of the problem is extremely important. Unless the problem is understood by everyone involved, the solution designed might not fit the problem, resulting in the potential for an enormous waste of time and money. Establishing a problem definition must be an iterative process, meaning that several changes are expected to occur in the definition before reaching the final version. People involved in the investigation all bring different perspectives to the problem-solving process, so that the proposal can be studied from many viewpoints before decisions are made.

Methods of gathering information to assist in determining the exact problem typically include interviews with people involved in the current process, people who would be involved in the new process (if this is a different group), and reviews of related organizational documents. The methods vary somewhat depending on the situation; for example, some proposals involve entirely new systems in which no employees are involved in a current process. The problem definition can continue to change while its feasibility is being studied.

Feasibility Study

As the name suggests, a feasibility study is conducted to determine whether the proposed project would be appropriate for the organization to pursue. One obvious part of a feasibility study is to compare the projected benefits with the expected costs. In addition, the project analysts must consider various aspects of the organization as a whole to see what areas would be affected. A proposed change might have considerable benefit for the person or people who suggested it, but analysis of the effect on the overall organization might show that it would be more detrimental to other parts of the organization than beneficial to the requesters.

One difficulty of a feasibility study is in determining a dollar value of the expected benefits to compare with the costs, particularly since the proposed system has not been designed at this stage. Some benefits, such as improved customer satisfaction, are hard to quantify in specific dollar amounts. In addition to monetary considerations, the study must determine that the project can be reasonably accomplished. Feasibility factors that are analyzed include:

▼ Financial or economic feasibility. What costs are involved (such as equipment, personnel, and supplies)? What are the benefits (such as improved performance or decreased costs of operation)?

▼ Technical feasibility. Can the project be accomplished with the hardware and software available in the marketplace?

▼ Schedule feasibility. Can the project be developed in the timeframe that is needed to make it useful?

▼ Operational feasibility. Can the system be operated by current personnel or by personnel that can be hired? Does it work with other systems already in place in the organization?

▼ Motivational feasibility. Are personnel available who are willing to support the change emotionally, as well as technically?

▼ Legal/ethical feasibility. Is the project one that violates no laws, such as privacy of data? Does it meet general guidelines of business ethics in cases where no laws exist?

After analyzing these and any other desired feasibility factors, the project team develops reports of the results and presents them to those people who will decide on the overall feasibility of the project. If approved, the project continues.

As shown in Figure 10.2, extensive communication must occur during the investigation phase. The problem is redefined, perhaps several times, after some investigative work is completed. The figure also shows that input comes from a requester and usually requires additional management input before the investigation phase begins. People responsible for initiating this investigation (and possibly other decision makers) typically "sign off" or agree that this phase has been completed to their satisfaction before the project continues. Larger, more expensive projects usually require sign off by high-level executives. Clear communication is extremely important at this stage; it is possible for managers or others to sign off on an interpretation of a project that could be quite different from a developer's interpretation of the project.

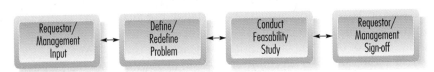

Figure 10.2 Initial Investigation Phase

REQUIREMENTS DETERMINATION

Once the feasibility study is completed and management approval to proceed has been received, the requirements determination phase can begin. Requirements determination is concerned with gathering facts about the current system, determining the requirements of the system users, and identifying any constraints (restrictions or problems). The objectives of this phase are

▼ analyze the existing system.
▼ determine system user requirements and constraints.

Study of Existing System

Before trying to create a new system, analysts must have a good understanding of the current system. Analysts concentrate on collecting as much information as they can, including what the current system does and does not do, as well as what works well and what does not. Those people involved in using and/or managing the current system are responsible for providing clear descriptions because the system analysts are not likely to have extensive knowledge of a particular system they are beginning to study. Details about the system components (hardware, software, data, procedures, and personnel) are included in the study. The new system may need to be compatible with other systems already in place. Even if no current system exists that does what is desired in a proposed system, the current situation must be analyzed, partly to develop an understanding of what is required and partly to identify areas in which a new system must be compatible with a current system.

Methods of acquiring information about the current system often include interviews, questionnaires, and observations. Written documentation within the organization is also used, such as procedures manuals, messages related to the system, and documents or reports related to the system. Information may also come from external sources involved in the system, such as suppliers and customers.

An important concept in reviewing an existing system is that a new system being considered is not necessarily a case of automating a current system. And if automating the current system is the goal, one of the most important questions then becomes, is the current system the best way to perform the task(s) involved? An inefficient system that becomes automated may still be an inefficient system compared with other available methods.

One tool used during the analysis phase is a data flow diagram (DFD), partly because it can be effective in providing feedback to users and managers. DFDs identify what happens to data items as they flow through the system. DFD symbols are simple to use and to understand. The terminology varies a little, but the symbols are often referred to in the following ways:

▼ an open-ended data store symbol for the location of data when it is not in use

▼ a data source/sink (destination) symbol to represent entities that either supply data or receive data as part of the system (these may be external entities)

▼ a process symbol for work that is to be completed that will transform the data in some way

▼ arrows to indicate the direction of data flow

As shown in Figure 10.3, data flow diagram symbols are easy to construct and to understand.

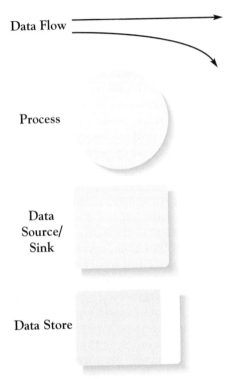

Data Flow

Process

Data
Source/
Sink

Data Store

Figure 10.3 Data Flow Diagram Symbols

DFDs are also used widely in other phases, especially design. Once the DFDs are defined correctly, they can serve as a basis for design and programming (coding) procedures. Some DFDs are developed to represent a general overview of the process; other DFDs are then developed to indicate more detailed procedures.

An entity-relationship (E-R) diagram is also a tool used in requirements determination. An entity is an item of interest (e.g., a person, place, or thing) about which data is accumulated. An E-R diagram shows relationships between or among various entities. A DFD gives a view of relationships of the processes or movement of data, and the E-R diagram supplies further explanation by describing the relationships of the data without regard to movement. The E-R diagram is used to obtain a clear understanding of the data relationships that exist. E-R diagrams may also be used as a basis for developing the actual database. Figure 10.4 illustrates a basic E-R diagram. The two entities are the customer and the order, and the relationship is the customer-order. This diagram also indicates a one-to-many (1:M) relationship—one customer may have many orders. Relationships could also be many-to-one or many-to-many, depending entirely on the situation.

Figure 10.4 Entity-Relationship Diagram

User Requirements and Constraints

Analysts must have a clear understanding of system users' needs, as well as any constraints—restrictions or problems to consider in analyzing the requirements desired by users of the system. The primary purpose is to determine what information or processes are needed. Analysts must work diligently with system users to develop accurate descriptions of users' requirements. Most systems have subsystems. Analysis of the requirements typically involves dividing the system into subsystems and working with these smaller parts individually. Analysts and system users usually find it much more efficient to work with individual aspects of the system. One characteristic of a good system analyst is the ability to identify the overall scope of a problem, along with appropriate subdivisions of the problem.

Figure 10.5 presents a general view of the overall process of requirements definition. Results of interviews, questionnaires, and any other sources serve as starting points for developing diagrams and other materials that define the current process. System users and managers typically review the materials. Once the users' requirements are clearly defined, a report is presented to appropriate managers for their approval. Considerably more work is involved in reaching a final analysis of user requirements than may be obvious from this introductory-level description of the process. Probably one of the major concerns to keep in mind is that system users and analysts are both responsible for ensuring that effective communication occurs throughout the process.

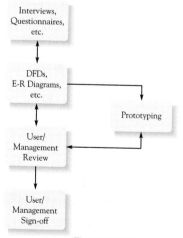

Figure 10.5 Requirements Determination

Additional information about prototyping is available at the Web site.

Prototyping is a tool that can be used to help identify user requirements. A prototype is a small working model of some aspect of the system, which can provide views to system users to help in identifying and clarifying their needs. Prototyping can also be used to enhance the overall system development process by getting users involved early in reviewing sample screens, reports, data, and so on.

Sometimes prototyping is used as a continuing part of the system development process, but sometimes it is used as a substitute for at least some of the system development phases. Types of prototyping include illustrations of proposed screens and reports, simple models that appear to do processing, and models that actually perform some process. The main feature of the use of prototypes is the ability to create a model that can be reviewed by users of the system and changed as many times as needed to meet their requirements. Prototypes used for requirements definition are sometimes of the "disposable" type, meaning that they are often developed quickly without necessarily following usual quality standards and without including other aspects that will be needed in the development stage. Some prototypes created at various stages of the system development process could become part of the final system, but many are intended for temporary review purposes only.

In general, prototypes can be used in four ways:
▼ As a description of requirements
▼ As a basis for additional prototyping
▼ As a working system
▼ As a determination that at least a part of the system should be discarded (which may sound negative but is a very useful result)

Advantages of the use of prototyping include:
▼ Improved capability of helping users and managers understand the problem and identify any areas needing further discussion
▼ Improved overall communication between developers and managers and/or users
▼ Better management of the project by dividing tasks into smaller units
▼ Reduction in risk of developing a system that is not what was wanted
▼ Improved acceptance of the new system

Disadvantages of the use of prototyping include:
▼ Difficult to explain the purpose and uses of prototyping (e.g., not a finished product, lacking in some functions, may be discarded)

▼ More effective for some projects than others, requiring project managers to have a good understanding of this methodology before deciding on its use and to what extent it is used

▼ Requires software tools for developing prototypes; the cost will vary depending on the system under development and the capabilities of the tools used

After approval (sign-off) of the requirements determination phase is received by the project manager, the actual design of the system can begin, assuming that the project continues to be feasible.

SYSTEM DESIGN

The requirements determination process identifies what is required to meet the needs of users, and the system design process describes how the new system will be implemented. System design includes development of a logical design and a physical design. The design process should focus on the people, the specific procedures, and the technology. Logical design is the basis for physical design. Designs are reviewed, perhaps several times, and revised as needed before being accepted. (Of course, a project can still be stopped at any time—the decision to accept and continue the process does not always occur at the end of each phase.)

Management Perspective

When developing a system application, designers must be careful to meet the needs of the organization without providing considerably more than is needed. For example, an insurance firm needed to develop a system that would be available on a 24-hour basis to provide automated answers to eligibility questions for several hundred thousand customers who might need assistance when traveling abroad. Options considered initially included satellite transmissions and cross-Atlantic fiber-optic circuits, with an estimated cost of $250,000 to $500,000. But after carefully analyzing the needs, designers determined that an easy-to-use system could be developed that could be connected to a public-switched data communications network, since use of the system would be intermittent and relatively infrequent. The cost was less than $100,000, and development time was reduced significantly.

Logical Design

Logical design identifies how all the components will work together through the input, processing, and output activities that will occur in the new system. Prototyping and other methods may be used to assist in identifying all the relationships that will occur. Data flow diagrams and similar design tools can be used in clarifying the logical design.

Specific considerations during logical design are related to the information systems components of hardware, software, data, procedures, and people. The first concern should always be to determine what output, such as specific reports, is needed. Here are some additional considerations:

▼ What data will be required as input into the system in order to get the desired output?

▼ What processing is required to proceed from input to output?

▼ What are the hardware and software requirements?

▼ How will the system be maintained?

▼ How will performance be monitored?

▼ What procedures will be needed for backup and recovery in case of loss of data?

▼ What are the personnel requirements, including required skills?

Did you notice that all these questions are clearly related to specific components of a system? The questions are all related to items that are needed for or by different components. Table 10.1 provides a brief summary of some typical logical design concerns, subdivided by people, procedures, and technology.

Component	Needs
People	1. Specific user skills
	2. Change management
	3. Quality control
Procedures	1. User procedures
	2. Applications
	3. Reports
Technology	1. Hardware
	2. Software
	3. Data

Table 10.1 Typical Logical Design Concerns

Change management related to people refers to the importance of giving sufficient consideration to the effect a change in any aspect of the hardware or software has on other current and new components of the system. Special emphasis should be placed on the effects of these changes on the people using the system. (Change management is also important as it relates to procedures and technology, not just to the people.)

Physical Design

Physical design is based on the logical design and involves the actual design of all aspects of the system. As with other phases, changes may be needed in previous parts of the process, including the logical design, as problems are encountered or as the situation changes.

As with logical design, physical design includes all components of the system. For example, physical design of hardware generally includes specifications of equipment. For software that is to be purchased, specifications must also be identified. For software that is to be developed, design would include specific details, such as data flow diagrams and other diagrams or descriptions that identify the needs of the software.

Figure 10.6 gives examples of physical design concerns related to system components. In the technology component, the concerns are always related to hardware, software, and data. In the people and procedures components, the concerns could be much more extensive than those listed here, depending on the specific situation, but are always based on the logical design.

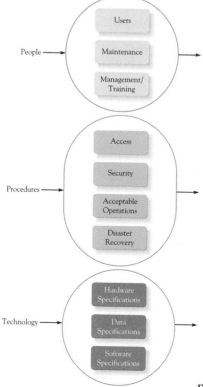

Figure 10.6 Physical Design

Concerns related to personnel include:
▼ an identification of who will use and maintain the system.
▼ who will handle all the various responsibilities involved with the system.
▼ what methods will be used to maintain quality of the work, including training.

Physical design related to process or procedures includes:
▼ descriptions of how users will access the system.
▼ what normal operations can be expected to occur.
▼ what methods will be used for unusual or exceptional occurrences.
▼ what disaster recovery measures will be included.

Physical design related to technology includes specifications of
▼ hardware
▼ software
▼ data

Hardware and software specifications are based on needs of other components of the system (people, procedures, and data), compared with the technological capabilities available.

Data specifications involve describing:
▼ what data will be included.
▼ how it will be organized.
▼ how it will be accessed.
▼ what methods will be used to be sure the data remains accurate and up-to-date.
▼ what procedures will be used to ensure security and privacy of the data.

Database development is described in further detail in Chapter 9.

SYSTEM IMPLEMENTATION

After a system design has been completed and approved, the process of system implementation can begin. This phase includes reviewing the possible sources for acquiring all the hardware and software needed for the system, as well as actual installation of the system.

Acquisition of Hardware and Software

Acquisition of appropriate hardware and software must be coordinated to be sure all software and hardware components are compatible. Hardware and packaged software under consideration must be evaluated and compared. Following their selection, they must be physically acquired so they can be installed, tested, and accepted. The software acquired may be custom developed rather than packaged software. If the software is custom developed, the development could occur internally or externally ("outsourced"), or could be a combination of both.

Several sources are available for obtaining hardware. If an internal staff is available whose members are knowledgeable about acquiring hardware, they can offer assistance in evaluating the best methods by weighing costs versus benefits of different methods.

Hardware Acquisition Considerations

In acquiring hardware, many questions must be answered. Here are a few examples:

▼ Will new equipment be compatible with existing hardware in the current system if it will continue to be used?

▼ Which sources would be best to use—manufacturers, distributors, or other companies that provide hardware components?

▼ If different vendors or suppliers are used, what problems may occur with coordination and compatibility?

▼ Is the desired equipment available? What is the length of time between order time and shipping time?

▼ What kinds of policies are provided for return of hardware, such as a 30-day, money-back guarantee? What is covered by the warranty?

▼ What technical support and repair services are available from the manufacturer and from other sources?

▼ How much training of employees will be necessary (and is it provided by the hardware supplier)?

Additional information on service-level agreements is available at the Web site.

Sources of Hardware

The manufacturers of computer equipment are the primary sources used for acquiring hardware for larger organizations. Large organizations typically send out requests for proposals (RFPs) to major suppliers indicating the items desired, including technical specifications. Smaller businesses, as well as individuals, often purchase equipment from computer dealers or mail-order companies.

Leasing companies should be considered as an option, since the cost of leasing may be lower than purchasing and can reduce the amount of cash invested in hardware that has the potential for becoming obsolete rather quickly.

Software Acquisition Considerations

In making software acquisition decisions, here are the general steps involved:

Determine what software (if any) is already developed and available commercially to fit your needs, then compare the purchase price plus any accompanying benefits with the cost of developing this software.

Determine the best sources for obtaining any remaining software, either from internal sources, external sources, or a combination of the two. Compare costs versus benefits in making the decision.

Make necessary arrangements for software to be purchased commercially, along with arrangements for software that will be developed, whether externally or internally.

Custom Software versus Packaged Software

Commercially available software packages (e.g., those available off-the-shelf in retail stores, mail order catalogs, etc.) have these advantages over custom-developed software:

▼ The overall cost is usually lower because the development cost is shared by many people or organizations.

▼ The package is usually available for immediate use.

▼ The package has already been tested.

▼ The use of already-developed, "packaged" software is usually the least expensive method when such software exists that can meet the organization's needs, even if some modifications are required.

One reason many organizations require custom-developed software is that they have unique needs that are not met by commercial packages. Many large programs that an organization needs in order to be competitive (and to distinguish itself from other businesses) must be developed individually because no one else has identical systems. Businesses can sometimes acquire or maintain a competitive advantage through specialized, custom software that may enable the business to provide a unique or better service.

When considering the purchase of commercially developed, packaged software, you should ask several questions similar to those for selecting hardware, such as:

▼   Does the software perform the desired tasks adequately so that the cost is less than the cost of developing unique programs to perform these tasks?

▼   Is the software compatible with other parts of the system to be used?

▼   If multiple vendors or suppliers are used, will there be problems with compatibility?

▼   How long will it take from order date to delivery date?

▼   What policies are provided for return of software, such as a money-back guarantee?

▼   What technical support is available from the vendor or supplier?

▼   Does the vendor provide training for users; if so, to what extent?

▼   Can the software be altered to fit unique needs of the organization now or later?

For most systems that have been designed, it is likely that some aspects will be unique to the organization and will require custom development of some software. This individual development aspect is the most time-consuming part of the acquisition phase, because some programs can be extremely complicated to write. Depending on the size of the project, development time can range from a few months to several years.

Internal versus External Development

Software is usually developed internally when the organization has staff members who have the time and the ability to develop the needed software. Otherwise, some or all of the software may be developed externally. This is often referred to as a build-versus-buy decision.

If an internal staff is available that could perform the work and if it is determined that developing the software internally would be the most cost-effective method, some additional benefits often occur. For example, the internal staff will be more knowledgeable about the programs once they are in use and therefore better able to handle changes as they are needed. In addition, using an internal staff gives the organization more control over what is developed. But internal staff should be used only if the members have adequate time to do the work and can produce the programs as efficiently and cost-effectively as an external organization. The needed internal staff will include a project management team in addition to those handling the actual program development.

Programs that are developed internally must be tested and corrected (debugged) as needed. The general process is depicted in Figure 10.7. Writing of programs begins based on needs developed during the design phase.

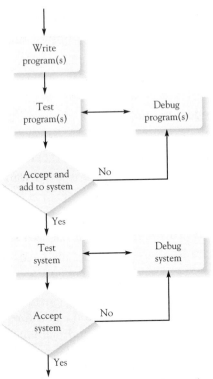

Figure 10.7 Program Process from Writing to Acceptance

Before a decision is made to use internal sources, it must be ascertained that the advantages of using the internal staff exceed those of an external staff. Often, some parts of a project can be performed better by internal staff, while external groups would be a better choice for other aspects. That is why many of these projects involve a combination of internal and external personnel.

When considering having the software programs developed externally, you should ask several questions, including these:

▼ What guarantee is there that the software programs will meet the organization's needs?

▼ Can a late fee be included if the programs are not fully operational and acceptable by some specified date?

▼ Can the programs be modified later as the organization's needs change, and can the modifications be made by internal staff?

▼ What is included in the price besides the actual programs—does it include installation, maintenance, and/or modifications?

▼ What provisions will be made to be sure the programs work appropriately with other parts of the system?

▼ How does the cost compare with the use of internal staff, assuming that such internal staff are available and qualified to perform the work, or could be hired?

▼ Have similar programs been written by the external source that have been tested and are working properly? Could visits be made to other organizations that are using the programs?

Global Perspective

One of the ways that U.S. businesses have been able to increase their programming productivity has been through the use of programmers in other countries. However, consideration must be given to some of the problems that occur before decisions are made to handle system development in this way. For example, some programmers lack knowledge of U.S. business practices, such as an understanding of what is meant by payroll deductions. Thus, businesses must be extremely careful and specific when setting rules and standards for foreign programmers to follow. Procedures for making changes and for meeting delivery dates must be clearly specified. A problem when time is critical is the difference in time zones and the difficulty of communicating over long distances, especially from countries with different standards for communications equipment. Videoconferencing and facsimile are being used more extensively to facilitate communications with programmers in some other countries. Another problem is the widespread occurrence of software piracy in some countries. Software is easier to steal than hardware, and in some countries there is less acknowledgment that programmers have intellectual property rights.

Most programs are expected to have some initial problems during development that require them to be debugged and altered. As the debugging process proceeds, the program must be retested. The testing and debugging process can occur numerous times before the program works properly. Sometimes, a change in one part of a program may cause a problem in another part of the program. In addition, multiple problems may be embedded in the program that will not become noticeable until other parts are corrected.

Once an individual program is working properly, it is added to other parts of the system being developed so that it can be tested with other programs. The testing and debugging process is repeated in this phase (refer to Figure 10.7). You must expect the testing and debugging process to require a considerable portion of the overall development time.

Another very important aspect of internal software development is to ensure that system developers, including programmers, provide adequate documentation, which refers to the materials that explain how the programs were written and how to use the system. Program documentation typically includes at least the following:

▼ An identification of the programming languages used for each program (combinations of programming languages may be used for the overall system).

▼ An explanation of the purpose and functions of each program.

▼ Detailed charts for each program that clearly explain the logical structure or flow of the program.

▼ Detailed explanations of all parts of the programs, often with comments or remarks included in the programs, so that a new programmer not involved in the original development could conceivably review the programs and the accompanying documentation and would then be able to work with the programs and make changes as needed.

System Installation

After all the programs have been developed, tested, and altered as needed, and all other parts of the system are in place, the system is ready for implementation. The implementation process includes integration of all factors in preparation for installation or startup, testing, and eventual acceptance of the system, including complete conversion to the new system.

Site Preparation

The physical facility where the system will be housed may need changes, such as new wiring, additional space, new air conditioning, or security mechanisms. In some cases, very little change is required; however, most major system changes involve alterations to the site. These changes must be completed before hardware is installed.

Hardware and Software Preparation

New hardware is often brought in and set up (installed) by the people who are the external sources of the equipment, with installation included as part of the purchase price. All software that has been purchased or developed must be installed on the hardware, if not installed during development.

Data Preparation

Data preparation (sometimes referred to as data conversion) is the process of converting current data files into a format that will work with the new system. Some data may require keyboard entry. Other data may have been stored within a different computer system and will require conversion or changes to the data before being acceptable for use in the new system. Any changes that have been made in hardware or software, including changes in programming languages, may cause a need for changes in some aspects of data files. Data preparation is sometimes the largest single factor in large systems preparation.

Preparation of System Users

Users of the new system must be given thorough training. Although this training is usually designed for the organization's employees who will be using the system directly, consideration should also be given to the need for training of other people who are affected by the new system, such as managers, customers, or suppliers. If the system was developed externally, training may be included as part of the cost.

After all preparations have been completed, system conversion or installation and testing occurs. As with the testing of programs during their development, individual programs must be tested as well as entire systems. Errors of any type must be located and corrected, along with any output formats or results that are different from what was desired. Every component is tested, including the procedures and the people involved in using the system.

Conversion

Several types of system installation or conversion plans exist, and deciding which to use depends on the situation. Advantages and disadvantages of each plan should be considered before the decision is made as to which plan to use. Variations in labels or names given to these conversion plans exist, but the typical plans are as follows:

1. Parallel approach. The old system is retained until the new system runs properly.

Advantages: It is very easy to make comparisons and determine if the results are the same with both systems. In addition, the old system can continue to be used until problems that occur with the new system are fixed.

Disadvantages: It is expensive because of large duplication of effort. Some old systems may not be adequate to produce results that can be compared with the new system, especially if the new system was designed for new needs such as a change from a batch processing system to an online system. There may not be an old system that does the new procedure. In addition, computer users may be reluctant to change to a new system as long as the old one is available.

2. Piecemeal approach. The new system slowly replaces the old system, often replacing only one part of the old system at a time; a phased-in approach.

Advantages: It has relatively low risk. Installers need to monitor or watch only a small number of changes at a time.

Disadvantages: Parts of the old system must be able to work with parts of the new system, which is not always possible. It is somewhat expensive because of duplication of effort. It only works well if the organization is one in which individual groups are doing different tasks that make division into parts possible for phase-in.

3.   Pilot approach. The new system is tried first with a small test (pilot) group, such as one branch or department of an organization; also a phased-in approach.

Advantages: It is less expensive to run than the phased approach that uses both systems tied together. It provides an opportunity to try out the entire system on a small scale.

Disadvantages: It is limited to situations in which a small group is available that can use the entire system. This method may take more time for implementation than some other plans and is difficult to coordinate.

4.   Plunge (direct cutover) approach. Change occurs all at once from the old system to the new system.

Advantages: No duplication of effort occurs. There is no need to worry about getting the two systems to work together.

Disadvantages: It is very risky, since there is no chance to compare results. No backup system is available if problems occur. This method is usually recommended only when the old system is not working or does not perform the same tasks as the new system and no longer serves the desired need.

Other variations of these approaches are used, depending on particular circumstances. Whatever approach is used, the eventual result is that the new system replaces the old system.

Testing

During testing, sample data is entered. Sample data should represent the types of data that will typically be used, as well as some unusual data that might occur, to test how the system handles anything that is incorrect or incomplete. System testing must include checking to make sure that the programs work correctly and that data flows through the system properly. Testing must also include the integration of any current programs with the new programs to be sure they will work properly together. Some attention should be given to system performance, such as the time it takes to run the programs and the memory requirements. The goal of testing is to have everything working satisfactorily so that the system is accepted by those who must agree that it is performing up to expectations.

SYSTEM MAINTENANCE

Maintenance refers to the process of making changes as they are needed, as well as adding new functions and fixing any problems. Although variation exists, the first review after the system has been implemented often occurs about three to six months after implementation. By that time, users of the system will be relatively proficient in using the system and can often help to identify problem areas. They can also better analyze by then how well the system performs compared with the old system and compared with what was expected. Adjustments to the system are then made as needed.

System Review

The system should be reviewed regularly, at least once a year, to be sure it is meeting the organization's needs. Additional reviews should occur whenever a need exists. Although some discussions are typically held with managers of particular operations, managers are not always the people who have direct contact with the system. The actual users of the system must be included in the review process, because they are an excellent source of specific information about the system's effectiveness.

Additional information about RAD and other design tools is available at the Web site.

System Alterations

Many changes that are needed in systems are caused by circumstances other than problems in the original development. As an organization changes, new types of information may be needed. As system users become more familiar with its capabilities, they may recognize additional features that would be improvements. In addition, government regulations change, often creating a need for change to a business organization's information system. Sometimes, changes are required to remain competitive.

Changes in systems are sometimes minor, perhaps requiring just a few alterations to programming code. But some changes that may seem minor have hidden relationships that may make the alterations more complicated. For example, changing to a new version of a software package may seem minor but might cause numerous changes to data and programs that were prepared for use with another version.

Maintenance is usually a large part of the overall cost of a system, typically a much greater part of the cost than the initial development of the system. But maintaining the current system is usually much less expensive than starting over with a new system every time changes are needed. Some systems can remain useful and effective for several years as long as they were properly developed and continue to be well maintained.

The traditional method of developing an information system that has been described above is referred to as the system development life cycle (SDLC). Some variation in terminology exists, but the general phases of the SDLC are identified in the blocks in Figure 10.8. Although not typically mentioned as part of the SDLC, project management is depicted in the center of the cycle because project management teams are at work throughout the process to handle staffing, benefits, priority setting, evaluations, and all the other events and crises that occur. Project management ties together all the aspects of the SDLC so that everything moves effectively from one phase to another.

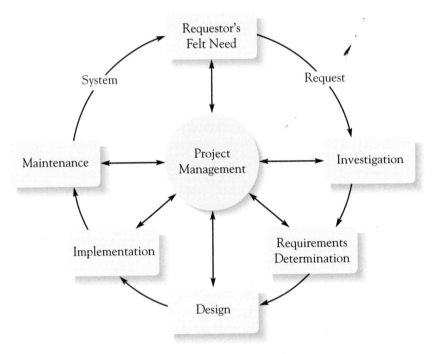

Figure 10.8 System Development Life Cycle

Social Perspective

Information systems design is a complex process, and systems designers sometimes have very few stated policies or guidelines to use when making choices that affect the systems being developed. In addition to designing systems to meet business objectives, information systems professionals are being asked by some people to take responsibility for social consequences of the systems they create. Design of systems may become even more complex as developers try to deal with the possibility of unforeseen social consequences of their designs.

TRENDS IN SYSTEMS DEVELOPMENT

Some trends related to systems development have occurred because of software that has become available in recent years that can enhance or improve the traditional system development life cycle. Some of the problems that have occurred with the SDLC include the following:

1. The new system was sometimes out of date by the time it had made it through all the phases to completion.

2. Users did not know exactly what they wanted at the beginning, so many changes were necessary that caused delays or the system did not meet users' needs.

3. Time constraints sometimes caused phases to be omitted or completed poorly.

4. Documentation developed early in the cycle needed constant changing during the process.

5. Following all the phases and creating a great deal of documentation does not guarantee that the final product will be successfully received.

One of the methods of improving on this cycle involves the use of rapid application development software that can speed up important parts of the process. Other trends related to systems are related to changes in businesses themselves, such as the use of Internet technology for business applications, or a desire to improve the overall operations.

Rapid Application Development

Rapid application development (RAD) tools are available to assist in the development of components needed during system development. Although some people initially suggested that RAD would replace the system development life cycle, many now suggest that it is currently useful only for more simple applications and is simply a tool to help with the development process.

Some of the RAD tools that are available include Powersoft's PowerBuilder, Microsoft's Visual Basic, Oracle's Developer/2000, and Borland's Delphi. These tools also are sometimes referred to as fourth-generation-language (4GL) tools. Tools of this type are relatively easy to use and allow for faster development of many types of applications. For example, user interfaces can be designed through the use of window painters, rather than starting with a paper-and-pencil design. Screen layouts formerly were a very time-consuming activity involving detailed coordinates for each field.

The use of RAD tools does not mean that the various system development phases are eliminated. For example, the requirements definition phase is still considered extremely important. The best tool in existence cannot create a desirable system if the problem has not been clearly defined so that the development fits the users' needs. The design phase probably derives the greatest benefits from RAD tools. Some of the applications can be developed more quickly, but the testing phase also remains at least as important. Some businesses are using RAD tools to speed up earlier phases so that more time can be allowed for later phases, such as testing.

Many developers today suggest that RAD is a great tool to use in conjunction with a very sound application development process.

Internet/Intranet Development

Development of Internet or intranet systems follows a process similar to any other system or application development. However, some changes exist. For example, people developing Internet sites are concerned with outsiders' perceptions. Requirements may be identified for an Internet site by viewing the sites of competitors. Prototyping for the specific organization would be useful before actually defining the requirements. One of the main concerns is to determine how the company's image is to be portrayed on the Web.

For intranet development, the emphasis changes from external to internal concerns. Human factors enter into the considerations when employees will begin receiving or using information in a different way. Technological considerations are also important considerations, and these and other topics must be weighed as with other development projects for their benefits versus the costs involved.

RAD tools may be available for assistance in the design of Internet or intranet projects, but overall development should be given as much concern as any other system in the business.

Business Process Reengineering and Other Management Strategies

Business process reengineering (BPR) was a very popular management philosophy in the early 1990s. Its basic emphasis was on radically redesigning business processes to achieve large improvements in productivity. BPR does provide useful information, such as an identification of how things work, how work flows, and how jobs should be organized. It is something like an overall system for an organization, and the results have typically included a decrease in the number of employees.

In the early years, use of reengineering was very high. However, by the mid-1990s problems occurred, such as a decrease in morale and a loss of innovation among employees. Now the trend in usage is declining. As with many new ideas, an initial rush to that idea occurs, followed by some decrease in use as problems begin to occur. A similar decline is occurring with total quality management (TQM), which generally tries to eliminate errors in order to reduce costs and serve customers better. Benchmarking is increasing in use currently; this methodology compares a business' activities to those of the best companies doing similar work.

As one or two methods decline, other approaches increase in usage; that pattern is expected to continue. You should expect that changes in systems development and management will continue to occur, whether they are overall business systems or very specific, user-defined systems.

Summary

The system development process begins when one or more people identifies a felt need—a need for a change in a current system. This proposed change then goes through several phases of development, as long as it continues to be perceived as a viable project. The development could be ended at any time if it were no longer desired or feasible.

During the investigation phase, the problem to be solved must be defined clearly, and a feasibility study is conducted to determine the appropriateness of the project for the overall organization. Financial, technical, schedule, operational, motivational, and legal feasibilities are considered.

The requirements determination phase includes an analysis of the current system and a determination of user requirements and constraints. Several tools may be used in this phase (as well as others), including data flow diagrams, entity-relationship diagrams, and prototyping. Prototyping may be used to develop a small working model of the system. Prototypes are often used to assist in determining user requirements.

During the system design phase, a logical design is created that identifies how all the components will work together to perform the input, processing, and output activities of the system. A physical design is developed based on the logical design and identifies specific features that will be included, such as hardware and software specifications and personnel needs.

The system implementation phase involves acquiring all the needed aspects of the system, as well as installing the system. For software acquisition, a build-versus-buy decision must be made. Consideration must be given to which aspects are to be custom developed and which are available as commercial packages. For custom development, additional consideration involves whether the development will occur internally or externally. During installation, site preparation occurs, hardware and software are installed, data is converted as needed into new formats, procedures are established, and personnel are trained. Then the installation or conversion occurs, which may involve one of several approaches, some involving phased-in conversions. Testing then occurs to be sure every component performs as planned.

System maintenance is an ongoing process of keeping the system running properly. It includes regular reviews of the system, the addition of new features as they are needed, and elimination of problems that may occur.

The traditional system development life cycle (SDLC) includes establishment of a felt need, followed by phases of investigation, requirements determination, design, implementation, and maintenance. Project management ties all the parts of the SDLC together and assists in creating a proper flow through the cycle.

Trends have occurred related to development of systems, including rapid application development tools. Changes have occurred in systems due to the use of Internet technology, as well as new management philosophies.

Questions for Review and Discussion

1. Discuss the importance of feasibility studies, including specific factors involved.

2. Describe the features and uses of data flow diagrams, entity-relationship diagrams, and prototyping.

3. Why is change management an important system design consideration?

4. Discuss the advantages and disadvantages of developing software internally rather than externally.

5. Identify and justify a situation in which the parallel conversion approach would be your preferred method of system installation.

6. Explain ways in which RAD tools can be used to assist in system development activities.

Selected References

Davis, Gordon B., and Margrethe H. Olson. *Management Information Systems: Conceptual Foundations, Structure, and Development*. New York: McGraw-Hill, 1985.

Garrett, Dave. "Internet Versus Intranet Development." *Data Management Review*, April 1997.

Hayes, Linda G. "Rapid Application Development; Collapse of the Development Life Cycle?" *Data Management Review*, September 1996.

Linthicum, David S. "The Good, The RAD, and The Ugly." *DBMS*, February 1997.

Linthicum, David S. "What's New With RAD?" *Byte*, June 1997.

Mayer, John H. "Avoiding a Fool's Mission." *Software Magazine*, February 1998.

Rigby, Darrell K. "What's Today's Special at the Consultants' Café?" *Fortune*, September 7, 1998.

Seligman, Dan. "College: A Reality Check" *Forbes*, July 27, 1998.

Wetherbe, James C., and Nicholas P. Vitalari. *Systems Analysis and Design: Best Practices*, St. Paul, MN: West Publishing Company, 1994.

Yourdon, Edward, and Larry L. Constantine. *Structured Design: Fundamentals of a Discipline of Computer Program and System Design.* New York: Yourdon, 1978.

Chapter 10 Key Terms

Felt need
the initial stage of system development, when someone feels that a change should be considered.

Initial investigation
system development phase in which the problem to be solved is clearly identified and a feasibility study is conducted.

Requirements determination
system development phase in which the current system is analyzed and system users' needs and constraints are identified.

Data Flow Diagram (DFD)
easy-to-use and understand tool that identifies the path data takes through the system.

Entity-relationship (E-R) diagram
a tool that shows relationships between (or among) entities, which are the items of interest.

Prototyping
a small working model of part or all of a system that can be used in evaluating various aspects during development.

Design
a development phase during which a plan is developed for implementing a new system.

Logical design
identifying ways in which system components will work together to accomplish the desired result.

Physical design
converting the logical design of a system to an identification of specifications for each component of the system.

Implementation
System development phase in which components of the system are acquired, installed, and tested.

Documentation
Explanatory materials identifying how a system was developed and how to use it.

Maintenance
system development phase that involves planned review of a system to keep it running appropriately, with adjustments made as new needs occur.

Rapid application development
tools used to assist in developing components of a system.

Online Activities

Refer to the companion Web site at www.wiley.com/college/simon for a variety of online activities: additional chapter content, *Wall Street Journal Interactive Edition* access, review materials, student assignments, and relevant links.

GO TO http://www.wiley.com/college/simon

THE WALL STREET JOURNAL.

Your four-month access to the Interactive Journal allows you to research articles published within the last 30 days in the Interactive Journal, Barron's Online, and Dow Jones Interactive. A Help feature is available if you need assistance in specifying your search topic.

For information on human resources, take advantage of the "HR Issues" link in careers.wsj.com. Management issues are often topics in "Today's Features."

Research each topic in the Interactive Journal and analyze the results of your search.

1. New design tools for system development, such as RAD. What new capabilities are available or under development?

2. Business process reengineering (BPR). How successful have these BPR activities been for businesses? What trends are emerging related to the use of BPR?

3. Total Quality Management (TQM). How has this been used successfully in businesses? What problems have occurred? What trends are emerging related to the use of TQM?

CHAPTER 11

Information Resource Management Strategies

LEARNING OBJECTIVES

After studying the contents of this chapter, you should be able to

1. Describe in general terms the importance of managing information resources for strategic advantage.
2. Identify and discuss management considerations related to the various components of an information system.
3. Explain the advantages and disadvantages of end-user application development, both to the organization and to the end user.
4. Describe types of end-user computing support and management considerations in providing this support.

INFORMATION RESOURCE MANAGEMENT OVERVIEW

The information resources of a business are its information system components–the people, procedures, and technology (the combined use of hardware, software, and data). To manage information resources effectively, the primary interest must be directed toward determining what is best for the organization as a whole.

Overall purposes of information resource management (IRM) include the following:

▼ Assisting the organization in making and executing appropriate strategic decisions to achieve and maintain a competitive advantage.

▼ Managing all aspects of the organization's information systems–the technology, the people, and the procedures.

Organization of Information Resource Management

Many medium-sized and large organizations have a top-level executive called a chief information officer (CIO), who oversees the entire information systems operation. The CIO typically needs both technical and managerial skills to coordinate information technology resources and to assist top managers. The major role of the CIO often involves matching current technologies with the strategic initiatives of the firm in both the planning and implementation phases of information systems development. Management of an organization's technology has become more complicated with the trend toward multiple systems that work together. The CIO is directly involved in strategic decisions related to an organization's information resources.

Some organizations place their IRM personnel within various individual departments. Other organizations have found it more effective to operate with a separate unit, usually referred to as Information Resource Management, Information Services, or something similar. By operating as an independent unit, this group can keep the overall objectives of the organization in mind by working regularly with other units and by being knowledgeable about the needs of different units.

Overview of Information Resource Management Decisions

Some management decisions occur during system development, when managers participate in planning and development related to information resources. One IRM decision might be to determine location(s) of an information system, including specific sites where data and facilities will be housed, and at which locations users of a system will access it. Additional decisions involve major equipment purchases, such as whether to lease or buy new computer hardware, or whether to replace an entire system or only part of it. A considerable amount of study and analysis is required to determine needs versus costs. Many IRM decisions are related to ensuring that resources are used appropriately. One such decision is concerned with setting priorities for the orderly use of information systems (e.g., identifying which computer processing jobs are most urgent). One of the easiest methods of establishing the order of performing work is to do everything in the order it is received. But this procedure does not necessarily let the organization make the best use of its information resources. The determination must be based on which combination of activities would be of most benefit to the overall organization.

A great deal of an information resource manager's time is spent in managing the various system components. In the following sections, you will find a description of typical concerns related to individual components. As you read, be aware that some types of concerns could occur in every section, but may be described only once.

MANAGEMENT OF HARDWARE AND SOFTWARE

With the continuing development of new options in hardware and software, keeping up with what is being used and how it is being used has become quite a large task. Major concerns include (but are not limited to):

▼ asset management
▼ performance monitoring
▼ configuration management
▼ security

Asset Management

Management of the information resource assets—primarily the investment in hardware and software—is of great importance, because the technology has to be managed as an integrated system of resources that must be coordinated to be effective for the organization as a whole. With distributed systems and multimedia capabilities increasing in use, knowing where each piece of hardware and software is installed is very important. This information is also needed when hardware or software must be replaced or upgraded. Trying to determine manually where every asset is located is quite time-consuming. In the past, microcomputers were not an important part of an organization's main operation. But with the use of high-powered microcomputers in many distributed systems, these assets have become increasingly important to the mission-critical work of many organizations, with the result that asset management has become essential. The various software programs, especially those that were custom-developed for the main operations or missions of the organization, are a valuable asset that must also be monitored.

Asset management software is available that can create an inventory of hardware, software, and peripheral equipment in use. Several products are available that can maintain an inventory of microcomputers and software applications. When the program is run, it identifies installed software packages, including versions and serial numbers, for leading software packages such as Microsoft's Word and Excel. Some asset management software focuses on the management reporting function. Products are available that can build a database containing lists of suppliers, installed desktop computers, and maintenance records, and can generate reports of the results. Some products provide inventories of computer assets other than desktop computers, including peripherals, minicomputers, and mainframes.

Creating an asset inventory has several other advantages to businesses, such as:

1. negotiating volume discounts with vendors for both hardware and software.

2. identifying software packages that are most widely used organization-wide and perhaps designating them as the company standards, partly so that a support program can be developed for those who use the programs.

3. discovering unauthorized copies of software that could cause the company to be liable in lawsuits related to software piracy.

Software exists that automatically inventories potentially hundreds of hardware elements (e.g., standalone computers, file servers, printers, external disk drives, and modems), as well as an unlimited number of software titles. Some of these tools can monitor and control the use of software and maintain license compliance of all applications. They can also provide usage reports and administrative information, such as version number, purchase date, and invoice number.

Table 11.1 identifies license options typically available for software purchases, although various combinations also exist. Businesses may use some or all of these options, depending on their needs for different software packages. And vendors continue to create different ways of providing licenses to meet varying needs. IRM personnel must maintain records of the types of licenses in use for every item of software and ensure that software purchased by the organization is used only as expected by the software vendor. Although the terms in this table may vary with different vendors, the general progression is the same, from purchasing individual software for each user to purchasing licenses for some specified number of users to purchasing a site license for everyone who has a computer.

Term	Description
Individual license	One user has software installed on a single machine for his/her own use
Concurrent license	An agreed-upon number of users can access the software from a server at the same time (actual users can vary)
Network license	An agreed-upon number of specific users can access the software from a server (actual users are specified)
Term	Description
Site license	All users at a particular location can have access to the software

Table 11.1 Software Licensing Options

Software metering tools are widely used by businesses that need to track the level of usage of software. These tools can help resource managers identify possible areas of cost reduction in license fees in cases where use of hardware and software is found to be lower than initial estimates. In addition, managers have a side benefit of being able to track users' activities and thereby do a better job of controlling a variety of desktop activities. Some of the numerous companies providing this type of software are McAfee Associates, On Technology Corp., and Tally Systems Corp.

Performance Monitoring

Managing today's applications has become more complex than in the earlier days, when most systems used a single mainframe. Applications today can work in a variety of subsystems, such as on microcomputers that are linked (networked) to share data and applications.

Additional information on asset management and performance monitoring tools is available at the Web site.

One trend in monitoring performance is toward giving more attention to applications and system workloads. Another trend is toward developing procedures for automating responses to application performance problems as they occur. By monitoring application performance effectively, IRM can help to ensure better quality, a more uniform level of service, and more satisfied system users.

Network performance monitoring is a concern that has become prevalent in recent years as desktop computers have become linked within and among businesses. Network monitoring packages are available that can generate custom reports. These monitoring tools typically collect usage information so that the reports generated can help to show the number of packets of data flowing over a specific segment of the network, the amount of extra bandwidth that is available, peak usage times, and similar data that can be used to describe network performance. Business such as Netops Corp., NetSolve Inc., and International Network Services have developed numerous performance monitoring tools for networks.

Configuration Management

Configuration management is concerned with collecting and maintaining data about the hardware and software being used in computer systems. Configuration has to do with how the hardware and software are set up to work together and possibly with other information systems.

Configuration management has become essential, because businesses often use multiple types of hardware and software in systems that sometimes operate independently but are also linked to other systems. When various systems are linked so that they can work together, additional management of the system components becomes necessary. Unless the system is well managed, one seemingly small change in software in one application could cause potential difficulties with other applications that rely on the old software. Effects of the change on the overall system can be considered and managed when adequate configuration management data is in place.

Think about all the purchases/developments that might occur in a large business of these items:

▼ Off-the-shelf software

▼ Custom-developed software

▼ Communications software

▼ Operating systems

▼ Hardware models, including peripheral equipment, such as monitors, printers, and scanners

Types of configuration data include names, versions or models, and uses of these assets. As purchases and developments continue to occur over a period of time, a wide variety of products must try to work together. Configuration data can be quite valuable in preventing problems that could otherwise occur if no consideration were given to uses being made of specific hardware and software distributed around an organization.

One trend today is toward the development of configuration management software that can automatically keep track of the components of a system and identify which parts are dependent on other parts and therefore would be affected by any change in any part of the overall system.

Hardware and Software Security

Hardware and software security issues involve the physical loss of the hardware and/or software programs, as well as concerns about the security of data. Data security is discussed further in the next section.

Hardware loss includes the disappearance or destruction of any part of the equipment. In the days when businesses used only mainframe computers, theft of hardware was less likely to occur. The physical size of the equipment made it pretty difficult for someone to carry it out of an office inconspicuously. In fact, most people working for an organization never actually saw the mainframe. Any contact was through terminals connected to the mainframe; most of these terminals had no processing capabilities of their own and were not of much value without the mainframe.

With the proliferation of desktop and portable computers, as well as other products such as laser printers and scanners, many people now have direct contact with computer hardware or related software. The equipment is small enough for one person to move it rather easily to other locations. A management concern, therefore, involves taking precautions to decrease the chance that computer equipment will be removed without authorization.

One method of ensuring hardware and software security is to institute procedures that control physical entry to the organization's offices, or to facilities where large quantities of valuable hardware and software

are contained. The value of the hardware and software is a factor (along with the value of the data) in determining the level of security needed for physical access to these facilities. Physical security may be provided through a combination of methods, such as card access to an exterior door, keypad access using a special code to an interior office door into the designated area, and additional procedures to actually use the equipment.

Methods of providing security are getting increasingly more sophisticated. Some systems can compare a fingerprint with an associated voice pattern, for example. The security systems that use information about various parts of the human body for approving access are referred to as biometric identifiers. In addition to voice and fingerprint data, palm prints (the ridges of the palm), hand geometry (size and shape of the hand), iris pattern in the eye, and ear shape are other possible identifiers. These methods have the advantage of convenience, because the person does not need to maintain ID cards, keys, and passwords. One disadvantage is that some of the body parts are likely to change over time.

Higher levels of security generally involve higher costs, so the expense must be weighed against the importance of ensuring security. For systems that include large investments in hardware and software in the same physical area, managers can often justify installing special devices that can monitor security of the room itself, as well as room temperature and air quality.

In addition to theft or intentional destruction of hardware or software, managers must be concerned with unintentional problems with these assets. Computers should be located in rooms that have temperatures in the 70-degree range. High temperatures can hurt performance and damage disks, and long exposure to cold temperatures can cause similar problems. Portable computers should not be left in places where they could be removed easily, nor in places that could be affected by extreme temperatures, such as car trunks.

Additional information on security issues is available at the Web site.

Many software programs are extremely important to the ongoing success of the business and require special security precautions. Specific procedures discussed in the next section related to data security also apply to security of software programs.

MANAGEMENT OF DATA

The management of corporate data—the data essential for the organization to continue to operate—has become an increasingly vital concern. Some of the most important concerns of data management include consistency, security, backup/recovery, and disaster recovery. IRM must treat data as a strategic resource of the organization and as a resource that must be coordinated so that it is compatible for people in different areas who need access to the data. The use of corporate databases must be monitored and managed carefully.

Data Consistency

IRM should develop methods of detecting errors or inconsistencies in data, from the initial entering of data, through the processing, to the output. Although some error checking can be performed through simple manual comparisons, more sophisticated error-checking methods should be developed. Results of error-checking routines should be monitored and included in reports. These results can then be used for evaluation of all resources.

Data Security

Managing information resources so that data is secure is becoming a very complex concern. With earlier systems, all the important data was housed in a centralized environment within a mainframe computer, and the primary concern was that the equipment and storage materials be kept in a safe location. But the current widespread use of large numbers of microcomputer-based networks has created a new set of data security concerns. Microcomputers are connected to each other as well as to larger computers, and sensitive information can be sent to every desktop in the organization. Unlike the old mainframe systems, these desktop computers are physically available to many people in the organization. Primary concerns of IRM related to data security include access and control, virus protection, and transmission protection.

Access and Control

Good information resource management includes specific procedures for accessing data. Several studies have indicated that unauthorized access to data is more likely to occur from insiders than outsiders (i.e., an organization's own employees should be considered a greater threat to the security of data).

Records should be maintained that list the data files critical to the operation (i.e., the business could not continue to operate successfully without these files). In addition, records should be kept that indicate which personnel are authorized to access and use each type of data file. Any system that is developed should monitor the data files and provide reports to management of how many times a file is accessed, by whom, for what length of time, and for what purpose. Systems are available that can also monitor which people have obtained printouts of data from sensitive files, as well as what data was involved.

For those who have authorization to use various data files, the most common form of identification is a password. IRM procedures should include guidelines as to how often these passwords are to be changed, such as monthly or weekly. Employees should be trained to follow good security policies, such as not writing down their passwords or giving them to anyone else. Many passwords can be guessed easily, and employees should be required to use unusual combinations of letters and numbers and not anything related to their name, house number, street name, or the words "password" or "secret," all of which are commonly used.

Many security systems have time periods built in, so that the user is required to change passwords at specified times before continuing to access the system. Other policies for password protection include locking out a user from the system if an incorrect password is entered three times in a row and requiring users to enter a password each time they log on to a system. Even though this is more trouble for the user, it can reduce the opportunities for unauthorized users to be able to gain access.

Other forms of identification include cards, signatures, and the biometric methods described in the previous section. Some systems containing sensitive data may include a call-back modem, in which the user calls in to the system with some form of ID, requests access, and hangs up. The system then calls the user back at the predetermined number for that user. This method reduces the chance of an unauthorized person being able to call in and access data.

Sensitive data usually requires a minimum of two forms of identification. You have probably experienced personal transactions that required identification. Making a purchase with a credit card is an example of a system that typically requires two forms of identification. You must have the card in your possession, and you must provide a signature that matches the one on the card. To use a bank automatic teller machine (ATM) for withdrawing cash, you must also have two forms of identification—the ATM card and the password that belongs with that card. Once users of a business system have gained access to data, other controls can be built into the system so that the types of data provided are limited to authorized files. One common method of limiting access to data is to develop menu choices indicating options; the computer user can work with only the items listed on the menu. Another method of limiting options is to provide an on-screen form. For example, if the system user is expected to enter data, the screen form is designed to indicate what data is to be entered and where. Many of these forms have built-in programs that compare input with expected data and can report immediately if the wrong type of data is entered.

Managers should regularly review the methods of control being used and evaluate their effectiveness. A method that is effective initially does not always remain effective; managers should expect to make periodic changes in methods.

Virus Protection

A virus is an unwanted instruction that can alter the programs or data of any system it enters. Several types of microcomputer viruses have occurred in recent years. A boot sector virus infects the boot sector of the disk, which is where the operating system records disk file information. When the computer is turned on, the virus becomes activated because the boot sector is accessed, and the virus may spread. Some viruses are designed to affect files on a disk (a file-infecting virus) and insert themselves into executable (e.g., .EXE or .COM) files. When one of these files is run, the virus is activated and may destroy data and infect other files on the disk. Contaminated software downloaded from the Internet has been one of the major sources of viruses in recent years.

Some viruses are designed to become active on certain dates and are named accordingly, such as the "Friday the 13th" virus. Unfortunately, new viruses continue to be developed as fast as methods are developed to discover and delete current viruses. There are, however, software packages that do a fairly good job of detecting viruses. Some are able to spot unusual changes to data on a disk even if they do not know the specific virus by name.

One of the first procedures that the IRM group should follow is to analyze their systems to determine which ones are vulnerable to viruses and how much impact a virus might have on the operation of the business. Appropriate virus protection measures can then be put into place in the areas that warrant it. A distributed system that is important to the company's competitive advantage should be expected to have the highest level of virus protection possible. A centralized system without links to other computers and without outside software being brought in has a lower risk of a virus. But with most companies' systems, the chances of a virus do exist, and adequate precautions must be taken.

Numerous software packages are available that provide some level of virus detection. Most of these products have additional options, such as the ability to clean detected viruses automatically. Each individual computer needs antivirus software, even if the computer is part of a network and similar software is used on a network server.

Many vendors offer regular updates to their antivirus software in an attempt to protect against new virus programs that are developed as well as to offer new techniques in virus detection; some of these updates can be downloaded free from the Internet. Newer operating systems for desktop computers usually include improved capabilities related to virus detection. Every computer in which a virus could disrupt the operation should have software that scans for viruses. Scanning software can also be installed on networks and can be set to regularly check each computer on the network. Procedures for computer users should be in place that reduce the likelihood of acquiring a virus, such as prohibiting use of disks from outside sources that have not been checked for viruses.

Transmission Protection

Transmission protection is an important aspect of IRM that involves supplying controls to ensure that data transmitted is correct and secure during transmission to its destination. Encryption (coding) methods are frequently used when it is important to convert data into a code that cannot be read and interpreted by people who might intercept the transmission. The intended destination must be able to decode the data to make it meaningful (sometimes referred to as decryption). Encryption software is available for data sent on a network as well as for individual applications. Many of these packages use a system that involves scrambling the data, then encoding it using a code or key that is unique to that transmission. Receivers of the data use a combination of the sender's "public key" and their own private encryption key, in order to decode the message. One well-known software package of this type is named Pretty Good Privacy, or PGP.

New procedures have become necessary in recent years because of the use of facsimile (fax) machines and cellular phones for transmitting business data. Fax machines are used extensively to send data, using unprotected lines and destinations that are not secure. In addition, employees have been known to dial the wrong fax number and send sensitive data to the wrong organization, where the employees could then do whatever they want with the information received. Employee responsibility should be stressed in relation to sensitive data.

Many companies fail to warn their employees about the hazards of cellular phones. Sensitive topics are sometimes discussed over telephone lines that are easy to tap into. Encryption service is available for cellular phones, but many businesses do not take advantage of it. But as we move to more digital technology, messages will be transmitted as 1s and 0s, hopefully making it more difficult (but certainly not impossible) to unscramble messages.

General Procedures

IRM personnel should establish general procedures for data management that will provide data security, communicate these procedures clearly to all personnel, and monitor the operations to be sure the procedures are followed. The suggestions that follow could serve as an initial list of procedures; the list can be expanded as needed to fit individual subsystems and new situations that arise within the organization.

Control the disposal of paper. Manuals and other materials should not be placed in trash bins where other people could retrieve them; these materials might sometimes contain sensitive data or names of passwords. Paper shredders should be placed beside photocopying machines to take care of any materials being discarded immediately.

Provide methods of limiting access to data, such as user IDs and passwords.

Provide security for on-screen data. Employees should not leave sensitive data visible on their screens for others to see. Screen-blanking mechanisms and keyboard locks can be installed for computers that might be unattended or unused for short periods. Passwords should not be written down and left visible to other employees.

Do not limit data security procedures to large data centers. Pay attention to cellular phones, fax machines, printers, portable computers, and magnetic tape.

Train employees in proper procedures to follow when accessing, using, or transmitting data.

Insist that desktop computers be turned off and physically locked when no one is at the desk, except in cases where they must be left on for processing activities. If not turned off, other procedures should be in place so they cannot be used without authorization.

Pay close attention to workers who are unhappy or who have been released from their jobs. Damage to data is sometimes done by disgruntled or dismissed employees.

Routine Backup and Recovery

Backup and recovery plans are established to ensure that business operations can continue if problems occur with any part of the computer system during day-to-day operation. Included are an actual backup system and a procedure for making regular updates to the backup system, along with a plan for recovering the system if a problem occurs.

Historically, backup systems have been maintained primarily for an organization's most important (mission-critical) data and programs. Now that desktop computers are widely used as a part of the overall system, backup systems are being included for desktop system users, too. Backups of user systems must be easy and quick to perform if the system user will be performing the backup procedures. Some backup systems for large systems have been developed to automatically create backup copies. For smaller systems, however, the system user typically must at least activate the backup program, sometimes performing additional tasks during the activity. Backup software can check to be sure data was copied correctly. This software may also be able to compress data, so less disk space is used, and be able to keep records of what was backed up and when.

Recovery is the process of restoring the database to a usable state after some shutdown or unexpected problem has occurred and usually involves using the backup data to reach some usable state. After it is determined that the database is in an unusable state due to some problem, normal processing should be halted while recovery steps are completed. The database needs to be restored to a usable state, with any invalid data removed and any other damage taken care of. Then any processes that were interrupted need to be executed before normal processing resumes.

Management of the backup system itself is very important. Here are some suggestions for managing a backup system:

▼ The backup process should be checked at regular intervals to be sure it is working properly and that it is able to contain all the required data.

▼ Data should be backed up at least once a week, using at least two different tapes or disks rather than using the same one over and over.

▼ Make sure at least two people know how to perform backup and recovery procedures properly.

▼ Keep at least one copy of important data offsite (away from the main business site) at all times.

Disaster Recovery

Disaster recovery refers to a plan for recovering quickly from a major disaster, such as a hurricane, flood, tornado, or fire. The potential for a major disaster usually requires a separate plan in addition to the plan for the daily or weekly backup system just described. Backups are precautions typically used in case of short-term problems with hardware, software, or data. The backup files would be needed in the case of a major disaster, too; but a completely separate, entire system might be needed. This separate system must be at a different site, since additional facilities in the same building would be useless if a fire or tornado destroyed the building. In many cases the disaster recovery system is in a different city, because it needs to be far enough away so that it is not affected by the same disaster.

An emergency equipment plan should be developed in case of a major regional disaster. One option, known as a hot site, is a similar computer system that is available and ready to use immediately if needed. Hot sites typically are ready to supply core functions and other important business functions. Several companies maintain hot sites for subscribers to this service. Disaster recovery services vendors currently include Digital Equipment Corp, IBM, several of the large accounting and consulting firms such as Andersen Consulting, and other firms that specialize entirely in this service. Some have hot site facilities in various locations worldwide.

One example of the use of a hot site involves Fiduciary Trust Company, an organization that handles portfolio management and other financial transactions. The company was located in the World Trade Center when the building was severely damaged by a bomb. Working with their hot site vendor, who housed duplicate equipment, company personnel were able to set up mainframe communications within one day. In addition, they were able to get workstations operational within a couple of days.

A second disaster recovery option, called a redundant system, lets companies mirror their data by keeping a second system at a different location. A redundant system is the most reliable but the most expensive disaster recovery method. However, it does give organizations the assurance of being up and running within 24 hours of a disaster.

A redundant system is typically maintained by the business that operates the main system. A hot site, by contrast, is a service provided by some other organization in which system capabilities are available when needed.

A reciprocal agreement is an agreement among companies with similar computing environments to provide backup. This method works reasonably well unless the disaster affects many companies in the same region, including the others involved in the agreement. Further, the other companies could be busy with their own processing. Nevertheless, reciprocal agreements are a comparatively inexpensive method.

A cold site is basically a shell that is a place to go in case of disaster and is less expensive than a hot site. But there is a delay in installing backup systems since the computer system is not already in place. This recovery method includes the room, electrical facilities, telecommunications links, and all arrangements other than the actual computer hardware, which can be brought in and installed whenever it is needed.

A service bureau can provide short-term backup but could be expensive for extended periods. A service bureau usually caters to companies that do not want to invest in their own disaster recovery systems and that have application-specific needs.

Additional precautions can be taken to reduce the difficulties from relatively small disasters. For example, you could have an uninterruptible power supply or a backup generator. Uninterruptible power supply (UPS) vendors can provide software that allows a central computer console to monitor the status of a UPS and its battery backups. This software also performs "managed shutdowns," which make sure that files are stored and all data is cleared out of input and output operations before a computer loses its power. Files are saved before the computer runs out of battery power.

Here are some general suggestions for disaster recovery:

▼   Store backup copies of data and programs off-site.

▼   Store a copy of the disaster plan on-site and off-site.

▼   Identify a nearby meeting place for employees in case a disaster occurs.

▼   Test your disaster plan regularly, and keep the plan up–to date.

MANAGEMENT OF HUMAN RESOURCES

Human resource management (HRM) refers to management of an organization's people—one of the most important resources of the business. The people involved in using information systems in an organization are generally referred to as end users. This term has been used widely ever since desktop computers became commonplace in business, with many employees using these computers as a regular part of their jobs. They perform work that sometimes is the "end result" of a system development project, so they are the end users of the programs. The general term referring to their use of computers to perform work is end user computing.

Sometimes the term has been shortened to user, which has caused difficulties with people who view that term negatively. Alternate terms have been used, such as computer user, system user, and knowledge worker, but end user is still the most widely used in journal and news articles. Terms such as user support and user groups are often used in referring to management of and assistance for end users. A general guide to proper terminology is to pay attention to current practices and to use whatever is accepted in your organization.

As the capabilities of computers have improved, so have the capabilities of end users. These people can access and use increasing levels of hardware, software, and data, in addition to communicating electronically with other end users. End users have also improved their abilities to develop their own applications. Traditional management concepts have not applied specifically to end users, since this is a fairly new category of employees. Because the management of end users is now extremely important, some of the major issues are described in this section, such as considerations related to:

▼ end users developing their own applications.

▼ types of assistance or support that should be provided.

▼ management controls that should be in place.

End-User Application Development

Companies have placed computers on individual desks for a variety of reasons, all of which are generally intended to improve the overall work of the organization. Several advantages are available to an organization that encourages its knowledgeable end users to develop some of their own basic applications rather than having all the development work performed by information systems professionals:

▼ Some applications can be developed in less time and at a lower cost by end users than by information systems professionals.

▼ End-user development of applications reduces the potential backlog of information systems projects and allows the systems development staff to concentrate on large projects that are most critical to the overall goals of the organization.

▼ An application developed properly by an end user is more likely to meet the exact needs of the end user, since that person is more likely to have a clearer understanding of the needs and does not have to try to communicate these needs to someone else.

Although there are distinct advantages of encouraging more application development by end users, there are also some disadvantages:

▼ End users may not be aware of similar computer activities in other departments or areas and may develop a system that duplicates one already in existence, thereby wasting considerable organizational work time.

▼ End users may not have information about the overall computer activities of the organization and could develop systems that would not be compatible with other systems in the organization or would not meet company standards.

▼ Systems development personnel often have had experience in developing similar systems, while an end user might have to use trial and error to develop a system. An end user could spend more time trying to solve problems in development and possibly produce an inferior or even erroneous system.

▼ Most end users are not trained in the use of systems analysis, design, and development techniques; they may omit very important procedures, such as requirements analysis, documentation, and backup that become essential if the system is to be used successfully for a long enough period to justify its development.

▼ End-user development activities increase the need for management, because additional controls and coordination must be provided.

Application development tools assist end users in writing standard programs. Programming tools, especially those available with graphical user interfaces (GUIs), are becoming easier to use. End users who are willing to take the time to learn them can put the products to use.

Support Systems for End-User Computing

End users must be given support (assistance) if their computer activities are to be used to the advantage of the overall organization. End users must learn how to use new hardware and software and may be given guidance and assistance in developmental tasks they undertake.

Some organizations have a separate department or unit that offers centralized support for end users. Most of these centralized areas are called "information centers," "help desks," "computing support," or something similar in concept. When an organization is deciding whether to establish a centralized support system or an individualized system, a primary consideration involves the number of end users who may need assistance as well as the frequency and type of need. Most organizations try to determine whether a coordinated effort by a centralized group would significantly benefit the overall operation of the organization compared with having individual personnel in each department help other people as needed. Some companies use a combination of these approaches.

Companies may also use outside sources ("outsourcing") for some of this assistance. The decision to outsource is usually determined by the level of need that exists and with the available staff on hand to provide the service, compared with the cost of obtaining equivalent services through the use of some other company.

People who provide end-user computing support must be able to learn new applications quickly, must be able to work well with other people, must be skillful in training others, and must have problem-solving and systems analysis skills. At the same time, they must be knowledgeable about the company's overall hardware and software systems. In other words, selection of personnel for end-user computing support is critical to the success of the operation. When these support groups have good personnel who give adequate support to end users as well as to the overall organization, the results are usually an increase in end-user productivity, fewer compatibility problems, and more operational efficiency within the organization.

Two of the most widely developed support systems for end users are
1. training
2. help desks or similar systems for answering individual end user questions.

Training

Studies have indicated that productivity of workers does not necessarily increase after organizations make substantial investments in hardware and software. One reason may be a lack of proper training.

End users can train themselves to a limited extent by taking advantage of materials such as tutorials, books, CDs, and videotapes. But these methods do not allow them to ask questions if a concept is not clear. Individual training is usually less expensive than organized group training sessions, especially if only a few people are involved. Group training sessions can be more cost effective than individual training, because several end users can be trained at the same time. They can also learn more in a shorter time if the training sessions are well designed.

If end users receive computer training on the premises, a training center with computer facilities is usually needed. Unless the organization needs to provide a considerable amount of training, the cost of the training center itself might not justify the expense. If only a few people need the training, it is usually more cost effective to send them to an offsite training session or to work with them individually at their work sites.

Information systems personnel and other system users who become proficient at some type of application find themselves responsible for developing training programs for others. Someone who starts as a basic "end user" of some system may eventually be responsible for training others to use the system. Here are some important considerations when developing a training program:

▼ When deciding on length of training sessions and types of training materials, keep in mind that training needs may vary for different people, even for those performing the same tasks. Consideration could be given to grouping participants into different sessions, based on needs and current skill levels.

▼ Short seminars are good for quick learning, but complete courses are better for learning basic skills.

▼ Courses with large numbers of participants may seem more cost effective, but may not address individual needs adequately.

▼ Hands-on training should be provided for computer applications, using computers set up as much as possible the same way the employees will use them in their jobs. Each participant should have access to a computer, rather than having two or more people sharing one computer. People who merely watch someone else will remember very little compared with those who actually perform the tasks. Very little information should be given in a lecture format.

▼ Training is more effective in short sessions. The same number of training hours spread out over several days typically produces better results than doing all the training in one day. For example, if eight hours of training are needed, four two-hour sessions would produce greater retention than one eight-hour session or two four-hour sessions.

▼ Training materials should include materials that end users can keep for later review. The materials should show all the content covered and contain illustrations of what will appear on the computer screen at designated times so that participants can confirm that they are following the procedures correctly.

▼ Participants should know what type of training is being offered before the training begins, and managers should ensure that participants are those who can most benefit from the particular training sessions. For example, if the participants are being trained in advanced applications, they should be at some stated minimum skill level before being accepted for this training.

▼ The training program should be evaluated by the participants at the end of the program. Participants should indicate what parts of the training they found most useful and least useful, and recommend changes to the training program.

▼ A follow-up evaluation of the participants is also useful. After a designated period of time, employees should be expected to be proficient at the desired skills that were introduced during training. Some may need additional training sessions, but employees who understand that a higher performance level is expected after training are more likely to implement new procedures into their work and become proficient without additional training. The follow-up plan may also include newsletters and other methods of reinforcing techniques learned or giving employees additional useful instructions.

A trend when many employees need to be trained is to use simultaneous interactive video for workers at various locations worldwide. Video-conferencing equipment and computer networks are used so that students and teachers can see each other during the training.

Another trend involves Internet-based training, which can be developed in-house by companies or can be obtained from many online sources. Advantages of Internet-based training include:

▼ Self-directed, self-paced instruction, so the user can participate whenever it is convenient.

▼ Availability from any location that has an Internet connection.

▼ Potential for quick updates to course content, as compared with printed materials.

Management Perspective

When developing or reviewing existing online training materials, keep these guidelines in mind:

Is interactivity included, in which the user provides input rather than simply reading on-screen materials?

Does the material make good use of multimedia (without overdoing it), such as graphics, animation, audio, or video, when appropriate?

Does it include methods of measuring progress of participants, such as questions to answer, along with some type of final evaluation of mastery of the content?

One of the disadvantages of Internet-based training is the lack of face-to-face, live instruction, which is sometimes needed for learning or motivation. Internet-based training can serve as an excellent method for preparing some employees to be at a minimum level needed for an upcoming classroom course, so that everyone taking the course has a similar level of knowledge.

Help Desks and Related Assistance

A basic help desk or similar assistance program provides a telephone number or electronic mail address that end users can access when they have questions about their hardware or software. The person at the help desk either answers the questions or tries to find someone who knows the answer. In larger organizations, a help desk may be available internally. Smaller organizations are more likely to obtain help externally because they are less likely to have their own support staff. Some organizations use an internal help desk for internally developed applications and an external group for applications that were not developed internally.

Help desk systems must be developed so that personnel are prepared to assist anyone who calls. In business organizations that operate worldwide, a major problem in providing end user assistance to their own employees is related to language differences. Some companies have instituted special language training for help desk employees. For example, a company with employees in Mexico would make sure that the help desk has a Spanish-speaking employee available at all times.

One reason for the trend toward help desks with their centralized assistance is that software is now available to assist in this activity. The capabilities of help desk software continue to expand and include a variety of capabilities:

▼ Automatic call direction sends the call to the proper support person for the type of assistance requested by the end user; some of these systems automatically send a "trouble ticket" describing the situation to a technician for resolution.

▼ A text retrieval system can be used to find information quickly on a desired topic (some of these systems use hypertext, which is a system that allows the help desk person to follow a chain of information to reach a solution).

▼ A call-tracking system can generate reports to indicate topics of inquiries and areas where problems occur most often.

Additional information on outsourcing is available at the Web site.

▼ A multimedia support system, so that help desk staff can look at a diagram of a process, for example, and help callers work step-by-step through the process.

▼ An online solution database that allows end users to try to find answers to their questions before calling the help desk.

The growth of distributed systems and the increase in remote or mobile users has increased the types of problems that now reach the help desk personnel. Remote users have additional problems not encountered by desktop computer users, such as communications difficulties and battery problems. Some companies have divided their help desk operations into at least two subgroups, such as one handling user services (e.g., training and materials), and one operating as a call center, usually with automated call distribution. Others are outsourcing at least part of the help desk operations. In addition to the cost of outsourcing, a problem some companies have encountered is that outsourcers, while technologically knowledgeable, are not always familiar with some of the specific ways in which the technology is used within a particular business; sometimes these little details can affect the decisions regarding appropriate solutions to problems.

Control Systems for End-User Computing

One purpose of control systems for end-user computing is to prevent the waste of time and resources that otherwise may occur. Ensuring the security of overall systems is another purpose of any control system.

Duplication of effort frequently occurs in many organizations because end users decide to develop an application for their own needs without finding out if similar applications have been developed within the organization. This situation arises from a failure to manage end-user activities, primarily those that involve application development. End users should not be expected to check with employees in other departments about their applications. Information systems staff and managers should be responsible for effectively coordinating activities among departments.

Control of Application Development

Specific controls are needed to assist in identifying which applications are appropriate for development by end users. Some end users have excellent application-development skills, while others may not realize that they do not have the technical expertise needed to develop a particular application. Some people know a particular aspect of an application very well but are not aware that there is much more to the application than the part they know.

Hardware and Software Controls

Hardware and software controls of end-user computing are primarily concerned with proper use and care. In addition to monitoring the procedures related to access and use (discussed earlier), managers must ensure that employees do not make unauthorized copies of software for their personal use ("software piracy"). Since companies are held responsible for unauthorized copies, they must establish controls for access to actual software. Sometimes the original software disks are never seen by the end users; information systems personnel may install the software on a hard disk or on a server and store the original disks in a secure location.

Software piracy is of serious concern to software developers. In some countries, a high percentage of software is pirated (i.e., stolen or obtained without permission of the publisher). A chart published in *USA Today* indicated that 77 percent of software installed in the previous year in Eastern Europe was stolen, compared with 65 percent in the Middle East/Africa, and 62% in South/Central America. The rate for North America was 28 percent.

Proper use of hardware and software also includes productive use of the computer. Some organizations try to measure the level of unproductive activities while using computers, although some unproductive activities may be legitimate efforts to get the computer to work properly. Some examples of hardware/software activities during scheduled work time that are considered wasteful and that require good management controls include:

▼ playing solitaire.

▼ personalizing the icons on the screen.

▼ regularly adding and changing screen wallpapers and screen savers.

▼ downloading "bootleg" copies of software.

▼ arranging a personal schedule through electronic mail.

▼ planning and arranging a vacation over the Internet's World Wide Web.

Some organizations have now installed controls related to the use of the Web by its employees. Software is available that can identify which Web addresses users access and for how long. Browsers can be set to access the Internet only through monitoring software, and this software can be set to prevent users from accessing certain designated sites. Other companies that are concerned about employee access to the Internet are using software that merely monitors usage and provides reports. If end users are aware that these reports are being produced, most will not need additional preventive measures.

Data Controls

Data controls are concerned with end-user access to databases, as well as database development guidelines in cases where individual development occurs. Data access was described earlier, but not in relation to applications developed by end users. End-user-developed systems that provide input of data to other systems must have the same level of controls as other systems, such as verification of data, program controls, documentation, and access controls (passwords or other security measures). Backup procedures are required for any systems that involve frequent changes to a database.

MANAGEMENT OF PROCEDURES

Some of the procedures requiring management are related to controls discussed earlier. The types of procedures requiring management vary depending on the company. Other specific procedural issues that are unique to the particular organization should be expected to occur. A few examples of major procedural issues include quality assessment, cost allocations, and usage logs.

Additional information on ISO 9000 is available at the Web site.

Quality Assessment

A survey reported in *Datamation* indicated that 92 percent of top executives who responded said their companies are using either the Malcolm Baldrige guidelines or the ISO 9000 criteria for quality assessment. The Malcolm Baldrige awards are named for a former U.S. Secretary of Commerce and are based on guidelines developed by the National Institute of Standards and Technology to help business organizations improve the quality of their goods and services. The International Standards Organization (ISO) has developed a set of standards numbered 9001, 9002, etc., referred to as ISO 9000 standards. These standards are designed to establish and maintain documented quality procedures and include areas such as planning and design, production, storage and delivery, and service. Information resource management groups may be involved in improving and monitoring quality by completely or partially overhauling some of their procedures, training users effectively to ensure that correct information is produced at all times, and overseeing the operation of the system and setting standards for its use.

Global Perspective

ISO 9000 standards are very important for U.S. companies that want to compete globally. Compliance with these standards is required for companies selling regulated products in the European Economic Community, as well as in some non-European countries. The standards indicate that a company must have a documented procedure that is in place and that works.

Efforts to compete better globally by improving quality can also result in an improved competitive position at home. Some U.S. businesses involved in improving their quality to compete in the international arena have found additional ways to improve what they do and are therefore improving their competitiveness worldwide. As they review their processes, they are not merely complying with the standards but are trying to further enhance their procedures when they find additional opportunities for improvement. The process of trying to meet ISO 9000 standards to compete globally has made managers more aware of additional benefits of improving the quality of their products and services.

Cost Allocations

Management of information procedures often includes determining and allocating the costs of performing different procedures. In many organizations, costs are charged to individual departments or units for whom operations or procedures are performed, as part of an overall approach of managing the resources and monitoring usage compared with costs. For example, the Payroll Department might be allocated the costs for running programs that calculate payroll records and produce paychecks. Cost factors can include items such as processing time, disk storage space, transmission time, and labor. In organizations where these costs are not actually charged to individual departments, records should still be kept that indicate the various costs for all activities and the units for whom the work was done, as part of the resource management goal of using resources effectively and efficiently.

Usage Logs

Usage logs provide data for cost allocation procedures and are also a source of other data used in managing information resources. Logs give managers information showing how the computer system has been used. The manager can analyze the lengths of time needed for different jobs, along with types of jobs involved, to determine what percentage of time each part of the computer system is being used for each type of work. Using data from the logs, the manager can determine how often problems are encountered with current procedures, along with the types of problems that occur most often. Log data can also be used to assist in determining if current capabilities and procedures appear to be adequate and to assist in scheduling future operations.

Usage log software is available for Internet or intranet operations. This software can provide reports on items such as:

▼ the volume of data that travels from Internet sites to employees.

▼ how much traffic was caused by electronic mail.

▼ how much traffic occurred from visits to Web sites.

▼ how much traffic occurred from downloading files.

While this software could also be used to some extent for controls of Internet usage, its primary intent here is to monitor level of usage as a means of monitoring the resources available for that purpose.

> ### Ethical and Social Perspective
>
> Technology available today makes it possible to monitor a wide range of employee activities related to work performance and proper use of equipment. Although monitoring of work is considered legal in many instances, some ethical and social issues should be considered. For example, is the monitoring activity accomplishing only the desired results and not unnecessarily invading an employee's privacy or decreasing the quality of the work environment.

Summary

Strategic management of information resources involves using these resources effectively to gain or maintain a competitive advantage. All aspects of the organization's information systems (the hardware, software, data, people, and procedures) must be managed appropriately.

A chief information officer (CIO) is a senior-level executive who coordinates information technology resources and assists in developing strategic systems that may include new technology. Management of procedures includes the use of quality assessment, cost allocations, usage logs, and inventory management.

Key considerations in the management of hardware and software include asset management, performance monitoring, configuration management, and security.

Important topics to consider related to the management of data are consistency of data, security of data, backup and recovery of data, and disaster recovery.

End-user computing allows individual employees to develop some of their own unique applications, which allows the information systems staff to concentrate on the needs of the overall organization. Unless end-user computing projects are properly managed, however, some problems can occur due to lack of coordination among individual end users and lack of systems development training of most end users.

Concerns related to management of end-user computing include ensuring adequate support and establishing appropriate controls. Proper management of end-user computing helps to direct information systems staff toward activities that are critical to continued success of the overall organization.

End-user support most often includes 1) training, and 2) help desks and other centralized support systems that aid end users in solving problems or in developing small-scale applications.

Several types of management controls for end-user computing are useful. Controls that can be implemented are related to application development, hardware and software decisions, data access, and acceptable procedures for use by specified personnel.

Questions for Review and Discussion

1. Describe options available for software licenses and situations when each might be an appropriate choice.

2. What is configuration management? Why is it an increasingly important concern?

3. What options are available for the physical security of hardware and software?

4. Compare backup and recovery systems with disaster recovery systems; describe their purposes and typical methods used.

5. Discuss advantages and disadvantages of allowing end users to develop their own applications.

Selected References

Blodgett, Mindy. "Remote Workers Stretch Help Desks." *Computerworld*, February 3, 1997.

"Cruise Control for Your Office." *PC World*, June 1997.

Dryden, Patrick. "'Futz Factor' Measurement Tough to Pin Down in TCO." *Computerworld*, April 13, 1998.

Francis, Bob. "Automate Your Asset Management!" *Datamation*, June 1, 1993.

Hall, Brandon, and Polly Sprenger. "Training." *Internet World*, July 1997.

Hibbard, Justin. "Monitoring Employee Access to Web." *Computerworld*, December 9, 1996.

Horwitt, Elisabeth. "Software Checks UPS Pulse." *Computerworld*, June 14, 1993.

Horowitz, Alan S. "'Net Train, Net Gain?" *Computerworld*, February 3, 1997.

Korzeniowski, Paul. "Monitoring Options Expand." *PC Week*, June 29, 1998.

Krzemien, Richard. "The Disaster Recovery Plan: Your Bridge over Troubled Water." *LAN Times*, October 18, 1993.

Mead, Jeff. "How ISO 9000 Quality Programs Affect IS." *Datamation*, August 1, 1993.

Mitchell, Robert B., and Rodney Neal. "Status of Planning and Control Systems in the End-User Computing Environment," *Journal of Computer Information Systems*, Spring 1993.

Picarille, Lisa. "Licensing Lessons." *Computerworld*, December 9, 1996.

Radcliff, Deborah. "The Danger Within." *InfoWorld*, April 20, 1998.

Rothfeder, Jeffrey. "Hacked! Are Your Company Files Safe?" *PC World*, November 1996.

Simon, Judith C., and Gregory C. Dennis. "Methods of Tracking Intersystem Configuration Management Dependencies." *Journal of Systems Management*, July 1993.

Taber, Mark. "Take Control of Application Performance." *Datamation*, May 15, 1993.

The, Lee. "Diagnostic Software Comes to the Rescue." *Datamation*, June 1, 1993.

"Up Front, Hackers' Delight." *Business Week*, February 10, 1997.

"USA Snapshots: Software Piracy Flourishing." *USA Today*, August 13, 1998.

Van Den Hoven, John. "End-User Access Tools: Self-Serve Data?" *Database Programming Design*, August 1993.

"Verbex Offers Voice System for Computer." *The Commercial Appeal*, March 13, 1994.

Whiting, Rick. "Panic at the Help Desk." *Software Magazine*, October 1997.

Wise, Elizabeth. "Body May Be Key to a Foolproof ID." *USA Today*, April 8, 1998.

Chapter 11 Key Terms

Information Resource Management (IRM)
effective decision making related to management of all components of computer systems.

Asset management
monitoring the location and use of the physical assets of a computer system.

Application performance
management procedure that is concerned with how well an application works, both in quality and quantity of results.

Network performance
management procedure that is concerned with how well a network is working compared with the level of data flow.

Configuration management
maintaining records and monitoring the ways in which components of a system are set up to work with each other.

Biometric identifier
security system containing comparison data about various parts of the human body.

Virus
unwanted instruction that can change or delete programs or data.

Encryption
a coding procedure often used for security purposes when data is to be transmitted.

Backup/recovery
regularly scheduled procedure of storing a copy of data and programs for recovery purposes in case of an unexpected problem such as a disk failure.

Disaster recovery
a plan of action used when a major disaster occurs (such as a hurricane, earthquake, or tornado), ensuring that critical computer systems can be available for use as quickly as possible.

Uninterruptible Power Supply (UPS)
protection against power failure in which files can be stored before power to the system is lost.

Human Resource Management (HRM)
management of the people as a valuable resource

End user
general reference to a person who uses computers for one or more common purposes, such as for office applications and decision-making activities.

Help desk
a centralized and sometimes automated system for assisting an end user.

Online Activities

Refer to the companion Web site at www.wiley.com/college/simon for a variety of online activities: additional chapter content, *Wall Street Journal Interactive Edition* access, review materials, student assignments, and relevant links.

GO TO http://www.wiley.com/college/simon

 THE WALL STREET JOURNAL.

Your four-month access to the Interactive Journal allows you to research articles published within the last 30 days in the Interactive Journal, Barron's Online, and Dow Jones Interactive. A Help feature is available if you need assistance in specifying your search topic.

For information on human resources, take advantage of the "HR Issues" link in careers.wsj.com. Management issues are often topics in "Today's Features."

Research each topic in the Interactive Journal and analyze the results of your search.

1.   Performance monitoring. How widely is this type of software used? Do you expect the use of this software to increase?

2.   Outsourcing. What are the advantages and disadvantages to a business in using outsourcing? Are there certain areas of a business that appear to rely on outsourcing more than other areas?

3.   Disaster recovery techniques. What technology is being used? Are some techniques more widely used than others?

INDEX

Access, data security and, 290–291
Access arm, 178
Access time, 181
Accounting/financial information system, 30–31
Accuracy issues, 39
Add-on package, 118
Address
   of database record, 233–234
   primary memory and, 189
   on Web, 58
AI. *See* Artificial intelligence (AI)
Aircraft manufacturing and use, information systems in, 4–5
Alphabetic symbols, 215
Alpha chip, 197
Alpha processor, 155
ALU. *See* Arithmetic-logic unit (ALU)
Amazon.com, 60
American Hospital Supply Corporation (AHS), 78
American National Standards Institute (ANSI), 186, 216
Americans with Disabilities Act (ADA), 170
America Online, 56
Analog computers, 10
Analog signal, 84
Analog systems, for transmission, 84
ANSI. *See* American National Standards Institute (ANSI)
Antivirus protection, 153, 292
Apple computers, 197. *See also* Macintosh
   chips for, 197
   Mac OS and, 159
Applets, Java programs as, 222–223
Application
   control of development, 303
   end-user development of, 297–298
Application generator, 219
Application performance, 287
Applications software, 12, 146. *See also* Office applications software
   evaluation of, 135–137
Arithmetic-logic unit (ALU), 191–192
ARPANet (Advanced Research Projects Agency Network), 54
Artificial intelligence (AI), 220
   data mining and, 244
   expert systems and, 130–133
   5GLs and, 224
   neural networks and, 134–135
   software, 130–135

ASCII (American Standard Code for Information Interchange), 154, 178
Assembler, 151, 215
Assembly language, 151, 215
Assembly-line systems, 7
Asset management, 285–287
Asynchronous communications, 86, 87
Asynchronous timing, 79
Asynchronous transfer mode (ATM), 96
AT&T. *See* UNIX system
ATM. *See* Asynchronous transfer mode (ATM); Automated teller machine (ATM)
Audio output, 176
Automated teller machine (ATM), 78, 291
   transactions, 53
Automatic call direction, 302
Automatic dialing, 52
Automation, office, 111–112
Automobile manufacturing, information systems in, 3–4

Back-end processor, 151
Backup
   cartridge systems, 179–180
   of data, 294–295, 296
   of shareware, 136–137
Bandwidth
   of coaxial cable, 88
   of communications channel, 86
Banking institutions, optical-disk storage systems in, 184
BASIC (Beginner's All-Purpose Symbolic Instruction Code), 217–218
Batch processing system, 24
Baud rate, 86
Behavior. *See* Ethics
Benchmarking, 276–277
Binary digit, as bit, 83
Binary system, 174, 177
   machine language and, 214
Biometric identifiers, 289
Bit, 80, 83, 86, 87
   bus width and, 195
   word size and, 194
Bitmap, 171
Bits per second (bps), 86
Block-at-a-time transmission, 87
Boot sector virus, 291
BPR. *See* Business process reengineering (BPR)
bps. *See* Bits per second (bps)
Branching, 130
Bridge, for data networks, 90–91
Broadcast radio, 88

Browser, 58
    software control and, 304
Bugs. *See* Debugging
Bus, 195
    lines, 195
    topology, 94, 96
    width, 195
Business. *See also* Automation;
        Electronic commerce; Software;
        specific systems
    changes in, 3–5
    information systems in, 7
    information technology in, 2–3
Business ethics, 37–38
Business process reengineering (BPR),
        276
Business-to-business sales, 61–62
Buttons, 115
Bytes, 87, 178, 189

C (language), 218
Cable. *See* Coaxial cable
Cable modems, 53
Cable TV, 89
Cache, 195
Calculations, with spreadsheets, 117
Calendaring software, 121
Call-back modem, data security and, 291
Call-tracking system, 302
Cards, for data security, 291
Careers, in information technology, 5–6
Carpal tunnel syndrome, 169
Carriers, communications, 90
Carrier-sensed multiple-access with
        collision detection (CSMA/CD)
        protocol, 96, 97
Carrier signal, 84–85
Cartridges
    magnetic, 179
    QIC, 179
Case-based reasoning, 132
CATV. *See* Cable TV
CCITT. *See* Consultative Committee on
        International Telephone and
        Telegraph (CCITT)
CD-R (CD-Recordable) disks, 185–186
CD-ROM (compact disk read-only
        memory), 181–186
Cell, 117
Cellular phones, data security and, 293
Central processing unit (CPU), 147, 179,
        188, 190–191
    arithmetic-logic unit, 191–192
    control unit, 192
    interpretation and execution of
        instructions, 192–193

large system processors, 193–194
    microprocessors, 194–195
    multiprocessing and, 150–151
Chain topology, 92
Change management, 264
Channel, in data communications, 80
Charts, creating, 120
Chief information officer (CIO), 284
Chips, 194
    memory, 196
    microprocessor, 197
    technology of, 195–197
CIO. *See* Chief information officer (CIO)
Circuit-switched service, 81
Citizens band (CB) radio, 82
Class, in object-oriented system, 239
Client/server model, 98
Clip art library, 120
Clock speed, 194
Coaxial cable, 87–88
COBOL (COmmon Business-Oriented
        Language), 216–217
Codec, 85
Code generator, 219
Codes, 212
    data security and, 292–293
    operating systems, language scripts,
        and, 154
    source and object, 151
Codes of Ethics, 38
Coding, 52. *See also* Encryption (coding)
Cold site, 296
Collaborating, 79
Color displays, 174–175
Command-driven systems, 156
Commerce. *See* Electronic commerce
Commerce Department, information
        from, 36
Commercial Internet use, 55–56
Commercial online services, 56
Common carrier, 90
Communication(s)
    direction of, 82
    infrastructure of, 100–101
    telecommunications as, 79–80
Communications carriers, 90
Communications channels, characteris-
        tics of, 81–87
Communications networks. *See* Network
Communications software
    requirements and features of, 52
    sources of, 53
Compact disks, 85
Competitive advantage, 7, 31
Competitive relationships, computer
        communications networks and, 78

Compiler, 151, 215–216, 219
Computer communications networks,
    78–79. *See also* Communications
    channels
Computers, 10. *See also* Internet
    chip technology and, 195–197
    communications software and, 52
    as data communications hardware, 90
    evolution of, 1–2
    input and, 168–173
    output and, 173–176
    processing and, 187–195
    secondary storage and, 177–187
    subcategories of, 10–12
Concentrators, 91
Concurrent processing, 147–149
Concurrent use, 240
Conferencing, on Internet, 69
Configuration management, 287–288
Connections, in data channels, 84
Consistency, of data, 290
Consultative Committee on
    International Telephone and
    Telegraph (CCITT), 95
Contaminated software, 292
Context-sensitive help screens, 115
Continuous composite standard, 186
Control(s)
    in communications software, 52
    over data, 290–291
Internet and, 55–56
    programs, 146–147
    systems for end-user computing,
    303–304
Control unit, of CPU, 192
Conversion, system installation and,
    271–272
Copyright
    Internet and, 55–56
    of software, 136–137
Corel, 121
Cost allocations, 306
Cost management, 125
Counterfeiting, scanners and, 171
C++, 222
CPM charts, 124
CPU. *See* Central processing unit (CPU)
Cray, Seymour, 12
Cray supercomputers, 155
Credit card transactions, 23, 53
Credit transactions, 23–24
Critical path, 124
Cross-functional relationships, 29, 33–34
CRT (cathode-ray tube), 174

CSMA/CD protocol. *See* Carrier-sensed
    multiple-access with collision
    detection (CSMA/CD) protocol
Cultures, global differences in, 116
Currency, global differences in, 116
Custom software, 266–270
Cylinder, 183

DASD. *See* Direct access storage devices
    (DASD)
Data, 12–13, 231–232
    accessing files in, 234–235
    backup and recovery of, 294–295
    in communications network, 78
    controls over, 304
    flow within management levels, 27
    information, knowledge, and, 13
    international transfer of, 242
    standards of usage, 239
    types of, 80
Database, 13
    concepts and terms, 232–233
    data models and, 235–240
    development of, 231–232
    distributed, 242–243
    file organization in, 233–234
    knowledge management and, 245–246
    online solution, 303
Database management system (DBMS),
    240–242
Database server, 98
Database software, 118–120
    for small businesses or individuals,
    119–120
Data communications, 77
    components of, 79–80
Data communications hardware, 90–91
Data communications media, 87–90
    broadcast radio, 88
    coaxial cable, 87–88
    infrared, 90
    microwave, 89
    optical fiber, 88
    wire pairs, 87
Data conferencing, 69
Data encryption. *See* Encryption (coding)
Data entry
    keyboard, health issues, and, 169
    word processing software and, 114
Data entry operators, 5
Data flow diagram (DFD), 257–258, 262
Data/information flow, 14–15
Data linking, 119
Data management, 289–296
    backup, recovery, and, 294–295
    consistency and, 290

disaster recovery and, 295–296
    security and, 290–294
Data mining, 244–245
Data models, 235–240
    hierarchical structure as, 236–237
    network structure as, 237
    object-oriented structure as, 239–240
    relational structure as, 237–239
Data paths, 83
Data preparation (conversion), 270–271
Data recovery program, 152
Data security, general procedures for, 293
Data sets, 232
Data source/sink (destination) symbol,
    257
Data specifications, physical design and,
    264
Data warehouses, 243–244
Date(s), global differences in, 116
Date-related viruses, 292
DBMS. *See* Database management sys-
    tem (DBMS)
DDE (dynamic data exchange), 158
Debugging, 219, 267, 269
DEC. *See* Digital Equipment
    Corporation (DEC)
Decimal system, 177
Decision making
    computer-mediated, 97
    degree of structure in, 27–28
— Decision-support system (DSS) software,
    125–128
Dedicated communications channel, 81
Defragmentation (defrag), 152
Delphi technique, 129
Demand chain, 33
Design, 261
Desktop database software, 119–120
Desktop publishing software, 114
DFD. *See* Data flow diagram (DFD)
Diagrams, creating, 120
Digital certificates, 61
Digital computers, 10
Digital Equipment Corporation (DEC),
    155, 197
Digital signal, 84
Digital subscriber lines (DSLs), 85
Digital systems
    digital events leading to, 10
    for transmission, 84–85
Direct access, to database file, 235
Direct access storage devices (DASD), 180
Direct file organization, 234
Direction of communication, 82

Disabled workers
    employment discrimination against,
        170
    information systems and, 5
    software for, 153
Disaster recovery, 295–296
Discrimination
    avoidance through network
        communication, 97
    against disabled, 170
Disk drives, 181–184
CD-ROM and, 185
Disk operating system. *See* DOS
Disk pack, 183
Disks
    floppy, 181–182
    hard, 182–184
    magnetic disk storage media and,
        180–184
    rewritable, 186–187
    write-once, 185–186
Distributed database, 242–243
Distributed systems, 98–99, 303
Distributed work, 79
DNS. *See* Domain name system (DNS)
Documentation, 270
Domain, 57
Domain name system (DNS), 57, 60
Domestic organization, 35
DOS (disk operating system), 53, 155, 156
Dot pitch (dp), 175
Drag-and-drop methods, 223
Dragon Systems, Dragon Naturally
    Speaking, 172
DRAM, 190
Drawing, 120
Drilling down, 130
Drives, 181–184. *See also* specific types
DSLs. *See* Digital subscriber lines (DSLs)
DSS. *See* Decision-support software (DSS)
Duplex system, 82
DVD-RAM, 186
DVD-ROM, 186
DVD-RW (CD-Rewritable) disks, 186
DVDs (Digital Versatile Disks), 186

Eavesdropping, electronic, 63–64
EBCDIC, 178
e-business. *See* Electronic commerce
e-commerce. *See* Electronic commerce
EDI. *See* Electronic data interchange
    (EDI)
Editing
    in spreadsheets, 117
    in word processing software, 114

Education, Global Schoolhouse Project
(GSH) and, 54
EEPROM (electrically erasable
programmable read-only memory),
190, 196
8-bit technology, 174, 177
EIS. *See* Executive information system
(EIS) software
Electronic commerce, 51–52
growth of, 61–63
security issues of, 61
Electronic data interchange (EDI), 24, 53
Electronic eavesdropping, 63–64
Electronic mail (email)
emoticons on, 64–65
privacy and, 38
Electronic mailing lists, 68
email. *See* Electronic mail (email)
Emergency equipment plan, 295
Emoticons, 64–65
Employees. *See also* Personnel
knowledge management and, 246
monitoring of, 307
Employment discrimination, against
disabled, 170
Encapsulation, 239
Encryption (coding), 52, 69, 90, 152
data security and, 292–293
on smart cards, 187
End result, 254, 296–297
End user, 296
application development and, 297–298
training for, 299–302
End-user computing, 297
control systems for, 303–304
support systems for, 298–302
Enterprise resource planning (ERP)
software, 33
Entity, in database, 233
Entity-relationship (E-R) diagram, 235,
258, 259
EPROM (erasable programmable read-
only memory), 190
E-R diagram. *See* Entity-relationship
(E-R) diagram
E-R model. *See* Entity-relationship
(E-R) model
ERP software. *See* Enterprise resource
planning (ERP) software
Error checking features, 52
Ethernet, 97
Ethics, 37–40
employee monitoring, 307
employment discrimination against
disabled and, 170
in hospitals, 41

program ownership and, 225
security and, 151
software shareware and, 136–137
European Computer Manufacturers
Association, 186
Execution cycle, 192, 193
Executive information system (EIS)
software, 129–130
Expert systems software, 130–133
Explanation facility, 133
Extended Binary Coded Decimal
Interchange Code (EBCDIC). *See*
EBCDIC
Externally-developed software, vs. inter-
nally-developed software, 267–270
Extranets, 68–69
communications via, 98

Fannie Mae. *See* Federal National
Mortgage Association (Fannie Mae)
FAQs, 67
FAT 32 (File Allocation Table 32), 157.
See also File allocation table (FAT)
Fax machines, data security and, 294
Feasibility study, for systems
development, 255–256
Federal Express, 59–60
Federal National Mortgage Association
(Fannie Mae), 53
Feedback, 15
Felt need, 253–254
Fetching, 189
Field, 13, 232
15-bit technology, 174
Fifth-generation programming (5GL)
languages, 224
File(s), 13
in database, 232
File access, in database, 234–235
File allocation table (FAT), 152
FAT 32 and, 157
File-infecting virus, 292
File linking, 119, 151
File organization
in database, 233–234
types of, 234
File server, 98
File transfer protocol (FTP), 66
Financial information system, 30–31
Find and replace, 115
Firewall, 69
First-generation programming languages,
214
5GLs. *See* Fifth-generation programming
(5GL) languages
Flash memory, 196

Flat-panel technology, 175
Flight management systems (FMS), 4
Floating-point operation, 195
Floppy disk, 181–182
    hard disks and, 182
Formatting
    in spreadsheets, 117
    in word processing, 114
Forms, 120
Forms processing software, 121
Formulas, spreadsheets and, 117
FORTRAN (FORmula TRANslator), 216
Fortune 500 companies, ERP software, 33
4-bit technology, 174
Fourth-generation (4GL) programming
        languages, 218–219, 220–221
Fragments, 152
Front-end modeling, 123
Front-end processor, 150
FTP. *See* File transfer protocol (FTP)
Full duplex channel, 82
Fully interconnected (plex) topology,
        91–92
Functional areas, 29

Gantt charts, 124
Gateways, 91
GB. *See* Gigabyte (GB)
GDSS. *See* Group decision support
        system software (GDSS)
Geographic area, of LAN, 96–97
Geosynchronous orbit (GEO), 89
GEO technology. *See* Geosynchronous
        orbit (GEO)
Gigabyte (G, GB), 157, 178
Gigaflops, 195
GIGO (Garbage In, Garbage Out), 9
Global organization, 34–35
    marketplace for, 35
    perspective of, 37
    strategies for, 36
Global perspective
    on data transfer, 242
ISO 9000 standards and, 305
    on operating system languages and
        sorting order, 154
    on programming, 269
    on software industries, 213
    word processing display differences
        and, 116
Global Schoolhouse Project (GSH), 54
Global village, 34
Goal-seeking analysis, 126
Goods (products), 32
Grammar/punctuation checker, 115

Graphical user interface (GUI), 58–59,
        157, 159, 219, 298
    choosing environment, 160
Graphics, 80
Graphics software, 120–121, 171
Group decision support system software
        (GDSS), 128–129
GSH. *See* Global Schoolhouse Project
        (GSH)
GUI. *See* Graphical user interface (GUI)

Half-duplex channel, 82
Hard copy, 173
Hard disks, 182–184
    removable, 183–184
Hardware, 9–12. *See also* Software
    acquisition of, 265
    controls over, 303–304
    data communications, 90–91
    preparation of, 270
    sources of, 265–266
Hardware management, 285–289
    asset management and, 285–289
    configuration management and,
        287–288
    performance monitoring and, 287
    security and, 288–289
Health, repetitive-motion injuries and,
        169
Help desks, 298, 302–303
Help screens, 115
Heterogeneous networks, 91
Heuristics, 127
Hewlett-Packard, 197
Hierarchical structure, of database,
        236–237
High-level languages, 214, 215
Holographic storage, 187
Home office, 35
    teleworking and, 65
Home page, 59
Honesty. *See* Ethics
Hospital information systems, 31, 32
    patient care in, 33
Host computers, 55, 60
Host sites, 295
Housekeeping programs, 152
HTML (hypertext markup language), 58,
        223
HTTP (hypertext transfer protocol), 58
Human resource management (HRM),
        296–304
Human resources information system,
        30
Hypermedia, 58
Hypertext, 58, 60

Hypertext Markup Language. *See* HTML (hypertext markup language)
Hypertext transfer protocol. *See* HTTP (hypertext transfer protocol)

IBM
    Intel chips and, 197
    parallel-processing technology and, 194
    ViaVoice, 172
IBM-compatible computers, 10–11, 156
Icons, 115
IDE (integrated drive electronics) drives, 182
Identification, data security and, 291
Identified need, 253–254
Images, 80
Implementation, of system, 264–272
Indexed sequential file organization, 234
Indexing, with database software, 119
Inefficient systems, 257
Inference engine, 132–133
Information, use of term, 13–14
Information centers, 298
Information flow, 14–15
Information reporting systems, 25
    in hospitals, 41
Information resource management (IRM), 283–285
    organization of, 284
Information resource management groups, quality assessment and, 305
Information sources, about global marketplace, 36
Information system
    accounting/financial, 30–31
    components of, 6–13
    definition of, 6–7
    design of, 274
    functional uses of, 29
    human resources, 30
    marketing/sales, 31
    production/operations, 32–33
    purpose of, 7
    strategic and other managerial uses of, 26–28
    transaction processing systems, 21–24
Information systems partnerships, retailer-supplier, 24
Information technology, impact of, 2–3
Infrared media, 90
Infrastructure, communications, 100–101
Inheritance, 239
Initial investigation phase, of systems development, 254–256

Ink-jet printer, 176
Input, 15, 168–173
    keyboard and, 168–169
    pointing devices for, 169–170
    satellite signals and, 173
    scanners and, 171–172
    smart card and, 173
    speech/voice recognition, 172–173
Input device, 168
Installation, of system, 270–272
Instruction cycle, 192, 193
Instructions, programming, 211
Integrated circuits, 194
Integrated Services Digital Network (ISDN), 95–96
Integration, 123
Intel chips, 197
Intellectual property, 40
Interactive systems, 127
Interactive videos, for training, 301
Intercom systems, 82
Interface. *See* User interface
Internally-developed software, vs. externally-developed software, 267–270
International Network Services, 287
International organization, 35
International Standards Organization (ISO), 186, 305
    network protocols and, 95
Reference Model for Open Systems Interconnection (OSI), 95
Internet, 54–59. *See also* Electronic commerce; Extranets; Intranets
    access to, 56–57
    advantages and disadvantages of, 55–56
    electronic commerce examples, 59–60
    electronic mail and, 63–65
Federal Express and, 60
    telecommuting and, 65
    terminology for, 60
    trends in usage, 69
Internet-based training, 301–302
Internet service providers. *See* ISPs (Internet service providers)
Internet systems, 276
Interpreter, 151, 215–216
Intranets, 68–69, 276
    communications via, 98
Iomega, 182
IRM. *See* Information resource management (IRM)
ISDN. *See* Integrated Services Digital Network (ISDN)

ISO. *See* International Standards Organization (ISO)
ISO 9000 criteria, 305
ISO-OSI reference model, 95
ISPs (Internet service providers), 56
Iterative process, 255

Java, 222–223
JavaScript, 224
Java Virtual Machine (JVM), 222
Jaz drives, 182
Jukebox, 185
Justified text, 114
Just-in-time (JIT) inventory, 24

Key, 235
Keyboard, 168–169
Kilobyte (K, KB), 178
Knowledge, use of term, 14
Knowledge acquisition facility, 133
Knowledge base, 132
Knowledge management, 245–246

Languages. *See also* Programming language
    operating systems and, 154
Language translators, 151–152
LANs. *See* Local area networks (LANs)
Laptop computers, 88
Large computer systems, operating systems and, 154–155
Laser, 88
    optical disk storage media and, 184, 186
Latency, 89
LCD. *See* Liquid crystal display (LCD)
LED (light-emitting diode), 88
Less-developed countries, software industries in, 213
License options, for software, 286
Line-sharing devices, 91
Linking
    data, 59
    file, 119, 151
LINUX system, 155, 158
Liquid crystal display (LCD), 174
LISP, 224
LISTSERVs, 68
Local area networks (LANs)
    bus and ring topologies in, 94
    characteristics of, 96–98
    protocols in, 96
    wireless, 90
Locking mechanism, 119
Logical design, 261–263
Loop topology, 93

Low-level language, 214

Machine cycle, 192
Machine language, 151, 214
Machine-language programs, 214
Macintosh
    chips for, 197
    sectors and, 180
Mac OS, 155, 159
Macro, 115, 118
Magnetic cartridges, 179–180
Magnetic disk storage media, 180–184
    floppy disks, 181–182
    hard disks, 182–184
Magnetic ink character recognition (MICR), 172
Magnetic tape
    data security and, 294
    reel-to-reel, 179
Magnetic technology, optical disks and, 184, 186
Magneto-optical (MO) technology, 186
Mail. *See* Electronic mail (email)
Mailing list, 68
Mail merge, 114
Mainframe computers, 10, 11
    operating systems, 154–155
    parallel-processing technology and, 194
    3GL tools and, 219
Maintenance, 273–274
Malcolm Baldrige guidelines, 305
Managed shutdowns, 296
Management
    communications networks and, 100
    of data, 289–296
    data access, transfer, and, 182
    electronic commerce and, 62
    expert systems and, 134
    GUI environment and, 160
    of hardware and software, 285–289
    human resource, 30
    online training materials and, 301–302
    programming language selection and, 221
    system application and, 261
    systems by level of, 26–28
Management decision-support software, 26, 122–135
    artificial intelligence software, 130–135
    decision-support system (DSS) software and, 125–128
    executive information system software, 129–130
    group decision support system software, 128–129

project management software, 122–125
Management information system (MIS), 25
Manager's Guide to Globalization, A (Rhinesmith), 36
Manufacturing
   automobile, 3–4
   information systems in, 7
Marketing/sales information system, 31
Marketplace, global, 35
Massively parallel processing (MPP), 194
McAfee Associates, 287
Measurement, global differences in, 116
Medical diagnoses, information systems in, 4
Medium (media), 79, 80
   data communications, 87–90
   magnetic disk storage, 180–184
   optical disk storage, 184–187
   tape storage, 178–180
Mega, 195
Megabyte (M, MB), 178
Megaflops, 195
Megahertz (MHz), 193, 195
Memory, 147
   partitions of, 148–149
   primary, 188–189
   virtual, 148–149
Memory chips, 196
Menu-driven help screens, 115
Menus, 52
Message, 79, 80
Metadata, 232
Metering tools, for software, 287
MICR. *See* Magnetic ink character recognition (MICR)
Microcomputers, 10–11
   3GL tools and, 219
Microprocessors, 194–195
   chips for, 197
Microsoft. *See also* Windows entries
   DOS and, 155, 156
   Internet Explorer, 58
   office suites of, 121
   VBScript, 224
Microsoft (MS) Windows, 155, 156–158. *See also* Windows entries
   OLE technology and, 171
Microwave transmission, 89
Middleware, 99
Midrange computers, operating systems for, 155
Minicomputers, 11
MIPS (millions of instructions per second), 193

MIS. *See* Management information system (MIS)
MMX™ technology, 197
Mnemonic devices, 215
Modeling, 123, 124–125, 127
Models, data, 235–240
Modem, 53, 85, 91
Monitors, 174
Moore, Gordon, 196
Moore's Law, 196
Mosaic, 58–59
Motherboard, 194
Motorola, 197
Mouse, 169
MPP. *See* Massively parallel processing (MPP)
MS-DOS. *See* DOS (disk operating system)
Multimedia, 85
   developers, 6
   support system, 302
Multinational organization, 35
Multiplexers, 91
Multipoint communications channel, 84
Multiprocessing, 149–150
Multiprocessor, 193
Multitasking capabilities, 148–149
MVS, 155

National Center for Supercomputing Applications (NCSA), 58
National Institute of Standards and Technology, 305
National Science Foundation, GSH and, 54
Natural language interface, 218
NCSA. *See* National Center for Supercomputing Applications (NCSA)
Needs, felt or identified, 253–254
Need to know, about data paths, 83
Netiquette, 67
Netops Corp., 287
Netscape
   Communicator, 58, 59
   JavaScript, 224
NetSolve Inc., 287
Network, 28, 77–78
   bridge for, 90–91
   computer communications, 78–79
   management issues and, 100
   scope of, 101
   social issues about, 97
   strategic issues for, 99–100
   topologies of, 91–94
Network managers, 6
Network performance, 287

Network protocols, 95–96
Network structure, of database, 237
Neural networks, 134–135, 244
Newsgroups, 66–68
Nonvolatile/volatile, 177, 189
Notebook computers, 11
NSFNet, 54
Numbers, global differences in, 116
Numeric symbols, 215

Object code, 151
Object linking and embedding (OLE),
    158, 171
Object-oriented database management
    system (OODBMS), 242
Object-oriented (OO) model, 235
Object-oriented programming (OOP)
    languages, 220–223
Object-oriented (OO) system, of
    database, 239–240
Object-relational database management
    system (ORDBMS), 242
Occupational Safety and Health
    Administration (OSHA), 169
OCR. *See* Optical character recognition
    (OCR)
Office applications software, 113–121
    database, 118–120
    graphics, 120–121
    spreadsheet, 116–118
    word processing, 113–115
Office applications systems, 26
Office automation, 111–112
Office suites, 121
OLAP. *See* Online analytical processing
    (OLAP)
OLE. *See* Object linking and embedding
    (OLE)
OLTP. *See* Online transaction processing
    (OLTP) systems
Online analytical processing (OLAP),
    244
    tools, 30, 130
Online business, 61–63
Online services, 56
Online solution database, 303
Online technology, 58–59. *See also*
    Internet
Online training materials, 301–302
Online transaction processing (OLTP)
    systems, 23–24, 213
On-screen data, security for, 293
On Technology Corp., 287
OO model. *See* Object-oriented (OO)
    model

OOP languages. *See* Object-oriented
    programming (OOP) languages
Open-ended data store symbol, 257
Open systems, 160
Open Systems Interconnection (OSI), 95
Operands, 214
Operating systems. *See also* System
    software
    for large computer systems, 154–155
    for midrange computers, 155
    programs for, 12, 153–156
    for small computers, 155–156
    software and, 53
Operational decisions, systems for, 26,
    27
Operation (op) code, 214
Operations information system, 32–33
Optical character recognition (OCR),
    134, 171
Optical disk storage media, 184–187
    rewritable disks, 186–187
    write-once disks, 185–186
Optical fiber, 88
Organizations
    information systems in, 21–26
    types of global, 34–35
OSI. *See* Open Systems Interconnection
    (OSI)
Output, 15, 173–176
    audio, 176
    printers and, 175–176
    screen displays and, 174–175
Output device, 173
Outsourcing, 299, 303
Ownership issues, 39–40

Packaged software, 266–270
Packet-switched service, 81, 91
Paper disposal, data security and, 293
Parallel communications, 83
Parallel processor, 194
Partitions, of internal memory, 148–149
Password, 52, 152
    data security and, 290–291
    for email, 64
    for Internet access, 56–57
    for screen security, 293
Path name, 58
Paths, for data flow, 237
PC-DOS, 156
PCs, 10
    sectors and, 180
PCSs. *See* Personal communications
    systems (PCSs)
PDAs. *See* Personal digital assistants
    (PDAs)

Pen computers, 170
Pentium chips, 196
Pentium II, 197
People, role in information systems, 9
Performance monitoring, 287
Personal communications systems
(PCSs), 88
Personal digital assistants (PDAs), 88
Personnel. *See also* Employees
change management and, 262–263
physical design and, 264
PERT charts, 124
PGP. *See* Pretty Good Privacy (PGP)
Physical address, 234
Physical design, 263–264
Piracy, of software, 304
Pixel (picture element), 171, 174
Plex topology, 91–92
Plug-and-play feature, 157
Point-and-click methods, 223
Pointing devices, for data input, 169–170
Point-of-sale (POS) terminals, 171
Point-to-point communications
channel, 84, 91
Polling, 95
Portable computers
data security and, 294
microcomputers, 11
POS terminals. *See* Point-of-sale (POS)
terminals
Posting material, to newsgroup, 67
POTS (plain old telephone service), 90
PowerBuilder, 223
Presentation graphics, 120
Pretty Good Privacy (PGP), 293
Priceline.com, 62
Primary key, 235
Primary memory. *See* Memory
Printers, 175–176
data security and, 294
Print server, 98–99
Privacy issues, 38
Privacy policies, on Internet, 61
Private certificates, 61
Problem definition, 254–255
Procedure oriented languages, 218
Procedures
in information systems, 9
management of, 305–306
Process, physical design and, 264
Processing, 15, 187–195
arithmetic-logic unit and, 191–192
control unit and, 192
CPU and, 190–191
in database, 235

interpretation and execution of
instructions and, 192–193
large system, 193–194
microprocessors, 194–195
primary memory and, 188–189
RAM and, 190
ROM and, 189–190
Processing programs, 147–151
concurrent processing, 147–149
simultaneous processing, 149–151
Process symbol, 257
Production/operations information
system, 32–33
Program, 211
Programmer, 5, 221
system analyst and, 252
Programming
concepts, 211–213
international business and, 269
Programming language, 151, 212–213
first-generation, 214
generations of, 213
second-generation, 215
third-generation, 215–218
trends in, 219–224
Programming language capabilities,
with database software, 119
Programming tools, 298
Programs. *See also* Software
documentation for, 270
Project accounting, 123
Project management software, 122–125
PROLOG, 224
PROM (programmable read-only
memory), 190
Prompts, 52
for Internet access, 57
Proprietary systems, 154
Protocols, 55, 91
network, 95
Web address and, 58
Prototyping, 260–261, 262
Public certificates, 61
Public domain software, 136

QIC (quarter-inch cartridge) data
cartridges, 179
Quality assessment, 305
Querying, with database software, 119
Query language, 218–219
relational structure database and, 237

RAD. *See* Rapid application development
(RAD) tools
Radio. *See* Broadcast radio

Radio receivers, for laptop computers, 88
RAID (redundant array of inexpensive disks/redudant array of independent disks), 183
RAM (random-access memory), 190, 196
Random access, 180
Random (direct) file organization, 234
Rapid application development (RAD) tools, 275–276
Reading, 189
Read/write heads, 181, 183
Receiver, 79, 80
Reciprocal agreement, 296
Record, 13
  in database, 232
  data control and, 290
Recovery
  of data, 294–295
  disaster, 295–296
Redundancy, 237
Redundant system, 295–296
Reel-to-reel magnetic tapes, 179
Reengineering, 276
Refresh rate, 175
Register, 193
Relational structure, of database, 237–239
Relative address, 234
Remote users, 303
Removable media, 183–184
Repetitive-motion injuries, 169
Report(s), features of, 125
Report generator, 219
  with database software, 119
Reporting systems, 25
Requests for proposals (RFPs), 265
Requirements determination
  for database, 235
  study of existing system, 256–258
  for systems development, 256–261
  user requirements and constraints, 259–261
Resource leveling, 123, 125
Resources
  IRM decisions and, 284
  of LANs and WANs, 97–98
Retailers
  credit systems in, 22–24
  information systems partnerships of, 24
Reusability, of object-oriented database design, 239–240
Rewritable disks, 186–187
Rhinesmith, Stephen H., 36
Ring topology, 94, 96
Robotic systems, 3
Robots, 130

ROM (read-only memory), 189–190
Router, 91

Sales. *See* Electronic commerce; Internet
Sales force automation, 31
Sales information system, 31
Satellite microwave systems, 89
Satellite signals, for input, 173
Scanners, 171–172
Scheduling, of tasks, 125
Scheduling software, 121
Screen
  data security and, 293
  resolution of, 175
  size of, 175
Screen displays, 174–175
Scripting languages, 223–224
SCSI (small computer system interface) drives, 182
SDLC. *See* System development life cycle (SDLC)
Secondary keys, 235
Secondary storage (storage), 177–187
  encoding systems and, 177–178
  holographic storage and, 187
  magnetic disk storage media and, 180–184
  optical disk storage media and, 184–187
  smart cards and, 187
  tape storage media and, 178–180
Second-generation programming languages, 215
Sectors, magnetic disk, 180
Security
  of data, 290–294
  for database software, 119
  of data transfer, 242
  ethics and, 151
  for extranets, 98
  of hardware and software, 287–288
  of intranets, 68–69
  system software and, 152
  virus protection and, 291–292
Security features
  of electronic commerce, 61
Internet and, 55–56
  of software, 52
Security issues, 39
Semiconductor circuits, 177
Semistructured problems, 125
Semistructured report, 27–28
Sender, 79, 80
Sequential access, 178
Sequential file organization, 234

Serial communications, 83
Serial processing, 147
Server, 98–99
Service bureau, 296
Services, 32
Sexual harassment, on computer
    networks, 97
Shareware programs, 136–137
Shielded twisted pairs, 87
Shopping, online, 61–62
Signal, in data channels, 84
Signatures, for data security, 291
Silicon chips, 196
Simplex channel, 82
Simultaneous processing, 149–151
Site preparation, 270
16-bit technology, 174, 177
64-bit microprocessor architecture, 197
Small businesses, database software for,
    119–120
Small computers, operating systems for,
    155–156
Smalltalk, 222
Smart card, 173, 187
Smart icons, 115
Social issues, 40
    computer networks and, 97
    employment discrimination against
        disabled and, 170
Social perspective
    on data usage, 239
    employee monitoring, 307
    on information systems design, 274
Soft copy, 173
Software, 12. *See also* Intellectual
    property; System software
    acquisition of, 265, 266
    backup, 294
    browser as, 58
    communications, 52–53
    controls over, 303–304
    custom vs. packaged, 266–270
    database, 118–120
    decision-support, 26
    for email, 64
    ERP, 33
    for FTP, 66
    graphics, 120–121
    internal vs. external development of,
        267–270
    management decision-support,
        122–125
    for offices, 113–121
    piracy of, 304
    preparation of, 270
    shareware programs, 136–137

    spreadsheet, 116–118
    text-search, 246
    for virus protection, 292
    word processing, 113–115
Software management, 285–289
    asset management and, 285–289
    configuration management and,
        287–288
    performance monitoring and, 287
    security and, 288–289
Sorting, with database software, 119
Sorting order, 154
Source code, 151
Speech synthesizers, 5
Speech/voice recognition input, 172–173
Spelling checker, 115
Spreadsheet software, 113, 116–118
    and what-if analysis, 126
SRAM, 190
Stalking, electronic, 97
Standards, for rewritable disks, 186–187
Star topology, 93
Statements, 211
Statistical techniques, in project
    management software, 123
Sticky-key software, 169
Storage. *See* Secondary storage (storage)
Strategic decisions, information systems
    and, 29
Strategic issues, for networks, 99–100
Strategic needs, systems for, 26
Strategic relationships, computer
    communications networks and, 78
Stride Rite, 24
Structured decisions, 27
Structured problem, 125
Structured reports, 25
Subsystems, 6
Sun transit, 89
Supercomputers, 12, 155
Super VGA (SVGA), 174
Supervisory needs, systems for, 26
Suppliers, information systems
    partnerships of, 24
Supply chain, 29, 33
Support systems, for end-user computing,
    298–302
Symbols, 120
Synchronous communications, 86, 87
Synergy, 128
System(s). *See also* specific types
    alterations of, 273–274
    definition of, 6–7
    preparation of users, 271
    review of, 273
System analyst, 5, 252

System board, 194
System design, 261–264
    logical, 261–263
    physical, 263–264
System development life cycle (SDLC),
    273–274
System operators, 5
Systems development, 251–253
    business process reengineering
        (BPR) and, 276–277
    felt or identified need and, 253–254
    implementation and, 264–272
    initial investigation phase, 254–256
    installation and, 270–272
    Internet/intranet development and, 276
    maintenance and, 273–274
    management strategies and, 276–277
    rapid application development (RAD)
        tools and, 275–276
    requirements determination for,
        256–261
    system design, 261–264
    trends in, 275–277
System software
    compatibility of, 160
    control programs, 146–147
    language translators and, 151–152
    processing programs, 147
    purposes of, 145–146
    utilities and, 152–153

Tables, in database, 232
Tactical decisions, systems for, 26–27
Tally Systems Corp., 287
Tape storage media, 178–180
TCP/IP (Transmission Control
        Protocol/Internet Protocol), 55, 96
Technology. *See also* Information
        technology
    automation and, 111–112
    computer evolution and, 1–2
    physical design and, 264
Telecommunications, 79–80
Telecommuters (teleworkers), 78–79
Telecommuting. *See* Teleworking
        (telecommuting)
Teledesic, 89
Telephones, 82
    circuit-switched service and, 81
Telephone twisted pairs (TTP), 87
Teleworking (telecommuting), 65
Temperatures, for computers, 289
Terminals, as data communication hard-
        ware, 90
Terminology, for Internet, 60
Terrestrial microwave system, 89

Testing, of system, 272
Text data, 80
Text-editing capabilities, 114
Text editor, 219
Text retrieval system, 302
Text-search software, 246
Thesaurus, 115
Third-generation (3GL) programming
        languages, 215–218, 220–221
3GLs. *See* Third-generation (3GL)
        programming languages
3GL tools, 219
Three-dimensional options, 121
Time reporting, 123
Token passing protocol, 96, 97
Token ring, 97
Topology, 91
    of LAN, 97
    of networks, 91–94
Toshiba, 196
Total quality management (TQM), 276
Touch pads, 170
Touch-sensitive screens, 170
Trackball, 170
Tracks, magnetic disk, 180
Training
    for end users, 299–302
    online, 301–302
    of system users, 271
Training and assistance personnel, 5–6
Transaction, 21
Transaction processing systems, 22–24
Transfer time, 181
Translation, into machine language, 215
Translators, language, 151–152
Transmission
    mode of, 86–87
    speed of, 85, 86, 97
Transmission Control Protocol/Internet
        Protocol. *See* TCP/IP (Transmission
        Control Protocol/Internet Protocol)
Transmission facilities, 84
Transmission protection, data security
        and, 292–293
Transmitter, 80
Transnational organization, 35
TSR (terminate-and-stay-resident)
        programs, 158
TTP. *See* Telephone twisted pairs (TTP)
Tunnels, for security, 69
24-bit card, 174

Unicode, 154
UNICOS, 155
Uniform resource locator. *See* URL
        (uniform resource locator)

Uninterruptible power supply (UPS), 296
U.S. and Foreign Commercial Service,
    information from, 36
Universal serial bus (USB), 157
UNIX system, 155, 158
Unstructured problems, 125
Unstructured report, 27
Upgrades, 115, 136–137
Upload, 59
    with FTP, 66
URL (uniform resource locator), 58
Usage logs, 306
USB. *See* Universal serial bus (USB)
Usenet, 66
    newsgroup categories, 67
User, 297
    requirements and constraints of,
    259–261
User-friendly applications, 213
User identification (ID), 60, 152
User interface, 127, 132, 133
Username, 57
Utilities, 152–153

Value-added carrier, 90
Value chain, 33
VAX processor, 155
VBScript, 224
VDT (video display terminal), 174
Very high-level language, 218
VGA (video graphics array) monitors, 174
Via Voice, 172
Video card support, 175
Videoconferencing, 69
Video data, 80
Virtual memory, 148–149
Virtual office, 65
Virtual private networks (VPNs), 98
Virus, 291
Virus protection, 291–292
Visual Basic, 223
Visual C++, 223
Visual J++, 223
Visual programming tools, 223
VMS operating system, 155
Voice conferencing, 69
Voice data, 80
Voice print, 172–173
Voice recognition input, 172–173
Voice synthesizer, 176
VPNs. *See* Virtual private networks (VPNs)

Wand reader, 171
WANs. *See* Wide area networks (WANs)
Web browser, 60
Web page creation software, 59

Web pages
    intranets and, 68
    scripting languages and, 223–224
Web server, 58, 60
Web site
    of businesses, 62
    developers of, 6
What-if analysis, 117, 126
Wide area networks (WANs)
    bus and ring topologies and, 94
    characteristics of, 96–98
Windows 95, 156–157
Windows 98, 157
Windows 2000, 157
Windows NT, 157
Windows system. *See* Microsoft Windows
Wireless local area networks (LANs), 90
Wire pairs, 87
Word processing, 113
    software for, 113–115
Word size, 194
Workbench tools, 219
Work flow software, 121
Work request system, 123
Workstations, 11
    networks and, 28
World Wide Web (WWW, Web), 55,
    58–59, 60
    company image on, 276
WORM (write once, read many) tech-
    nology, 185, 186
Write. *See* Read/write heads
Writing, 189
WWW. *See* World Wide Web (WWW, Web)

X.25 protocol, 95

Y2K problem, 217

Zip disks, 181–182